The Erosion of Faith

THE EROSION OF FAITH

An Inquiry into the
Origins of the Contemporary Crisis
in Religious Thought

by
Thomas A. Idinopulos

Chicago
QUADRANGLE BOOKS
1971

For ZAHARIA, *my mother, and my wife,*
CHESSIE

Contents

Preface

Theologians in the twentieth century have sought to discern the meaning of faith as it relates to the turbulent experiences of our "modern" world. It was not always so. Faith once rested secure, and theology, then "queen" of the sciences, was the basis of ethics, law, government, and art. But the great transformation that began in Western culture in the 1500's liberated the intellectual disciplines from the a priori truths of Bible and church and hastened the break with the old religious order of life. This movement enriched theology. From the time of the Reformation on, religious thinkers have leaned away from organizing and applying timeless truths about God, and have instead addressed the more human problem of man's struggle with faith. The theologians I have chosen to treat in this book—Karl Barth, Paul Tillich, Jacques Maritain, Nicolas Berdyaev, and Martin Buber—are "giants" in the present era because they have shown more vividly than most the gains and losses for man in this struggle.

Modern theologians view their task not so much as the word would suggest—*theo-logy*, an understanding of God—but rather as an understanding of the *problem* of God; their task is not God but man, for the problem of God is *man's* problem. At a time when other disciplines have become academic exercises, theology continues to take man himself as its object and to respond to the uniqueness and mystery of the human experience. In Barth, Tillich, Maritain, Berdyaev, and Buber, the question of man's humanity in the struggle with faith is raised as nowhere else. For this reason, the study of these thinkers is not only worthwhile but perhaps even indispensable.

My selection of the theologians discussed in the pages to

follow, and my plan for this book, seek to avoid the old pseudo-literary practice of approaching this subject as a matter of "telling the story of" modern theology. My efforts are directed toward understanding these theologians' respective bodies of thought, not with formulating some convenient framework in which they can be introduced as "exemplifications" of something called "modern theology." Although each thinker is treated separately in order to give maximum attention to his particular system of thought, I shall compare and contrast authors and their ideas as I proceed, the cumulative effect of which is to create, I hope, a lively dialogue among major theologians on the crisis of faith in the modern world.

Selection assumes omission. The authors I have selected are major representatives of different religious traditions and of different theological methods; economies of space and method force me to omit such formidable figures as Rudolph Bultmann, Emil Brunner, Reinhold Niebuhr, Abraham Heschel, Teilhard de Chardin, and Karl Rahner.

Although the titles of the chapters suggest different "types" of theology, this is correct only to a point. The particular religious tradition of each author, and the different philosophical presuppositions of the milieux in which they wrote, create concrete differences in theological method and outlook which must be taken into account in analyzing and assessing their contributions. But these differences are in themselves extremely instructive, for they allow the examination of the very same problems of God and faith to be seen through the eyes of, say, Barth in and through the tradition of reformed Protestant thought, or of Buber in and through the wisdom of Hasidism.

The roots of twentieth-century religious thought lie in nineteenth-century European philosophy and theology, particularly German, and reach back to Immanuel Kant in the eighteenth century. In such figures as Kant, Hegel, Schleiermacher, Schelling, Feuerbach, Ritschl, Nietzsche, Kierkegaard, Dostoevsky, Marx, and Freud are to be found the formative ideas, issues, and methods of the theology of the twentieth century:

the critique of speculative reason, the abandonment of metaphysics, the clarification of religion's distinctiveness, the beginning of theological anthropology, the insight of the "death of God," the discovery of the irrational, the defense of the uniqueness of revelation, the critique of religiosity, the understanding of the relation of religion and the unconscious, and the discernment of the existential meaning of faith.

Any effort at summarizing this important and complex formative era invites superficiality and distortion. Rather than summarize we have chosen to analyze two figures from the nineteenth century who are seminal to the twentieth century: Friedrich Schleiermacher and Søren Kierkegaard. In Schleiermacher's theology of feeling is to be found the basis of the modern effort to relate faith to culture. Kierkegaard's discovery of the primacy of the individual has guided the modern theologian in redefining the meaning of his faith. Schleiermacher and Kierkegaard are both keys to the two principal directions in modern theology: the one direction, the primacy of revelation taken by Barth in the early period of his thought; and the other direction, the inseparability of religion and culture, taken by Tillich, Maritain, Berdyaev, and Buber.

The final chapter of the book aims to relate the theology of the first half of the twentieth century to newer developments at mid-century which point to the direction of theology in the second half of the century. I analyze several representatives of these new developments, then critically examine their ideas in the light of the theologies that went before them.

Every book reflects the influence on its author of his teachers and friends; this one is no exception. I take pleasure in acknowledging the faculty of the Divinity School of the University of Chicago, where I was a doctoral student, and particularly Professor Bernard M. Loomer, who was my adviser during those years. Professor Lois Von Gehr Livezey offered criticism of Chapter I, as did Professor Karen Brown of Chapter II and Professor Joseph E. Hathaway of Chapter III. Conversations with Professor Daniel C. Noel helped to deepen my understanding of issues dealt with in Chapter VIII. The Faculty Research Committee of Miami University (Ohio) made a grant available to me in the summer of 1969 to continue research on this book. I am grateful to all these people for their help; at the same time I take responsibility for whatever errors and inadequacies appear in the text. I also wish to acknowledge my indebtedness to Samuel Freifeld, without whose encouragement this book would not have been conceived. The unfailing courtesies and attention of Ivan Dee, managing editor of Quadrangle Books, made it possible for me to complete the manuscript without anxiety. Chessie Idinopulos, my wife, read, edited, and typed the manuscript.

The Erosion of Faith

I

The Theology of Feeling: Friedrich Schleiermacher

At the beginning of the nineteenth century, Friedrich Schleiermacher rejected the prevailing view that the task of the theologian is to reflect on the eternal object, God, that supernatural being fixed for man's faith by the dogmatic truths of church thinkers, or fixed for his intellect by the deistic diagrams of Enlightenment philosophers. In place of this view, Schleiermacher held that the *experience* of God— man's religion—is the proper concern of the theologian; for only in the "living" experience of God can the theologian be assured he has before him the reality of God Himself and not some historical *idea* of God.

Friedrich Schleiermacher was born in 1768 in Breslau, Germany, the son of an army chaplain of the Reformed, or Calvinist, Church.[1] At the age of fifteen he was sent to a seminary of the Moravian Brotherhood, a Christian sect known for its simple piety. To the Moravians, the essence of Christian existence consisted not of expressed beliefs and ideas but of the living experience of God, the spontaneous recognition of and response to God in worship, which imparted a confidence of God's presence in a Christian's day-to-day life.

Schleiermacher studied classics at the Moravian seminary, and, in 1787, continued this study at the University of Halle. Greek philosophy proved a profound influence on Schleiermacher's religious ideas, particularly Plato's notion that at the heart of man's most creative or "spiritual" vision is an eternal oneness of man and the divine.

His appreciation for religion as an experience of the heart was intensified when, in 1796, he went to Berlin as a chaplain of the Reformed Church and came into contact with a group of young Romantic poets and philosophers. The Romantics preached a joyful unity of man and the universe, an emotional unity expressed through the infinite possibilities of poetry. Their attitude was emerging in intellectual circles throughout Europe, counteracting the influence of the older rationalism.

Schleiermacher became a close friend of the poet Friedrich Schlegel, a leader of the Romantic movement in Germany, and defended him when one of his literary works was attacked by church leaders as indecent. This was one of many times Schleiermacher was to find himself at odds with church officials. His willingness to think freely on theological subjects, to employ the newer philosophical views in place of the official teachings of the church, and his frequent use of the pulpit for dealing with sensitive political issues of the day, made him a constant object of official ecclesiastical disapproval.

Schleiermacher taught at the University of Halle from 1804 until the outbreak of the Napoleonic War in the winter of 1806–1807 forced him to leave. When he saw the devastation of German people and lands wrought by the invading French armies, he involved himself in underground movements opposing the French. He made frequent political speeches to encourage the establishment of a unified, free German state. Germans have since regarded Schleiermacher as one of the benefactors of the modern German nation. It is interesting to note in this regard that he was the pastor who prepared Otto von Bismarck for church confirmation.

By the time he died in 1834, Schleiermacher had achieved one of the most penetrating analyses of the nature of religion, and showed the subtle depths which unite religion to all the other dimensions of human experience. H. R. Mackintosh, the late Scottish theologian, wrote:

> It was Schleiermacher's peculiar gift to unite in an exceptional degree the most passionate religion with the unbending rigour of a scientific thinker. The human, for him, is one at bottom with the Christian, and the fear perpetually haunted him lest the line of communications between religion and intellectual life should be cut, and piety little by little become synonymous with barbarism.[2]

In response to the request of his friends in the Romantic circle in Berlin, Schleiermacher undertook to write a set of essays concerning the role of religion in human life. The result was the publication, in 1799, of a book which almost immediately brought him fame as an original author on the subject of religion. The book's purpose was to defend the integrity of religious experience and to show the validity of its expressed meanings. That religion needed defending was never in doubt, for the book's title stated plainly the problem: *Discourses on Religion to the Cultured Among Its Despisers.*

To understand what Schleiermacher meant by religion's "cultured despisers," it is necessary to understand the intellectual atmosphere in which he worked. The publication of the *Discourses* occurred in Germany at that period which the twentieth-century phenomenologist of religion, Rudolph Otto, calls "the high noon of that stirring springtime which saw the germination and the blossoming of modern intellectual life."[3] Otto's words are hyperbole, but justifiable if one remembers that this was the time of Johann Wolfgang von Goethe, "that civilization in himself." German ascendancy in the cultural life of Europe could be argued by the achievements of Goethe alone. But add to Goethe's the names of Kant, Schiller, Herder, Fichte, Hegel, and Schelling, among others, and one supposes that only in the Golden Era of Greece could one find a comparable array of philosophical and poetic genius. "A mighty pulsing torrent of the powers, talents, and strivings of the human spirit surged forward," says Otto, but he goes on to observe: "Only one human interest seemed to be laggard, and it was precisely the interest which for so long had been the first, indeed almost the only one: religion." [4]

At the turn of the eighteenth century, the attitude toward religion among German intellectuals, religion's "cultured despisers," was less deliberate antipathy than it was apathy. The vigorous anti-clericalism so common to the French educated elite of the eighteenth century never spread to Germany, nor was the materialistic basis of French philosophy ever shared by German thinkers. No German intellectual, even at his most skeptical, ever matched the great Voltaire in the creativeness, militancy, and influence of his atheism. In fact, philosophical arguments for either skepticism or atheism were quite alien to German thought.

The prevailing attitude among German intellectuals seemed to say: One need not take up arms against religion if one does not regard it as an enemy or a threat, especially since one expects to surpass the best that religion had to offer. What directed and justified the mind-set of the educated elite was the classical concept of the transcendental unity of beauty, truth, and goodness. Whether in art, philosophy, science, or in moral behavior, one could achieve that spiritual wisdom and virtue which the Greeks called *arete*, a nobility of mind and soul, which made religion, by contrast, unquestionably inferior. Further, if religion could make any creative contribution to life, it would have to be in relation to the "higher" value of moral goodness.

A generation earlier, Kant had formulated a view of religion as the watchdog of morality, a view that was reflected in the thought of German intellectuals of Schleiermacher's day. Kant had argued that the church's vast store of dogma contained certain truths which reason could independently recognize as valid. He identified these truths as the reality of God, the immortality of the soul, and the freedom of man's will. Each of these truths had a definite relation to an ethical philosophy whose ultimate basis was a rational recognition of duty. A man's actions can be regarded as moral, Kant argued, not by the presence of his desire to act morally, nor by virtue of his conformity to the church's commands on morality. Rather, a man is understood to behave morally solely through his willingness to do what his reason is able to recognize and report to him as right and therefore a matter of duty.

Kant nonetheless realized that the man of moral virtue is seldom if ever rewarded for doing his duty. And without the expectation of reward, what would be the incentive for moral behavior? This was not a theoretical but a practical question of great social moment. One could not look forward to orderly society—and, for Kant, there was no other valid society—if one could not expect men who are educated to their duties to perform them. The question of incentive or motive may not have been relevant to the theoretical character of the good, but it was essential to the practical possibilities of the good.

Kant, then, saw the relevance of religion in terms of its ability to inspire one to do his moral duty and, by so doing, take his place in an orderly society.

Because of the biblically based Christian religion, it was possible to say that, despite the uncertainty of worldly rewards, the virtuous man could look forward to a reward in the "after life." Thus the moral justice of the universe itself could be defended by the belief in a God who created the universe and who rewarded the just and punished the unjust in the after life. Moreover, if religion permitted one to say that there is for each man a final judgment from God after this life, then there should be no question that the soul lives on after death and can continue to perform its moral duties indefinitely.

And, further, there would be scant reason to believe that virtue is rewarded and wickedness punished, unless one were also prepared to believe that man had freedom bestowed upon him by God to choose to do his duty and obey the will of the author of both his freedom and his life.

Religion, then, where it was not despised as intellectually insignificant, was made to seem a persuasive force of social morality. It was in the face of this practice that Schleiermacher presented his thesis on the nature of religion.

His strategy was "to defend and foster religion by a new examination and statement of its essence." [5] Religion, he argued, should be identified neither with morality nor with knowledge. The religious man may be moral and he may be wise, but it is not by virtue of what he does or knows that he is religious. To appraise religion on its moral and intellectual content implies a basic error about the meaning of religion. To examine the religious consciousness is to discover that religion possesses a quality of its own, and this is what Schleiermacher set about to find. In so doing he almost singlehandedly reversed the trends of a priorism and rationalism which had marked theological reflection in Germany since the fires of the Reformation had died. Schleiermacher explored what was actually present in the religious consciousness, not what the dictates of reason or the church's authority said should be present. His empirical method, albeit in primitive and not always consistent form, set the pattern for a continuing serious, scientific study of religion.

The findings of Schleiermacher's own study of religion was that religion consisted essentially of *feeling*—though he was not always clear about this—*a* feeling in which one experiences his oneness with everything and everyone about him. By *feeling* Schleiermacher did not mean emotion as we ordinarily think of it today: an outward manifestation of an inner experience. In fact, he meant the very opposite: feeling is a passive experience, the experience of receiving. The religious consciousness is a tool by which the subject remains open to impressions received from without. Schleiermacher definitely regarded feeling as a faculty of human consciousness. The view of psychology at this time was that the mind, in the general sense of consciousness, consisted of a set of distinct but related faculties. Logical thinking comprised one faculty, the activity of will in moral acts or decisions comprised another. Since religion was a genuine experience, Schleiermacher concluded that there must be a faculty to which religion corresponded— and that was feeling.

But, one might wish to ask, is this not equating religion with the subject's experience only? If so, that would make religion little else than a peculiar quality of a person's self-experience. But it would be wrong to think that Schleiermacher's view of religion amounted to making religion merely an aspect of human psychology. For him there had to be an object which was perceived in the experience of feeling. That object was God: a feeling was religious if it had God as its object.

Religious feeling consisted of an experienced object as well as the experiencing subject. "Remember in the first place," he wrote, "that any feeling is not an emotion of piety because in it a single object as such affects us, but only in so far as in it and along with it, it affects us a revelation of God." [6] Yet it is misleading to assume that Schleiermacher would have been satisfied with referring to God without careful attention to the active meaning God held for its believer. Here, as almost everywhere else, Schleiermacher approached the meaning of God from the beginning point of the believer's experience.

God is experienced as the transcendent order of the universe. Religious experience is the grasp of this order through feeling and the recognition of one's relation to others. Schleiermacher called this close, internal relation between God and the world "Universe." To be religious is to intuit the "Universe" in everything; it is to see that relation of the finite to the Infinite, to find the place of each thing within the ultimate order. For Schleiermacher, religious experience became experience not just of

9

the world but of the divine depths of the world. It is the intuition of the subtle but real presence of divinity in every portion of the world.

The relationship of God to the world is most adequately manifested by the feelings one experiences with other human beings. For sensitive persons, the experiences of art and of the natural world may provide some vision of the Infinite; but only when one experiences love, joy, and compassion for other persons does one come into contact with God.

Schleiermacher would allow no easy philosophical differentiation between man's experience of other men and his experience of God. His view of the interpenetration of the Infinite and finite simply would not permit it. The influence of Spinoza's pantheistic philosophy may be seen here, but Schleiermacher was no pantheist. He maintained a vivid sense of the difference between the pantheistic equation of the divine and the worldly and his own view that the divine constitutes an extra dimension of the world, a "depth" in all things.

Emotions like love and joy could be regarded as religious by Schleiermacher because at the depths of man's humanity, he possesses a link with God. Man's humanity at its highest or noblest is divine. To see this humanity in everyone, to understand the deep relation between the individual person and the indivisible wholeness of divine humanity, was, for Schleiermacher, a religious obligation. He wrote:

> . . . humanity and religion are closely and indissolubly united. A longing for love, ever satisfied and ever again renewed, becomes religion. . . . the pious feelings are most holy that express for [the individual] existence in the whole of humanity. . . .[7]

> Work on individuals, but rise in contemplation, on the wings of religion, to endless, undivided humanity. Seek this humanity in each individual.[8]

In the above lines, Schleiermacher came very close to the attitudes of Plato and Spinoza. Schleiermacher had undertaken

to translate Plato's *Dialogues* into German, and he shared with
Plato the belief in the unity of the divine and human, a unity
experienced through the infinite depths of the human soul. According to both Plato and Spinoza, man is conceived as a participant in divinity by virtue of his relation to that universal
humanity which is in each man. This recognition—the recognition of the particular in its relation to the universal—was for
both Schleiermacher and Plato an experience of self-transcendence, the self's recognition of its relation to that which is
greater and deeper than itself but yet utterly congenial with
itself. This—the experience of religion—is the experience of
unity or wholeness.

Schleiermacher described the "Universe" as follows:

> The Universe is ceaselessly active and at every moment is
> revealing itself to us. Every form it has produced, everything
> to which, from the fullness of its life, it has given a separate
> existence, every occurrence scattered from its fertile bosom
> is an operation of the Universe upon us. Now religion is to
> take up into our lives and to submit to be swayed by them,
> each of these influences and their consequent emotions, not
> by themselves but as a part of the Whole, not as limited and
> in opposition to other things, but as an exhibition of the
> Infinite in our life.[9]

As these words make clear, no part of the world is devoid of
divinity, though the human portion of the world most dramatically reflects the divine presence. This is due, clearly enough,
to the greater "depths" that man enjoys by virtue of his powers
of conscious feeling. The beast of the field can feel, but he
cannot be conscious of himself in feeling, and therefore is
devoid of the capacity to see himself in relation to transcendent
ideals. In the depths of man's experience of the world, through
the feelings by which he receives the world into his consciousness, man comes into immediate awareness of his fundamental
unity with God. This is the experience of the omnipresence of
divinity, prompting Schleiermacher to say, "To a pious mind

religion makes everything holy. . . ." That unity which underlies the world's constant movement is not anything man can
seek; rather, it comes to him in the moment of piety, when
he releases himself through feeling to the impressions produced
by the world. Through the passivity of feeling he recovers
that unity of which he was originally a part:

> . . . however we exhibit the World and God they cannot be
> divided. We do not feel ourselves dependent on the Whole in
> so far as it is an aggregate of mutually conditioned parts of
> which we ourselves are one, but only in so far as underneath
> this coherence there is a unity conditioning all things and
> conditioning our relations to the other parts of the Whole.
> Only on this condition can the single thing be, as it is here put,
> an exhibition of the Infinite, being so comprehended that its
> opposition to all else entirely vanishes.[10]

Thus Schleiermacher was communicating to his learned contemporaries what he thought to be true about religion: that
religion was not action or knowledge but feeling; and that when
the feelings of men are deepest, they come closest to recognizing
the central truth governing their lives: their dependence upon
each other because of their common ground in God. Religion is
not to be confused with externally imposed dogmas and
commands; rather, it proceeds spontaneously and naturally from
the innermost capacities of man's sensibility.

Schleiermacher sought to convince his audience that the fine
sentiments of the poets are resonant with the sound of the Universe—that divine Whole which exists underneath all and
thereby unites everything with it. Before this holy presence
the proper stance should not be that self-assurance and optimistic humanism which Schleiermacher's contemporary, Johann
Gottlieb Fichte, was espousing, but rather a humility, a receptive and sensitive awareness of one's nearness to all creatures
and to God. Rudolph Otto was right to observe that for
Schleiermacher, without the humility of religion, "the mood

and culture of the time with all its lofty inspiration was
naught but pride (hubris), naught but a 'Promethean arrogance
which timidly steals what it might have demanded and waited
for with calm and confidence.' " [11] Not morality, not knowledge, but religion was the source and guarantor of true
humanity; for only in religion was there possible the perception
and appreciation of that universal humanity which makes
it possible to avoid the narrow egotism and self-sufficiency
which stifles the spirit of each man. To take the religious
posture toward life and toward other human beings was to
endow one's life and experience with "value, significance,
content and depth."

Naturally, Schleiermacher's unorthodox way of relating God
to the world and man provoked criticism from established
theological and ecclesiastic quarters. The principal criticism
was that he was advocating pantheism, that he had replaced the
integrity of the personhood of God with vague talk about
a cosmic whole and man's psychological responses to it.

In fairness, it must be said that Schleiermacher provided the
occasion for much of this criticism. Indeed, he had avoided
theistic ideas and the traditional theological language which
would have established for his critics the distinctness of the
divine personality. Moreover, his method of analyzing religious
experience militated against most of the traditional theological
notions of the personality of God, including the basic conception that God is a person.

Schleiermacher's tendency in the *Discourses* was to regard the
experience of religion as the experience of a felt unity with other
men and with the world, a unity whose basis is God. God is
not perceived directly or independently, and, therefore, no
relationship of a personal sort could describe the content of the
subject's religious experience. God is always felt "in" things
or as a fundamental part of men; the ground upon which they
stand; and the love they share with others. God is not experienced as a distinct isolated being:

The sum total of religion is to feel that, in its highest unity, all that moves us in feeling is one; to feel that aught single and particular is only possible by means of this unity; to feel, that is to say, that our being and living is a being and living in and through God . . . it is not necessary that the Deity should be presented as also one distinct object.[12]

It would be incorrect to suppose that Schleiermacher did not appreciate the question of the personhood or identity of God. He accepted the biblical belief that God as Creator is distinct from the world of his creatures. What he declined to accept was the traditional mode of understanding this distinctness. Medieval philosophers had spoken of God as one, simple, omniscient, omnipotent; and theological language could not escape the tradition of rational arguments about God's nature, existence, and relation to the world.

Schleiermacher regarded such notions as speculations which may or may not have any correspondence to the actual *experience* of God. He was not prepared to say that the medieval theology of God was in error, or that any particular concept of God was wrong. His entire concern with theological ideas was directed not against their contents, but against all rationalistic, a priori, and speculative *methods* by which theologians arrived at their ideas. All ideas of God—philosophical or otherwise—should be held responsible to the examination of their experiential content. An interpretation of God's character is sound only when it accurately describes actual religious experience. Any preoccupation with the oneness or distinctness of God falls victim to the kind of thinking that disregards living experience and favors preconceived notions about transcendence, eternity, and the absolute. Man's experience of God is always mediated by our feelings. Hence, the religious content of our feeling is always God *and* world, always some perception of divineness *in* the world. Thus, any narrow focus on God's own nature, or the way in which he differs from the world, diverts us from the *encounter* with God as a sacred wholeness in the world. We become bogged down in less fruitful, rationalistic conjectures about a historic God as he is in himself, independent of our encounter with him.

Yet, as Schleiermacher saw it, God's self-manifestation in the world as divineness need not be confused with the world. God is not the world nor the world God, as Spinoza had thought. It is hard to see, at times, how Schleiermacher differs from Spinoza's pantheism and mysticism. But clearly, Schleiermacher's notion of religious feeling is that it is a fundamental perception of a divine dimension of reality, identifiable for the subject as a meaning distinct from other meanings, but experienced through the world:

> The contemplation of the pious is the immediate consciousness of the universal existence of all finite things in and through the Infinite, and of all temporal things, in and through the Eternal. Religion is to seek this and find it in all that lives and moves, in all growth and change, in all doing and suffering. It is to have life and to know life in immediate feeling, only as such an existence in the Infinite and Eternal. . . . [Religion] is a life in the infinite nature of the Whole, in the One and in the All, in God, having and possessing all things in God, and God in all.[13]

In short, said Schleiermacher, "Your feeling is piety insofar as it is the result of the operation of God in you by means of the operation of the world upon you," with little doubt in his mind that in the experience of feeling, God was distinguishable from the world.

When Schleiermacher was not accused of equating God with world, he was accused of reducing the meaning of God to the contents of man's mental or spiritual life. When not accused of pantheism, he was charged with psychologism. The latter would be harder to refute, for Schleiermacher's methods of analyzing religious meaning, by his own account, rested entirely on discerning the content of the religious consciousness. While the first edition of the *Discourses* stated clearly that religious feeling is based upon the perception of an external being, subsequent editions were not so clear on this.[14] And, in any event, the only way to talk about this being, objectively real though it be, was through the subject's experience. Hence, it was virtually impossible to demonstrate that Schleiermacher did not identify, or at least confuse, the meaning of God with the meaning of one's experience of God. But if this is a substantial confusion in Schleiermacher's thought, it seems to be a price he was quite willing to pay in order to introduce the only mode of analyzing religion that successfully counteracted the prevailing rationalism in theology and philosophy.

On the whole it can be said that Schleiermacher's subordination of doctrines to felt experience was of a piece with his effort to describe the structure of religious experience, as distinguished from the moral and intellectual aspects of human experience. If there are to be doctrines and dogmas, they must be utterly faithful to the experiential mode of religious meaning. The meanings we receive from felt experiences are the criteria for evaluating the soundness of every effort to provide conceptually precise terms for these experiential meanings. Thus, in assaying such traditional theological notions as grace and miracles, Schleiermacher ignores what was traditionally believed, and instead focuses exclusively on whatever experiential content they could possess. Of miracles, he says:

> Every event, even the most natural and usual, becomes a miracle, as soon as the religious view of it can be the dominant. To me all is miracle. In your sense the inexplicable and strange alone is miracle, in my mind it is no miracle. The more religious you are, the more miracle would you see everywhere.[15]

And grace is not a supernatural infusion of blessedness and illumination; rather, grace is that dual movement in which the presence of God in the world is felt with sufficient vigor to impel a person into a deeper relationship with his fellow human beings in the world.

It may be said that this experiential criterion for religion compelled Schleiermacher to abandon the theology of transcendence in favor of the theology of immanence. While this is in a sense true, it is perhaps truer to say that he was substituting the concrete, vivid language of personal experience for the abstract language of the official theology of the church. If, in this substitution, the objective character or personality of God seems to be inadequately defined, Schleiermacher was prepared to argue that in the final analysis it is the *experience* of God, and not a defensible definition of God, that really matters. The following lines make this eminently clear:

> . . . the manner in which the Deity is present to man in feeling, is decisive of the world of his religion, not the manner, always inadequate, in which it is copied in idea. This rejection of the idea of a personal Deity does not decide against the presence of the Deity in his feeling. The ground of such a rejection might be a humble consciousness of the limitation of personal existence, and particularly of personality joined to consciousness. He might stand as high above a worshipper of the twelve gods whom you would rightly name after Lucretius, as a pious person at that stage would be above an idolator.[16]

> The usual conception of God as one single being outside of the world and behind the world is not the beginning and end of religion. It is only one manner of expressing God, seldom entirely pure and always inadequate. . . . Yet the true nature of religion is neither this idea nor any other, but immediate consciousness of the Deity as He is found in ourselves and in the world.[17]

In 1821, twenty-two years after the appearance of the *Discourses*, Schleiermacher published his magnum opus entitled *The Christian Faith*. It was the first effort on the part of a Protestant thinker, since Calvin's monumental *Institutes of the Christian Religion*, to state in systematic fashion the essential meaning of the Christian religion. In the *Discourses*, Schleiermacher discovered religion to consist of the experience of feeling. He regarded this experience to be universally true of religion, irrespective of different religious traditions or of the differences in religions imparted by history and culture. This did not mean, however, that religion was to be equated with just any feeling. The experience of religion could be differentiated from other types of feeling-experience by the presence of a God-object, and in *The Christian Faith* Schleiermacher further amplified this differentiation. The result was that a particular feeling, "the feeling of absolute dependence," was held up as the most adequate criterion for the experience unique to religion.

Schleiermacher argued that feeling is generally a passive experience. In most cases, the experience of feeling carries with it the sense that one can influence, by his own action, that object which is acting upon him. This is true in the case of love; it is true also of fear and anger. The subject and object always interact to some degree. But, Schleiermacher argued, this is not the case with respect to religion. The experience of the Christian, for instance, shows that he has no sense of influencing that being—God—which exercises power over him. He finds himself totally dependent upon it, completely at its mercy, without any sense of the freedom to influence it by any thought, action, or feeling of his own. This feeling of unconditional dependence, and this alone, is the genuine experience of religion.

In *The Christian Faith,* Schleiermacher refined his definition of religion as feeling, and, in the process, gained greater clarity about the thought-content of religion—a troublesome problem occasioned by his definition of religion and never finally resolved by any of his subsequent statements. In the *Discourses,* Schleiermacher had counteracted rationalistic treatments of religion by emphasizing the centrality of immediate experience. This emphasis was continued in *The Christian Faith,* where he came to regard the subject's experience as the only reliable method for ascertaining religious meaning. Theological doctrines, he claimed, are expressions of the content of the religious consciousness. Where no connection can be shown between the theological idea and the concrete datum of religious experience, then the idea has no basis in fact and should be abandoned. This is empiricism as applied to Christian theology; and it heralded a new era, in which the great metaphysical and dogmatic theologies of the periods just before and after the Reformation were to give way to empirical studies as found in the history, sociology, and psychology of religion.

If theological doctrines are, as Schleiermacher said, accounts of the subject's religious experience *alone*, what of the doctrines relating to God himself? With respect to such doctrines as the power, love, and justice of God, is the believer to be told that, when speaking of God's compassion, he is speaking not about God (for he is unknowable in himself) but about his own religious experience, that is to say, about *himself?* Surely the view that doctrines have to do not with objective realities but with subjective experiences exposes that psychological subjectivism of which Schleiermacher was continually accused, does it not?

Schleiermacher's answers to these questions are difficult to discern in his writings. He certainly acknowledged that God is a reality distinct from one's experience of him; how else could this experience prove religiously meaningful? But he was reluctant to allow that the *meaning* of God could be rooted in something other than the believer's lived, immediate experience of God. Schleiermacher thought of the meaning of God as a distinct meaning, but one included within the complex experience of religion as an integral part of it. In *The Christian Faith* as well as in the *Discourses,* he looked on feeling as containing the direct perception of a reality adequately described by the verbal symbol "God." In the feeling of absolute dependence, the subject is immediately and continually aware of a relationship to something transcending himself which again can be adequately expressed by the word "God."

By "God" did Schleiermacher think of anything more than the logical source of the feeling of absolute dependence? If so, then his notion of God is at variance with that image of a personal being which is conveyed by the Bible, an image which has guided Jewish and Christian theologians for hundreds of years. And it seems to be so if we take Schleiermacher at his word: ". . . the Whence of our receptive and active existence . . . is to be designated by the word 'God,' " [18] and, "God signifies . . . simply that which is the co-determinant in this feeling [of absolute dependence] and to which we trace our being in such a state." [19] Schleiermacher in fact rejected the notion of God as person because it basically contradicted his notion of the passive character of religious experience. The result of rejecting personality as a fitting symbol for God meant that Schleiermacher could speak of God as an undifferentiated power which is related to the world as its eternal cause, a concept which implicitly denies the biblical belief in a divine creation of the world ex nihilo, and unmistakably indicates Schleiermacher's heavy indebtedness to Spinoza's pantheism.

Spinoza's equation of God and nature which hovered over the pages of the *Discourses* continued to be present in *The Christian Faith*. God is the "Whence," an impersonal but eternal causal efficacy of whatever has come to be in the world of nature and history. So closely was this causal efficacy identified in Schleiermacher's mind with the causal nexus in the natural world that one wonders if there is any room left for human freedom and responsibility, or how sin and evil could have entered a world so completely governed by the divine causality. Schleiermacher's answer to the latter question was pure ad hoc theorizing. God, he argued, permitted sin in order to provide a suitable object for the event of redemptive grace in the person of Jesus Christ. This meant, in effect, that God himself was indirectly responsible for the presence of evil in the world.

Thus is revealed that inescapable weakness in Schleiermacher's experiential method of analyzing religious meaning. When Schleiermacher rejected all theological ideas that were not literal descriptions of religious experience, he was left with a notion of deity so meager in content as to prove unworkable exactly at the point of elucidating the content of the religious consciousness. In supposing that he could identify the meaning of religion solely in terms of what one supposes is contained in the consciousness of the religious subject, he eschewed just the type of theoretical ideas which are necessary to make sense of the existence of the religious consciousness. Without such ideas, questions such as the relation between divine creation and the reality of evil would forever beg answer, or be expressed in such contradictory and otherwise unacceptable forms as we in fact find in Schleiermacher's writings.

For the divine "Whence," however adequately it corresponds to the passive experience of feeling, appears wholly inadequate in light of the sense of interpersonal communion expressed in the experience of prayer, or the deeply personal experiences of God's judgment and forgiveness—experiences which form part of the classical structure of the religious consciousness in all monotheistic faiths. The inadequacy of Schleiermacher's notion of deity means finally that the feeling of absolute dependence, while certainly genuine as a "moment" of the religious consciousness, proves itself too meager and incomplete as a criterion of the essence of the richness and complexity of the religious consciousness. As H. R. Mackintosh wrote: ". . . in stressing the fundamental importance of felt dependence, as a factor in religion, Schleiermacher certainly did not err. . . . But this feeling is not the only one involved; to mention no more, there is the feeling of shelteredness, of creatureliness, of unworthiness, of obligation." [20]

It followed from Schleiermacher's experiential understanding of religion that the differences between various theological ideas could be traced to basic differences in the experiences of the individual communities. No critical evaluation could be made of theological ideas beyond the question of the correspondence of the ideas to experience. This meant the presupposition of relativism in any effort to understand and appreciate various religions, although Schleiermacher himself was less ready to recognize this presupposition than later thinkers proved to be. For example, Ernst Troeltsch (1866–1923), the distinguished German historian of the Christian church, was prepared to argue that there is no way outside the given religious community to speak of the truth or falsity of its beliefs, and, therefore, no way in which one can effectively speak of superiority and inferiority of different religious ideas, claims, and convictions. This meant that the Christian claim for the universality of its revelation could be authoritative only for those within the fold—and there, presumably, only insofar as the claim for universality adequately expressed certain aspects of the actual experiences of the community. As Troeltsch saw it, a religion could be adequately understood only in view of its unique historical development and its present practices as they have been shaped by its history.

If Schleiermacher himself did not draw the relativistic implications of his own view, it is probably because his experiential method was never made the sole principle of his analysis of religious meaning. It was one of two principles, the other being evolutionary monism.

The concept that history shows evolutionary changes in all societies, moving from lower to higher forms—movement reflected in art, politics, morality, philosophy, and religion—had been first advanced in Germany by J. G. Herder, but received its most brilliant and systematic expression at the hands of Hegel (who, it is thought, may have been influenced in this respect by Schleiermacher [21]). The notion of social and historical evolution was the product of the rationalism of German philosophy from the time of Kant on—a notion which fed the humanistic optimism and moral idealism of German philosophy. It influenced Schleiermacher in ways which he seems not to have recognized; having once established to his own satisfaction that religion consists of the feeling of absolute dependence, Schleiermacher then set about "evaluating" the authentic experiential content in different religions, grading them on the degree to which they inspired in their adherents that which is essential to religion, the feeling of absolute dependence. But his effort amounted to a comparison of various religious traditions with Christianity, showing the latter to be superior at every point of comparison.

Schleiermacher began with the observation that monotheistic

religions are superior to polytheistic religions, because the belief in one God more adequately conveys the sense of unity which is implicit to the experience of absolute dependence than does polytheism, where the subject's feelings are divided by different and often competing deities; for similar reasons, he found polytheism to be superior to fetishism or animism. Within the sphere of monotheistic religions, Christianity is found to be superior to Judaism and Mohammedanism, because in Christianity there is realized the purest experience of absolute dependence. In Christianity everything is referred to God, whereas in Judaism and in the religion of Islam there are vestiges of "lower" religions in that a certain sensuousness remains which obstructs the perfect consciousness of God (though, in this respect, Judaism is "higher" than Islam). With respect to Christianity, Schleiermacher stated that among the three great traditions —Roman Catholicism, Eastern Orthodoxy, and Protestantism— none could be said to have a superior form of the Christian revelation; yet his discussion of the other two traditions in relation to Protestantism leaves little doubt of his feeling for the superiority of the latter.

Throughout this analysis of the religions of the world, Schleiermacher was influenced by the perspective of evolutionary monism to such an extent that he was compelled to seek in the data of a community's experience some way to justify the rank which was assigned to it in his scheme, a practice which contradicts at every point his own experiential method as applied to religion. He judged Christianity to be perfect, by which he meant there could be no historical evolution of religion "after" Christianity, nor a more perfect form of the Christian religion itself. Christianity has achieved the true goal of religion, which is to liberate men from sinful God-forgetfulness and impart to them that feeling of absolute dependence in which God's presence is felt in every facet of their lives. For in the Christian religion, unlike every other religion, Schleiermacher wrote, "everything has relation to the redemption accomplished by Jesus of Nazareth."

Schleiermacher was prepared to argue that other monotheistic faiths were inadequately redemptive, and therefore less than perfect religiously. His reasoning was that founders of other faiths, such as Moses and Mohammed, were arbitrarily selected, and were not very different from the other men in their communities. This was not true, however, of Jesus. The religious superiority of Christianity could be seen in the unique spirituality of its founder, Jesus of Nazareth, and the extraordinary power he possessed to communicate this spirituality to others.

Schleiermacher spoke of this spirituality as the *sinlessness* of Jesus. Jesus had been born in the world, lived, and died as every man; but, miraculously, unlike any other man, he kept himself from sin. His consciousness of God, by which Schleiermacher meant his relation to God, was perfect. God completely filled his heart so that every feeling, thought, and act proved a witness not only to the presence of God but to the presence of God *in him*. As Schleiermacher put it: ". . . the constant potency of His God-consciousness . . . was a veritable existence of God in him." [22] Thus, anyone who comes into contact with Jesus comes into contact with God. Schleiermacher also implied that Jesus is able to communicate God to man since he, Jesus, by virtue of his spirituality, awakens that spirituality or God-consciousness in man which lies dormant and obstructed by sin.

Much of what Schleiermacher had to say about the redemptive power of Jesus Christ reflected his own personal experience. In his early years he had lived with the Moravian Brotherhood and had drunk deeply of their spirituality. The Moravian piety was based on a sense of the love of Christ for man, and this piety left an indelible impression on Schleiermacher. In addition, Schleiermacher's view of Christ reflected a warmth and sense of personal relationship which his more philosophical view of God lacked. Mackintosh observed in this respect: "It is hardly too much to say that, so far as piety is concerned, Christ for him took the place of God." [23]

Schleiermacher's unique achievement is that his influence on modern theologians is just as great on those who have rejected his Romantic theology as on those who have constructively appropriated its basic insights. A number of thinkers come to mind, who can be separated into two camps. Kenneth Hamilton, in his defense of theological orthodoxy, shows that Schleiermacher's thought has had a positive impact on theologians as otherwise diverse as Henry Van Dusen, H. Richard Niebuhr, Nels Ferre, Paul Tillich, Daniel Day Williams, and Rudolph Bultmann.[24] One should add to this list the name of the distinguished American theologian Bernard Eugene Meland, who, in his definition of religious faith as "sensitive awareness," and in his understanding of the structure of experience which underlies faith, reveals his indebtedness to the fundamental concept of feeling and Universe in Schleiermacher's thought.[25]

Among those theologians whose positions have been formulated in negative reaction to Schleiermacher's theological liberalism, the most prominent are the Swiss thinkers Emil Brunner and Karl Barth, whose brand of neo-orthodox theology has held sway on the European continent for over forty years.

We will deal with Karl Barth and Paul Tillich in separate chapters, because each man is a distinctive major voice in modern theology. But were it not for the writings of Schleiermacher, the form of thought in Barth and Tillich would not have been what it is, and the shape of modern theology would therefore have been different. So great has been Schleiermacher's influence, positive and negative, that most of the problems that now preoccupy theologians either have their roots in his thought or can be shown to parallel important aspects of it. We shall come to deal with these problems in the remaining parts of this study. For now, we shall identify the five primary claims of Schleiermacher's Romantic theology upon which the "modern" theologians have developed their outlooks.

First, in claiming that religion consists of feeling, Schleiermacher has influenced theologians to avoid both moralism and rationalism in the understanding of the essential character of religion. Thinkers such as Barth, Tillich, and Bultmann insist that while faith should find expression in morality and thought, faith itself is a relation to God more primary than what a man thinks or does. This was a fundamental relation which Schleiermacher himself was seeking to articulate in his notion of feeling. Schleiermacher's definition of religion also influenced thinkers to regard religion as a distinctive type of *human* experience. In this Schleiermacher refuted supernaturalism and established the pattern for all subsequent refutations of it. Religion is to be understood not as the intrusion of the divine into the natural world, but rather as a natural quality of human experience, in which expressions such as "God," "grace," "heaven," and so on, can be meaningful. Schleiermacher taught others to look on religion not in terms of the biblical, a priori conviction about what God does, but rather in terms of what man undergoes. The presupposition, for Schleiermacher, was not divine action but man's religious experience. We shall see the influence of this presupposition when we discuss Tillich's notion of religion as "ultimate concern," and again in Barth's vigorous reaction to the presupposition in his own effort to defend anew the concept of divine action.

A second influential claim of Schleiermacher's is that theological doctrine must have religious experience as its source. In this claim, Schleiermacher broke cleanly with supernaturalism and its own claim of the biblically revealed (or philosophically reasoned) truth about God. Schleiermacher set forth a vigorous brand of religious naturalism. Theological truth is truth about God, man, and the world from the point of view of man's experience; thus, theology becomes inescapably anthropocentric. The Bible is no longer the source of theology; rather, it is understood as a manifestation of the religious consciousness— a record of a distinct type of religious experience. Schleiermacher thereby provided the impetus for the new investigation of scripture on the part of liberal scholars who were not compelled to regard the Bible as a repository of supernaturally revealed truths but who saw it as a unique product of the religious history of a community.

Schleiermacher: The Theology of Feeling

A third claim influencing modern theology is Schleiermacher's metaphysical concept of God. One of the assumptions of his analysis of religion as feeling is that man has a religious nature, that religion is not, therefore, something which is imposed upon him but is the expression of what is most vital in his nature. It followed that whatever object inspired religious affection, that object was a real part of human existence. This means that man has a capacity for God; it means, conversely, that the divine is not a deviation from reality as we experience it, nor totally dissimilar to man, nor confronting him as a wholly alien being. There is a structural or ontological continuity between the divine and the human which Schleiermacher expressed in speaking of man's inherent "God-consciousness." The facts of man's religious experience were meaningful to Schleiermacher only through the ontological notion of God's infinity, to which man, by virtue of his very finitude, has an underlying relationship. Man, for Schleiermacher, is, by virtue of the capacity of feeling, God-prone; God is part of his very nature. Thus, any fundamental explication of the meaning of God must include a philosophical explication of all finite reality, including the reality of man. Here Schleiermacher's thought is at the root of the natural theology which is closely identified with Tillich.

The fourth claim of Schleiermacher's theology lies in his interpretation of the meaning of Jesus Christ. Schleiermacher is the father of all subsequent "liberal" Protestant treatments of Christ, in that he saw Christ not as a redeemer sent down from heaven to a grossly sinful and unsuspecting world by the miraculous action of God, but as a person who, by virtue of his unique spirituality, was better able to manifest God than anyone else, and who therefore constitutes in his own person a rallying point of redemption. Jesus is the Christ not by virtue of supernatural decree but by virtue of his *manifest* power to relate men to God. In grounding his Christology on Jesus' own experience of God and his redemptive activity, Schleiermacher provided the orientation for a new appreciation for the

27

personality of Jesus, which was to figure so prominently in the thought of Albrecht Ritschl, the second great "liberal" Protestant theologian of the nineteenth century. Karl Barth and the school of neo-orthodox theology aggressively rejected the view that the meaning of Jesus Christ could be based on the idea of Christ's personality, or on any supposed capacity of Jesus himself to communicate the gracious power of God to man. But quite recently New Testament scholarship has reopened the question of the human Christ.[26]

As we have seen, Schleiermacher sought to convey the essential meaning of religion to those who had rejected it as a culturally inferior expression of the human spirit. His fifth influential claim is this unique apologetic. Schleiermacher's strategy was to show that religion was a function of the "higher" capacities of man, and that when man was expressing himself most creatively, he was in fact expressing himself religiously. Schleiermacher influenced others to think of religion not as a special realm of meaning apart from culture and identical only to ecclesiastic forms of meaning, but as a quality of meaning pervading all life. Religion can be found wherever and whenever the human spirit rises in feeling to moments of exalted, creative self-expression, whether it be in art, philosophy, science, morality, or religion. For it is in those moments that man comes into contact with the abiding presence of the Infinite. Schleiermacher's concept of God is developed in terms of what Tillich, Berdyaev, Maritain, and Buber regard as the organic relation of religion to culture. By articulating that relation, Schleiermacher sought to lead religion, and particularly religious thought, out of that parochialism which centuries of "church religion" had generated.

In specifying these five claims of Schleiermacher's thought as the basis of his influence on modern theology, we do not assume that we have exhausted the nature of that influence, nor have we characterized it in other than the most general terms; we have tried merely to delineate the essentials of that influence. The full theological implications of Schleiermacher's theology of feeling were seen by Ernst Troeltsch. Troeltsch argued that if Schleiermacher was right, that there was no basis for the knowledge of God apart from the subject's experience, then there was no way in which one religion could be shown to be superior to another. If one takes seriously Schleiermacher's theory of religious knowledge, then there is no truly objective basis from which to compare and grade the different religions of the world. Each religion has its own way of expressing the nature of the divine, based on the distinctive way in which the divine is experienced in that religious community's life. For Troeltsch, this meant that the only adequate philosophical viewpoint for the study of religion was relativism: to acknowledge the unique values of any religion in relation to the cultural possibilities and limitations through which that religion develops. The immediate implication of this position for Troeltsch was that Christianity could make no universal claims for the truth of its revelation and means of redemptive grace. Schleiermacher did not see this implication, but Troeltsch did, and employed it as a new, surer way to interpret the historical meaning of the Christian faith. It was also seen by Karl Barth, who firmly rejected it in favor of what he regarded as the sovereign biblical authority underlying Christianity's unique revelation.

The conclusion that Troeltsch was to reach—that the truth of Christianity was historically relative and therefore subjective —had also been reached by the great Danish thinker, Søren Kierkegaard. In the middle of the nineteenth century, Kierkegaard, independently of Schleiermacher, had constructed an interpretation of the meaning of Christian existence from the point of view of its subjective truth. This interpretation was to have so great an impact on twentieth-century religious thought that it placed Kierkegaard with Schleiermacher among the most influential thinkers of the nineteenth century.

II

The Theology of the Individual: Søren Kierkegaard

The purpose of Søren Kierkegaard's work was directly opposite that of Schleiermacher: Schleiermacher's aim was to show the relevance of religion to culture, Kierkegaard's was to liberate religion from culture. Schleiermacher felt that the cultural leaders of Europe, and particularly of Germany, had ignored religion; Kierkegaard's feeling was that religion, at least in Denmark, was unnecessarily entangled with culture so that nothing identifiably *religious* remained. Though the purposes of these two authors differed, their procedures for achieving their respective aims were identical. Kierkegaard, like Schleiermacher, sought to restate the essence of religion, though Kierkegaard's effort dealt with Christianity alone. He did not share Schleiermacher's interest in providing a general or philosophical theory of religion, although what he did finally say about Christianity was applicable to a general philosophical theory of human existence, including its religious dimension.

Kierkegaard: The Theology of the Individual

Søren Kierkegaard was born in 1813 in Copenhagen, Denmark, and died there in 1855. His was a life whose appearance of ordinariness hid an immensely rich interior. Most scholars are agreed that he lived an intense, unusual, perhaps neurotic emotional existence, and that the urge for his brilliant, varied, and tremendous output of books and essays stemmed from his internal states.[1] Two details of biography should be mentioned here, because they suggest the quality of Kierkegaard's inner life and provide a vivid perspective from which to appreciate crucial aspects of his thought: his belief in the arduousness of Christian existence, and in the sacrifice which God requires of the one who wishes to live by faith.

The first incident has to do with Kierkegaard's father, to whom Kierkegaard dedicated the bulk of his work. Hermann Diem, the German scholar of Kierkegaard, has given an admirable treatment of the impact of the elder Kierkegaard on the younger:

> All that we know about Kierkegaard himself suggests that his father's life, and one event in it particularly, was of extreme significance for him. Once when he was a poor shepherd boy twelve years old, on the moors of Jutland, Kierkegaard's father had cursed God on account of his wretched life. The memory of this event hounded the melancholy man, even when he later achieved respect and prosperity in Copenhagen; it drove him into a form of religious devotion in which only the sternest image of the crucified Lord could afford him comfort. In Søren, the "child of his old age," the father saw with clairvoyant dread his own history about to repeat itself. Then he did what he had to do: he brought his son, so perilously like him, under the same image of the crucified Lord; in the presence of this image he laid his own fate upon the shoulders of his son. When Kierkegaard is informed of this secret in the life of his father, suddenly, as he says, there is forced upon him "a new, infallible principle by which to interpret all phenomena": God's punishment lies upon the family as a curse. Even the most brilliant intellectual gifts must spell doom; only

31

the Christian faith in its strictest form can open up new possibilities for a life weighed down by such a burden. From this moment on in Kierkegaard's life, the entire struggle of and for faith focused on this one point. . . .[2]

The second detail of Kierkegaard's biography concerns his engagement in 1840 to Regine Olsen, the seventeen-year-old daughter of a prominent Copenhagen family. A year later, without explanation, he broke the engagement. Some time later he accounted for his action as a sacrifice which he felt compelled to make in order to pursue his writing, whose declared aim was to communicate to his contemporaries what he referred to as the problem of "becoming a Christian in Christendom." There is every reason to suppose that Kierkegaard entered into his engagement with sincerity and that he never ceased to love Regine. He later admitted that if he really had had that faith which his view of Christian existence demanded, he would never have had to give up Regine. No reason finally proves entirely satisfactory in explaining Kierkegaard's action, but that the loss of Regine weighed heavily on his mind for the balance of his life and helped shape his ideas is evident in his repeated reference to the affair. The "aesthetic" and "ethical" modes of existence about which Kierkegaard spoke were developed in careful reflection upon the meanings of his decision. The sacrifice of Regine was later to be rationalized by the third, "religious" mode of existence, whose model Kierkegaard found in the biblical story of Abraham's sacrifice of Isaac. Of Kierkegaard's broken engagement, Diem writes:

> The way he broke off his engagement without any apparent reason or concern scandalized the respectable citizens of Copenhagen. No one, not even his bride, could be allowed to suspect that he had been wrestling with God over the knowledge of his duty, and this struggle had taken him through hell and brought him to the very edge of insanity.[3]

As Schleiermacher's thought cannot be adequately understood without knowledge of the "cultured despisers" of religion,

Kierkegaard's thought must always stand in relation to that body of cultural ideas which he thought put the Christian religion in bondage. The source of these ideas was the philosophy of Hegel, and particularly the Hegelianism which had captivated intellectuals in Kierkegaard's Denmark.

It was H. L. Martensen, a renowned Danish religious thinker and contemporary of Kierkegaard's, who introduced Hegel's philosophy to Denmark. According to Reidar Thomte, one of Kierkegaard's most astute American interpreters, Martensen's ideal was to achieve a creative synthesis of humanistic culture and the Christian religion, and in Hegel's philosophy he saw the intellectual basis for such a synthesis.[4] Martensen spoke of this synthesis in words that are reminiscent of Schleiermacher:

> There must be a view of the world and of life in which everything that has meaning in existence (*Dasein*)—nature and spirit, nature and history, poetry and art and philosophy, harmoniously unite to form a temple of the spirit in which Christianity is the all-governing and all-explaining center.[5]

We are told by Thomte that when Kierkegaard attacked Hegelianism, he frequently had Martensen's use of Hegel in mind. Kierkegaard was angered at what he thought to be Martensen's inability to recognize the integrity of the expressions of humanistic culture as distinguished from the integrity of Christian religion. Martensen, he thought, did not really synthesize the two into a higher unity; he simply threw them together into a mishmash, without adequate differentiation and therefore without adequate respect for their respective meanings and values. Kierkegaard had a profound respect for Greek culture, Shakespeare, Goethe, and Mozart, but he was not about to allow the genius of Christianity to be confused with cultural humanism.

If Martensen was guilty of confusing Christianity with culture, the fault lay with Hegel's philosophy as much as with Martensen's use of it. Indeed, in the sustained attack on Hegel's philosophy which Kierkegaard launched in the *Concluding*

Unscientific Postscript, his large work of 1846, it is hard to know when he had Martensen in mind and when he had Hegel. Kierkegaard seems to have discerned in Hegel's philosophy a propensity for rationalization, for reducing life to the most convenient intellectual terms at hand, a propensity which surely would have tempted Hegel's followers to ignore altogether the uniqueness of Christianity in their efforts to find the place for everything in a rational system of philosophy. We cannot take one step toward understanding the theology of existence which underlies Kierkegaard's view of Christianity without first knowing those elements of Hegel's philosophy which are in back of the claim that Hegelianism made a perversion of Christianity.

The heart of Hegel's philosophy is the proposition that "the real is the rational." This means that a comprehensive and logically sound system of ideas would reveal the complete structure of reality. Hegel spoke of this union of thought and being, or of reason and reality, as the "Absolute Idea." The aim of his philosophy was to show the historical unfolding of the Absolute Idea in every aspect of existence: nature, art, society, politics, religion, and philosophy. Toward this aim he employed a principle which he considered unique in philosophical reflection: the *dialectic*, or the view that every idea passes into its opposite.[6] The implication of this view is that contradiction does not frustrate or subvert thought, as conventional understandings of logic had held, but rather advances it creatively.

Hegel sought to show the nature of the dialectic by concentrating first on the most basic of all ideas, the idea that something is: *isness*, or the idea of being. He argued that if being is carefully considered independently of any particular being, then the conclusion is inescapable that being-itself is *nothing*. The idea of being logically contains its opposite, the idea of nonbeing, or nothing.

Hegel schematized the relation which these two ideas suggest by speaking of a *thesis* which necessarily generates its *antithesis*. He recognized, however, that if the structure of thought consisted only of a proposition and its antithesis, knowledge would not be possible. He therefore postulated that a third stage of the movement occurs, wherein a *synthesis* takes place of what is simultaneously presented as thesis and antithesis. The synthesis of being and nonbeing is to be found in *becoming*. Only in the vibrancy of existence, only in the coming-to-be and passing away, can something and nothing (being and nonbeing) occur simultaneously. The character of thought, Hegel concluded, is the movement from thesis to antithesis, and thence to a "higher" synthesis which itself becomes a thesis for a new dialectical movement.

Hegel believed that this dialectical movement expressed the true character of the actual world as well as of thought. It is frequently overlooked (though probably not by Kierkegaard), that the motivating force of Hegel's philosophy was his perception of the varied fullness of life, in which nothing exists alone. It was the relational character of existence that fascinated Hegel and drove him, to whatever exaggerations, to state the inner unity of life through a comprehensive system of ideas. Once embarked on the task of giving a philosophical account of the nature of reality, Hegel's assumption that the innermost character of reality is rational and can be expressed by logically formulated ideas gained power, though, as the Danish historian of philosophy, Harold Hoffding, remarks, ". . . the triad (position, negation, higher unity) is only a *schema* into which [Hegel] pressed the empirical content more or less arbitrarily." [7]

Hegel developed the schema itself in three parts: the Logic, which dealt with the purely formal character of the dialectic, in other words, the Absolute Idea as manifested in thought alone, without empirical content; the Philosophy of Nature, which dealt with the application of the dialectic to the physical world, or the Absolute Idea manifested in matter alone; and, finally, the Philosophy of Mind, which aimed to "synthesize" the Logic and Philosophy of Nature, to synthesize thought and matter by dealing with their highest actual exemplification—this was the Absolute Idea as manifested in the life of the human spirit, in the historical development of man's culture.

The Erosion of Faith

Hegel ranked the achievements of the human mind in ascending levels of significance: art, religion, and philosophy. With philosophy, he argued, the human spirit becomes one with the divine spirit; philosophy is the highest manifestation of the Absolute Idea, and with the application of philosophical wisdom to human society, that freedom will be achieved which was man's true aim and the inner aim of reason at every moment of history.

What was arresting in Hegel's philosophy of history was his readiness to argue that the high civilization that he and his European contemporaries enjoyed, and that was adequate witness to the culmination of history in freedom, was the result of the rational rule of law as seen in the modern political state, particularly Hegel's own Prussian state.[8] Hegel did not share the British "positivistic" concept of the state as a useful device agreed upon by people to achieve certain limited ends such as personal security and protection of property; instead, he saw it as the natural manifestation of the rational character of history itself. When he applied the dialectical method to the rise and fall of world civilizations, it gave ample evidence of the progress made in history by the emergence of the state. The great civilizations were three: the Greco-Roman, which expressed the Absolute Idea through art; the medieval-Christian, which expressed the Absolute Idea in a form superior to the Greco-Roman by replacing the sensuousness of art with the "more perfect" reflective, nonsensuous consciousness of religion; and, finally, the modern German civilization, which was a truly perfect expression of the Absolute Idea, because within it came to flower philosophy, the ideal expression of the human spirit.[9] Hegel seems to have thought that the state provides that social and political stability in which philosophical reflection thrives, thereby manifesting the highest cultural expression of a people.

Philosophy, according to Hegel, is a stage higher than religion in the self-manifestation of the Absolute Idea, because it takes religion's truth about the divine and expresses it in "purer" form—*rationally*.[10] Art possesses the truth about the divine *sensuously;* religion possesses the same truth in a "higher," non-sensuous, historical form; but philosophy, which expresses the truth by reason alone, transcends the inherent limitations of history by possessing the truth in its eternal essence. After 2,500 years of continuous philosophical reflection, the quest for a true account of reality had evidently come to an end with Hegel's rational system, a system which had to be regarded finally not as *a* philosophy but as *the* philosophy—as the Absolute Idea expressing itself philosophically.

In evaluating Hegel's system, especially in relation to the Christian religion, Kierkegaard seems to have thought of himself as David before Goliath. The weight and size of the system showed only how terribly vulnerable it was to well-aimed rocks. Kierkegaard argued that Hegel's philosophy had committed one serious mistake, a mistake which simply could not be corrected within the terms of that philosophy: in his effort to bring the whole of reality within the scope of a rational system of philosophy, Hegel had neglected the reality of the philosopher himself, the thinker who cannot be equated with or reduced to the content of his thought. Kierkegaard asked, What is the relation of the philosopher to the system of philosophy? [11] Was the philosopher, as a human being, part of the rational system, too? If this was so, we have reached the ridiculous stage, Kierkegaard concluded, where a grand system of philosophy is conceived not by a real-life philosopher, a spiritual descendant of Socrates, but by a bloodless abstraction; we have reached the stage wherein philosophy is something contemplated not by individuals but by itself.

In taking the philosophy of Hegel as his adversary, Kierkegaard was attempting to affirm the unique and irreducible reality of individual human existence. Hegel's philosophy had raised for Kierkegaard the life-or-death matter of the individual versus the system, the concrete versus the abstract, passion versus reason, the lonely, private self versus the glamorous heroes of history—the Alexanders, Caesars, and Napoleons of Hegel's philosophy of history. Speaking of the philosophers of his own day who, in their "Hegelian" fascination with the movement of history up to their own age, seemed to have forgotten the eternal value of the individual, Kierkegaard said:

> Each age has its own characteristic depravity. Ours is perhaps not pleasure and indulgence or sensuality, but rather a dissolute pantheistic contempt for the individual man. In the midst of all our exultation over the achievements of the age and the nineteenth century, there sounds a note of poorly concealed contempt for the individual man; in the midst of the self-importance of the contemporary generation there is revealed a sense of despair over being human. Everything must attach itself so as to be a part of some movement; men are determined to lose themselves in the totality of things, in world-history, fascinated and deceived by a magic witchery; no one wants to be an individual human being.[12]

The Hegelian philosopher was blinded from seeing that he was first a man, first an individual, and second a thinking individual; moreover, he could not legitimately be a thinker without constantly taking his individuality into account. Speaking of the Hegelian philosopher, Kierkegaard wrote: "If the logical thinker is at the same time human enough not to forget that he is an existing individual, even if he completes the system, all the fantasticalness and charlatanry will gradually disappear." [13] The model of philosophical thinking, Kierkegaard claimed, has always been Socrates; and Socrates was constantly aware of the relation between philosophy and life, that inner connection between one's thought and his individual self. To forget this relation on the fantastic assumption that life is somehow nothing but pure, logical thought, is not only to do an injustice to the worth of individual humanity but to wrong philosophy itself by separating it from the concrete particularities of real existence.

Kierkegaard's conflict with Hegel's philosophy came to focus over the Christian religion. Hegel had, in his fashion, defended the truth of Christianity.[14] He claimed that Christianity was not only religiously true but truer than all previous religions because

Christianity had come into being as a synthesis of all previous religious truth, expressing in its uniqueness the truth about God himself. Moreover, the truth of Christianity was incontrovertible, since it was established objectively by the historical dialectic of reason. For was not Jesus Christ, as the Evangelist John proclaimed, the divine reason itself made flesh? Christianity was absolutely true because it superseded all other religions, and it was objectively true because it was shown to be true by reason. Hence, Christianity was the absolute or final revelation of God. At least, so Hegel thought.

Kierkegaard was scornful of the claim that one could establish the truth of Christianity through reason. His argument was of a piece with what he had said of the Hegelian system, namely, that what was ignored was the individual. Christianity speaks essentially of sin, judgment, grace, and forgiveness, and these are available not to the understanding of impersonal, objective reason but rather to the individual in the inward depths of his personality. If one seeks to understand Christianity and forgets the individual, one confuses Christianity with something it is not.

The truth of Christianity, Kierkegaard claimed, is not an objective truth which can be grasped by the mind, independent of the thinker-as-person. Christianity's truth is subjective.[15] It is vouchsafed only to him who has personally committed himself to Christianity and whose understanding of Christianity comes as reflection upon that commitment. What subjective truth means in relation to Christianity is that the individual, by the passion of his commitment, does not *discover* Christianity to be true, he *makes* it true. No other type of truth mattered for Kierkegaard, nor was thought really possible. The truth of Christianity is subjective because it holds only for the believer's total subjectivity: passion, decision, seriousness, and personal reflection. The truth of Christianity was, in a word, *faith*.

At a time that he thought it was most necessary because it had been forgotten, Kierkegaard reintroduced the great insight of Saint Paul: faith is not something one is born with, nor something one inherits from others, it is a deeply personal quality of existence in which one lies nakedly open before God. In resting his case for the truth of Christianity on Paul's doctrine of the personal character of faith, Kierkegaard was arguing that Christianity was no other than a claim that in Christ God has judged each individual man to be sinful and has simultaneously offered the grace of forgiveness. This is a claim that cannot be received except personally; that is, by each person as an individual, *in faith*, alone—without the securities otherwise provided him in family, nation, culture, and education, and without the securities of the established practices of religion and morality.

The great error concerning Christianity which the Hegelian philosophy of culture had fostered was the belief that one's relation to Christianity could be established independent of his personal decision. One should not suppose that simply because he was born a Christian, or baptized one, or because he was counted a respectable member of a Christian church, that he could therefore assume he was a Christian. Nothing could be further from the truth. Kierkegaard was antagonistic toward his own Danish State Lutheran Church and toward all established Christianity because of the tendency of organized religion to ignore the voluntaristic basis of religion in favor of a socio-cultural basis—to make of religion a matter not of passionate avowal but of lineage and social responsibility. When Kierkegaard spoke of how hard it was to be a Christian in Christendom, where everyone claims to be a Christian, he was expressing his disgust for that practice of the church which robs the Christian of his individuality and makes it impossible for him to become a Christian.[16]

If the truth of Christianity was the quality of one's relation to it, and not any objective truth about it, it followed for Kierkegaard that Christianity could not be verified by arguments based on the inerrancy of scripture, nor by the authenticity of the witness of Christ's disciples. Arguments such as these missed the fundamental point about Christianity, which was to inspire what Saint Paul called the "new life." Objective truth has nothing to do with Christianity, for Chris-

tianity is a matter of choosing to become Christian. So convinced was Kierkegaard of the value of personal commitment
in Christianity over any question of objective content, that he
was prepared to assert:

> If one who lives in the midst of Christianity goes up to the
> house of God, the house of the true God, with the true con-
> ception of God in his knowledge, and prays, but prays in a
> false spirit; and one who lives in an idolatrous community prays
> with the entire passion of the infinite, although his eyes rest
> upon the image of an idol: where is there most truth? The one
> prays in truth to God though he worships an idol; the other
> prays falsely to the true God, and hence worships in fact an
> idol.[17]

> . . . objective truth is a question of the object: whether one is
> related to something true or not; subjective truth is a question
> of the subject's relationship, whether the relationship is in the
> truth, even if what one is related to is not the truth.[18]

Where truth is subjective, a question of passion or the "how"
in opposition to a passionless "what," the object-content of
truth is secondary. Thus an ignorant man may worship an idol
in utter sincerity and be closer to the truth than one who, in
having before him the true God, worships halfheartedly. Truth,
for Kierkegaard, is subjectivity; and Christian truth is a matter
of *becoming* Christian, not of *being* Christian; thus Christianity
must be constantly repossessed, reaffirmed in passion if it is to
remain true for the individual.

The truth of Christianity is personal, what we would call
today (and as a result of Kierkegaard's writings) *existential.*
In the light of the existential meaning of truth, it followed for
Kierkegaard that he who chooses to reject Christianity, recognizing in it a burden too heavy to bear, establishes a truer relationship to the claim of the Christian revelation about God's
forgiveness of sins in Jesus Christ than he who assumes the
correctness of his relationship to Christianity by virtue of his

"parentage" or other such "objective" means. That person is unmindful of the burden which Christianity imposes upon its believers.

One of the implications of Kierkegaard's understanding of Christianity is that there cannot be, in the strict sense, a rational or "systematic" statement of Christianity's essential meaning. Hence, there cannot be a philosophy of Christianity. Christianity is a matter not of thinking but of doing—a matter not of the mind but of the will. Christianity means *existing*, and, as Kierkegaard said, where "a logical system is possible . . . an existential system is impossible." [19]

In considering Kierkegaard's unswerving rejection of a rational, objective knowledge of Christianity, it would be wrong to suppose that Kierkegaard meant that one becomes a Christian at the cost of all knowledge. The knowledge of Christianity is always the knowledge of *oneself becoming a Christian.* Therein is the subjective knowledge of Christianity, a knowledge of what it means to become Christian. [20]

Christianity directs its claim, Kierkegaard said, to the heart, not the head: the central teaching of Christianity forever defies reason because it claims that God became man! This is the claim of the Christian revelation; it is the absolute paradox which the Christian religion puts before man. As one commentator put it, "This doctrine [the Christian doctrine of the Incarnation] by its very nature raises the passion of faith to its highest pitch, because to the human understanding it is absurd and repels the believer." [21]

The role of passion in Kierkegaard's view of Christianity suggests a concept of man which is basically at odds with the concept of man in Hegel's philosophy. To Kierkegaard, the essence of man is his freedom, which consists of what he calls "striving." With striving, the individual creates and re-creates himself; with striving, one renews his worth as an individual human being through the personal creativeness of decision, passion, and seriousness. But by its nature, striving is continuous, always unfinished.

The hallmark of Hegel's philosophical system, on the other hand, is precisely the opposite of striving; it is totality and completeness. Hegelianism, in its assumption of universal truth, was positing in its proponents the wisdom of divine vantage point. Christianity's obligation for the individual, Kierkegaard said, was more modest: in place of universal truth it put striving-for-the-truth; not the possession of truth, which belongs to God, but the pursuit of truth. This is well expressed in a passage from Gottfried Lessing, the eighteenth-century German critic and dramatist, which Kierkegaard quotes with enthusiasm: "If God held all truth concealed in his right hand, and in his left hand the persistent striving for the truth, and while warning me against error, should say, Choose! I should humbly bow before his left hand, and say: 'Father, give thy gift; the pure truth is for thee alone.' " [22]

By denying striving, Hegelianism had no philosophy of man but only of anti-man. Kierkegaard said that Hegelianism was an immoral philosophy, because, in seducing man into thinking he was part of the necessary movement of reason in history, it prevented him from making those decisions that contribute to the quality of his own life. ". . . We owe to Hegel," Kierkegaard said, "the completion of the System, the Absolute System—without the inclusion of an Ethics." [23] In place of the real life of decision and passion, the Hegelian philosopher promoted the empty life of abstract reason; the life not of living in history through personal decision but of viewing history from the detached perspective of philosophical contemplation.

For Kierkegaard there is no continuity between will and reason. Reason, in fact, operates to postpone indefinitely any action of the will. Kierkegaard said: "Only when reflection comes to a halt can a beginning be made, and reflection can be halted only by something else, and this something else is something quite different from the logical, being a resolution of the will." [24] According to Kierkegaard, no decision is made rationally; it is made by an act of will which puts an end, an "arbitrary" end, we should say, to the reflective process. Unless such an end is reached and existence begun, life loses its quality in endless abstractions of the mind.

In the hero of the book *Notes from Underground*, Dostoevsky gives us a memorable portrait of an individual whose life is actually emptied of meaning by a sacrifice of will to the security of endless reflection on the meaning of life. Dostoevsky agrees with Kierkegaard that there is no continuity between thought and decision, only discontinuity. When a person decides to put his whole life on the path of striving and existence, he does so by suspending for one precious moment the collective moral, social, political, and religious wisdom of his day. Every such choice represents a leap from the known securities of his life into the insecurities of the unknown. But it is only by such leaps that man can achieve worth as an individual and his life take on quality of meaning.

Kierkegaard's understanding of Christianity as striving or the act of *becoming* Christian reflects his preoccupation with the question of human existence generally. He analyzed existence in what he called three modes or "life-styles": the aesthetic, the ethical, and the religious. These are life-styles because they involve fundamentally different approaches to the meaning of life. Kierkegaard postulated a graded hierarchy, with these three modes ranked according to the contribution they make to man's individuality. By this test, he ranked the religious mode highest, because it regards individuality more highly than do the aesthetic and the ethical modes. The modes of existence were regarded by Kierkegaard both as distinct stages one can ascend, leaving behind one for the higher, and as three "moments" coexisting in a single human life, which could be alternated.

Kierkegaard claimed for himself none of the styles; he declined to admit he was a religious man, and strenuously denied being a Christian. Christianity, he said, was too high an ideal, and therefore too hard a burden for him to bear.[25] His works were written, he alleged, to communicate the essence of the different modes of existence, leaving it to others to make up their minds for themselves. Accordingly, each of his works can be located in one or another of the modes, and since they did not reflect Kierkegaard's own inclinations, they were published for the most part under pseudonyms. Another reason for his use of pseudonyms was his wish that, if his effort to convey the meaning of Christian existence proved of value to the reader, the reader should not be distracted from the task of becoming Christian to preoccupation with the author and the author's ideas. Kierkegaard, like Socrates, wanted no disciples; and, like Socrates, he claimed that the truth was not his to give, therefore no praise was due him for helping to convert men from ignorance to truth.[26]

Kierkegaard's aesthetic style of life is based on feeling; by feeling Kierkegaard meant the sensuous, not Schleiermacher's passive experience of the depths of life, those experienceable "unitics" of friendship, kindness, beauty, and love. The aesthetic style of life consists of immediacy, change, pleasure, and "carelessness" or the feeling of abandon. The man who pursues life aesthetically, Kierkegaard argued, fears permanence, for it dulls his pleasure. Therefore, he avoids commitments of any kind, and permits no relationship longer than a moment. The aesthetic attitude toward women is clearly expressed by these words in a dramatic episode in *Stages on Life's Way:*

> Just as one man finds his amusement in balancing a cane upon his nose, in swinging a glass of water in a circle without its contents flying out, or in dancing among eggs, and other similar exercises which are as entertaining as they are profitable— so and not otherwise has the lover in commerce with his lady the most incomparable amusement and the most interesting study.[27]

Don Giovanni, the hero of Mozart's opera, was regarded by Kierkegaard as the aesthetic hero *par excellence*. Don Giovanni derived pleasure not from loving a particular woman but from any and every woman. His source of pleasure was not the woman, but *different* women. Don Giovanni is the aesthetic hero, the consummate sensualist, because he established an eternal relationship to variation, affirming change for its own sake. Kierkegaard argued that Mozart brilliantly expressed the sensualism of Don Giovanni through music, for music is a wordless medium which gives rise to no verbal thought, and thereby to no moral discrimination. Void of reflection of any kind, music exists at the level of pure, sensuous immediacy. Kierkegaard stated:

> The genius of sensuality is the absolute subject of music. The sensual genius is absolutely lyrical and it comes to expression in music in all its lyrical impatience. It is, namely, spiritually determined, and therefore it is force, life, movement, constant unrest, perpetual succession. . . .[28]

Sensualists, Kierkegaard claimed, suffer from boredom; it is from boredom that they seek change, spurning any permanent attachment. The sensualist lives the life of frivolity. He is incapable of making a choice, for any such choice would commit him to a course of action and therefore to a relationship of substance—and if there is anything the sensualist fears it is attachment. Hence, the sensualist is forever contemplating the great "either-ors," the moral alternatives which are put before each human being in the course of his life. Aimlessly, without hope and direction, he sifts the alternatives, secure in the knowledge that he will go no deeper than what strikes his most immediate feelings.

Kierkegaard argued further that the aimless energy of the sensualist suggests ultimately that his aesthetic mode of being is born of despair. In his unwillingness to make decisions, and thus to create for himself a course of living, he is subject to whatever alluring object comes before him. He is the seducer who is himself seduced: the one who has no hope for life because he is hopelessly at the mercy of his whims. By losing the power of decision, the sensualist has lost the power of self-determination, and rapidly becomes what the objects of his sensuousness make of him. He is the hollow man, the man who is always the observer of life (very much like Hegel's "world-historical" or cultural philosopher), but never the participant in it.

According to Kierkegaard, the aesthetic despair induced by a life of sensuousness is overcome by choice alone. But there is no smooth transition from aesthetic indecision to ethical decision; it requires a leap. Choice is, by its very nature, discontinuous with all that goes before in the life of the individual, for what is really chosen, finally, is not "this" or "that" but the self. The individual in his choice determines himself—and this is what makes his choice essentially ethical—not *what* he chooses.

The ethical individual is no longer at the mercy of the external world; he is self-creative and therefore able to shape the world through his decisions. For Kierkegaard the crucial difference between the two modes of existence was that the aesthetic individual loses himself through his indecision and falls victim unwittingly to external powers, whereas the ethical man attains selfhood through decision, by exercising power over the external.

The mark of the ethical mode is responsibility and duty. The prototypical ethical man possesses a sense of responsibility related to the values of continuity and stability in society: marriage, family, friendship, work, and civil responsibility. The ethical individual can be contrasted to the aesthetic in viewing marriage, for example, as a decision requiring the utmost seriousness, a question which each individual has the duty to answer for himself. The aesthetic man avoids even entertaining the idea of marriage. The ethical order of life consists of sobriety, maturity, and responsibility. The ethical individual must sacrifice the immediate delights of the senses, but he is willing to do so in order to gain the "higher" value of selfhood.

As contrasted to ethical existence, the unwillingness of the aesthetic individual to accept the "either-or" as a real dimension of his personal existence meant for Kierkegaard that he was not immoral but rather amoral. The aesthetic man is neither good nor evil; by virtue of his indecision, he is in danger of losing his selfhood and becoming, humanly speaking, "nothing," a condition far worse than moral evil. In distinguishing between the two modes of existence, Kierkegaard seemed to be saying that a man remains in the aesthetic mode because he fears the struggle in being a self, for it is easier to yield to the powerful allure of the senses than it is to oppose the senses through the agony of reflective decision. A man transcends the aesthetic mode only when he begins to regard selfhood as a value so precious as to be supremely worthy of the struggle.

The aesthetic mode of existence is based on feeling and consists of enjoyment; the ethical is based on decision and consists of struggle; but the religious mode, which Kierkegaard considered the "highest," is based on faith and consists of suffering. Kierkegaard provided a brilliant illustration of religious faith in his analysis of the biblical story of Abraham's sacrifice of his son, Isaac.[29]

God commands Abraham to sacrifice Isaac as a proof of faith. Poignancy is given to Abraham's predicament because Isaac is Abraham's only son, the son which his wife Sarah bore him in her old age, long after they had both abandoned hope of children. Isaac is the child they had dedicated to God, for they regarded his birth a miracle; now God has commanded Abraham to slay him. Obedience to this command would in fact mean disobedience to the moral law which holds for all and is expressed by the injunction "that a father shall love his son more dearly than himself," not to mention the injunction against murder. In issuing his command to sacrifice Isaac, Kierkegaard wrote, God was compelling Abraham to commit an immoral act. One must consider, too, the author continued, that the birth of Isaac occurred in relation to God's promise, which for many years seemed so vain but which was now on the verge of fulfillment—that from Abraham's seed all the nations of the world would be blessed. In demanding the life of Isaac was God now going back on his word? We are told in the Bible, Kierkegaard said, that Abraham could not answer this question.

Abraham's love for Isaac was unbounded, and he knew the sacred power of the moral law; but he also knew that God had spoken to him alone. God, who authored the law and gave him the precious gift of a son, had spoken to him. Caught between the feeling of a father and the moral injunction against murder, and the religious authority of a command placed upon him as an individual person by God, Abraham's experience, Kierkegaard tells us, was one of fear and trembling. Obeying God and disobeying his holy law, *or* obeying the law and denying the sacred will of God—contemplating the alternatives, Abraham was filled with fear and trembling. The author of the biblical story informs us that Abraham chose to obey God and prepared to offer Isaac as a sacrifice required of him by God.

According to Kierkegaard, Abraham's decision shows the true character of faith and discloses the inner meaning of religion. He calls Abraham "the knight of faith." Abraham's faith has two parts: There is first the act of resignation whereby Abraham carries out the will of God. Here Abraham experiences great suffering, for he knows that in each moment of his obedience to God he is disobeying the law, and thereby violating the moral sensibility of all men, and most particularly of himself. This is the act of resignation, Kierkegaard says, which is indispensable to faith but is not faith itself. Faith or belief is in a second act.

Abraham not only resigns himself to the divine will; he also believes that somehow, some way, by the miraculous power of God, God will not break his promise. Abraham has a faith that he who takes Isaac will also give him back. Abraham believes that what is not humanly possible is possible for God. He believes in that which, from the point of view of human experience, is absurd. Dead men are not restored to life—at least not by human beings! Abraham's faith is founded on the absurd, on the abandonment of the securities of human reckoning and expectation, and on the entrusting of oneself completely to God. The scriptural reader is told that when God saw the strength of Abraham's faith he was pleased and withdrew his command from Abraham, thus sparing Isaac. Thus Kierkegaard observed, "By faith Abraham did not renounce his claim upon Isaac, but by faith he got Isaac."

Kierkegaard argued that the story of Abraham and Isaac reveals the meaning of the "teleological suspension of the ethical," wherein something higher than the ethical is disclosed, and this is the religious. The religious does not abrogate the ethical, it *suspends* it for the purpose of showing that the ethical is itself founded on the religious. The story of Abraham's sacrifice of Isaac shows that the law governing murder, and a father's duty toward his son, continue to hold; but a higher obligation intrudes, an obligation which sets aside for one extraordinary moment the ethical law. In that moment, Kierkegaard was saying, God is shown to be higher than morality, the lawgiver higher than the law. In fear and trembling, Abraham perceived the meaning of this moment and made the leap of faith. He not only obeyed God's command, he also took the step indispensable to faith: he was willing to trust that Isaac would be given back, that God would fulfill his promise to make of Abraham's seed a universal blessing. It is the absurdity of the trust that God can restore Isaac after he is slain that makes Abraham, in Kierkegaard's eyes, the "knight of faith." Faith meant for Abraham the absurd, it meant cutting oneself off from the moral and rational securities of ordinary human living. Thomte makes the same point when, in interpreting Kierkegaard's meaning, he writes:

> Abraham's relationship to God was of a private nature. It was a relationship which dispensed with such universal intermediaries as community, state, humanity, and tradition. Because of his absolute relationship to God, the ethical consciousness with its obligation to the universal requirements as expressed in the social and institutional life of man was suspended in favor of a *religious consciousness*.[30]

"Faith begins precisely where thinking leaves off," Kierkegaard said.[31] By "thinking" he meant the moral-rational conscience, as well as that rationality which characterizes human beings and their relationships in their normal efforts to exert an influence over the physical world. Kierkegaard was saying that faith consists of the act whereby the believer puts himself nakedly before God, without human supports, utterly alone, exactly as Abraham was alone in his act of faith, unable to whisper even to Sarah that in slaying Isaac to fulfill the divine will, he believed God himself would restore Isaac to life.

Faith, for Kierkegaard, is an act that man can commit only as the "lonely individual." In that respect, religion, demanding as it does the act of faith, is a mode of existence higher than ethics, to which it is otherwise closely related, and certainly higher than aesthetics, which suppresses individuality. In recognizing that through the meanings of faith and the absurd religion puts the highest value on the individual, we are at the gate to Kierkegaard's understanding of the meaning of the Christian religion.

Kierkegaard understood Christianity in its essence to be a supreme affirmation of the value of human individuality. Christianity and individuality were inseparable in his mind. He did not, however, think that to become an individual one first had to become Christian, though the opposite was true: being Christian meant *becoming* Christian. That was in Kierkegaard's mind identifiable by the meaning of individuality alone.

The claim of Christianity, according to Kierkegaard, is that one's eternal happiness is decided by virtue of the fact that at a certain moment in time God became man; the eternal became temporal! The proper response to this claim must be the decision either to accept it or reject it; which means, existentially speaking, to live as if it were true or to live as if it were false. Improper responses to the claim consist of aimless philosophical or speculative reflections on whether or not God could become man, or to what degree and in what sense God became man; or of vain historical investigations of the question whether or not God *actually* became man in the person of Jesus Christ— investigations which, as we said earlier, focus on the authenticity of the scriptural record, the veracity of the disciples, and so on.

The Erosion of Faith

As Kierkegaard saw it, the claim of Christianity—that one's eternal happiness is based on God's becoming man—is plainly contradictory to human reason; it is "the paradox," that which, with respect to reason at least, is unacceptable, just as unacceptable as God's command to Abraham. In light of this it is not only useless to engage in philosophical and historical proofs or disproofs of the Christian revelation, it is misguided. For the assumption in such efforts is that the so-called objective truth of Christianity must first be decided before the question of one's personal relation to Christianity is answered. Kierkegaard's indictment against the church Christianity of his day was that the objective question was being raised and debated precisely in order to avoid the infinitely more arduous subjective or personal question.

Kierkegaard argued that two claims fundamental to the meaning of human existence are embedded in Christianity's assertion that God became man in the person of Jesus Christ. The first claim is that man is a sinner; the second, that his sins have been forgiven in the atoning death of Christ. Both these claims are no less objectionable to man, no less an offense to his intelligence and conscience than the paradox of the God-man. Most so-called Christians are willing to believe that they are sinful, but they understand this to be a human condition into which they are born and which is therefore inescapable. They avoid individual responsibility by the comforting thought that all are sinful. But the revelation of the God-man, Kierkegaard said, asserts that all men exist in sin because each sins and continues to sin. The emphasis falls on the individual who is in sin; thus the God-man cannot but be repulsive to men who would spurn disclosure of their individual selves. And no less repulsive is the thought that the forgiveness Christ brings is for the human race *only because it is for each man, individually.*

Men refuse to acknowledge the real meaning of sin because they exist under the illusion that sin is a case of "this" or "that" act, acts of moral impropriety which could be controlled by a greater willingness to engage in correct behavior. But what is the real meaning of sin? Kierkegaard's answer is that sin is the "yawning abyss" between God and man, showing each man's abject refusal to obey the will of God. This abyss cannot be closed by man; it could only be closed by God, who, doing so in Jesus Christ, revealed the existence of the abyss. Graciously, out of an infinite concern for his creatures, God became man, that in the person of Jesus Christ, the God-man, the miraculous forgiveness might be given and man rescued from the abyss of his own making.

According to Kierkegaard, he who fails to crucify his reason on "the paradox" which is Jesus Christ, is the very same one who persists to believe that the sin and forgiveness of which the scriptures speak have nothing to do with him *personally*. But he who so crucifies his reason, who thereby puts himself into continual conflict with the world, represented by the civilizing values of learning, patriotism, morality, and church religion, and by the cultural values of philosophy, art, and science—this man, who is now alone, who is now the "lonely individual" before God, this man can truly understand that the scriptures speak to him of sin and forgiveness, and that Jesus Christ has to do with him personally. In that act of resigning himself from the world, in that act which Abraham knew must be repeated every moment lest the temptation of the world's security prove too much, one is naked before God—that condition wherein God alone can grant the raiments of faith, the gift of trust in which the God-man can be received without offense. To Kierkegaard, only faith ultimately can receive the word of sin and forgiveness contained in the paradox, Jesus Christ; and faith is the gift of God, of which the precondition is that "infinite resignation" which the story of Abraham teaches.

What does it mean to have Christian faith? What does Christian existence mean? Kierkegaard's answer was that in his struggle to become Christian, the individual becomes a contemporary of Christ. History no longer stands between the individual and Christ, the disciples are in no closer relation to Christ than he, for the issue is not, was Jesus the Christ? but rather, to become like Christ. Christian existence is what is meant by "contemporaneity with Christ." It consists of what comprised the life of Christ: suffering, or that quality of love which inevitably leads to conflict with the world. "God's love is expressed in the cross of Christ which is love's collision with the world." Though Christian existence takes place in the world, it is not monastic withdrawal from the world. Yet Christian existence is not *of* the world, it is not equatable with the forms of moral and religious existence as they appear socially or publicly. On the contrary, those are called into question by Christian existence. Kierkegaard spoke of people who follow those forms as "the crowd" from which the individual must extricate himself in order to become "the individual" and which he must in turn denounce. Christian existence, or contemporaneity with Christ, is possible through "inwardness" or subjectivity, and this means for Kierkegaard the constant concern of the individual for his individual self, that constant vigilance against the danger of confusing what Christ says with what the world says, and thus failing to see that Christ has to do with him alone. "Inwardness" is, in a word, *becoming* Christian.

Kierkegaard's notion of Christian existence is founded on the struggle to become Christian in opposition to the objective determination of Christian truth and meaning. This being the case, one can very well understand that Kierkegaard was indifferent to the efforts to ascertain from the Gospel accounts an accurate record of the person of Jesus. The basis of Kierkegaard's notion of faith, and hence of Christian existence, is not *who* Jesus Christ was but *that* he was—the basis is the absurd claim that God became an individual man. This claim alone makes possible the paradox, the "offense" to man's understanding that guarantees the meaning of faith as the individual naked before God. Any concern for the biography of Jesus, for so-called Gospel history, would dilute the power of faith by making "the paradox" less paradoxical. This is what Kierkegaard meant when, in relation to the object of Christian faith, he said, with calculated exaggeration:

If the contemporary generation had left to posterity nothing more than the words, "We have had faith that in such-and-such a year God appeared in the humble form of a servant, lived and taught among us, and then died," it would be more than enough.[32]

Both Schleiermacher and Kierkegaard engaged in analyses of religion that produced normative definitions of religion, but those definitions were substantially different. Schleiermacher sought to show the relevance of religious meaning to the intellectual climate of the Germany of his day. To do so, he made great use of metaphysical philosophy and its capacity for providing general concepts for the interpretation of all experience, including the experience of religion. Through the metaphysics of Plato, Spinoza, and others, supplemented by his own brilliant analysis of the Christian religion, Schleiermacher produced a persuasive account, though not acceptable to all, of the relation of religion to morality, art, philosophy, and science.

Kierkegaard's task, however, was to extricate religion from culture. At the close of the eighteenth century, Schleiermacher was arguing that the unique genius of religion was overlooked because of failure to recognize its meaning for culture. Forty years later, in Copenhagen, and largely as the result of the spread of German "cultural" Christianity to other Protestant countries, Søren Kierkegaard undertook to rescue the unique genius of the Christian religion—to rescue it, in particular, from what he saw as the confusion and error created by theories of religion like those of Hegel and Schleiermacher.

Kierkegaard's rejection of Hegel's philosophy was at heart a rejection of metaphysical philosophy as relevant to the understanding of religion. The aim of metaphysical philosophy is to provide a comprehensive understanding of reality through general concepts applicable to all experience, including religious experience. For Kierkegaard, however, religion was unlike other experiences, or at least should be so regarded. The moment one began to think of being a Christian as an occupation, such as that of a teacher, one ceased to be a Christian. This was precisely what was happening to Christianity in Denmark in Kierkegaard's day: Christianity was identified with Christendom and the state church, and people no longer worried about whether they were Christians because their birth, parentage, and nationality reinforced their sense of identity in this respect. But he who seeks to become Christian, according to Kierkegaard, soon discovers the utter uniqueness of Christian existence and its absolute discontinuity with all other forms of existence. For this individual, intellectual efforts to compare Christianity with other things, to seek some sort of scheme in which it can be shown to be like this but not like that, would be to avoid the practical struggle of becoming Christian. Christianity, for Kierkegaard, was not thinking, and therefore it was not philosophy. Christianity was "becoming" Christian, it was a form of existing, day by day, each moment. Everything in Christianity, as Kierkegaard saw it, was intended to reinforce this "existential" meaning.

The difference in theological outlook between Schleiermacher and Kierkegaard should not obscure, however, an important point of similarity. Schleiermacher was no less concerned to distinguish religion from intellectual activity than was Kierkegaard. For him, too, the genius of Christianity, as of religion generally, lay not in the dogmas or preached ideas of the church and her theologians, but in "existence," in the vividness and immediacy of experience. Kierkegaard himself regarded Schleiermacher's view of religion as an authentic and inescapable "moment" in the religious development of an individual. But Kierkegaard held that that general religious "feeling" which all Christians share is a secondary stage which is put aside when that warm feeling of religion of which Schleiermacher spoke is shattered by the awareness of one's sin—the "yawning abyss" which separates man and God. The genius of Christianity is found in the declaration of sin and the forgiveness of sin by the miracle of the God-man, not, as Schleiermacher held, by participating in a general religious consciousness with other religions.

Schleiermacher's theory of religion demands that sin be regarded as an arrestment of man's spiritual development, which can be overcome by occasions of inspiration and enlightenment. Thus he understood the role of Christ in Christianity as the one who inspires man, who sets him going again toward a greater or more sensitive spiritual awareness. To compare Schleiermacher with Kierkegaard on the meanings of sin and Christ is to understand why the former should be considered the father of modern "liberal" theology, whereas the latter should be identified as one of the sources, if not *the* source, of the "neo-conservative" theology which has determined the course of twentieth-century Protestant thought.

For Kierkegaard, sin is not arrestment of man's spiritual development; rather, it signals man's utter incapacity to obey God, and is the basis of what Kierkegaard called "the infinite qualitative difference between God and man." Sin means the opposite of Schleiermacher's theology of divine immanence, it means the absolute "otherness" of God. For Kierkegaard the meaning of "Christ" is not that of an inspiration for man; sin has destroyed any such possibility. Christ represents the forgiveness of sins, the act of God for man languishing in sin. Redemption, for Kierkegaard, is entirely the work of God, who took pity on man and graciously interceded in his behalf.

In the stress on the helplessness of sinful man before God and the sheer mercy of God's act in Christ, one perceives in Kierkegaard a resurgence of Luther's emphasis on the same questions. The "realism" about the sinfulness of the human condition rooted in Saint Paul, moved Luther to reject the rationalism and morally optimistic view of human nature, which had been developed by Roman Catholic scholastic thinkers influenced by Greek philosophical ideas about the rationality of man. Similarly, Kierkegaard revived Luther's "biblical realism" to strike out against the rationalism and morally optimistic view of man that began in German philosophy in the late seventeenth century and came to a head in the idealistic philosophy of Hegel.

Kierkegaard has had an enormous influence on twentieth-century thought in general, but most particularly on philosophy and theology. He is commonly regarded as one of the principal sources for the philosophy of existentialism. Contemporary existential thinkers such as Jean-Paul Sartre, Martin Heidegger, and Karl Jaspers all acknowledge a great debt to his thought. Kierkegaard's notion of the uniqueness of human existence, consisting of individual decision and not reducible to the categories of reflection, was generalized by these thinkers and others into a distinct theory of reality.

So great has been the influence of Kierkegaard on modern religious thought that no theologian in the twentieth century could have done his work in ignorance of Kierkegaard's ideas. Certainly this holds true of all the thinkers we treat in this study. In the case of Karl Barth, Kierkegaard became the figure upon whom Barth was able to formulate his own theological position against Schleiermacher and the notion of the continuity between the Christian revelation and man's culture. Tillich, by contrast, sought a way to synthesize the insights and theological methods of Kierkegaard and Schleiermacher in a unique interpretation of the religious experience of the twentieth century. Jacques Maritain attempted a comparable synthesis, drawing his insight not from Schleiermacher but from the intellectual traditions of Thomistic philosophy, on the one hand, and Kierkegaard's existentialism on the other. Nicolas Berdyaev and Martin Buber are two major modern religious thinkers who have been influenced by the sort of existential theology represented by Kierkegaard; in the case of Buber, this is quite explicit. Although each thinker in his own way chooses to interpret the wider meaning of faith along the lines followed by Schleiermacher, Tillich, and Maritain—as an affirmation which can only be expressed through the symbols that man's culture provides —they all accept the basic Kierkegaardian insight that faith is a matter of "existing."

III

The Theology
of the Word:
Karl Barth

Karl Barth is perhaps the most important figure in the transition of religious thought from the nineteenth to the first half of the twentieth century. Knowledge of his thought is essential to understanding the impact of secularization at mid-century.

In his early writings Barth revealed a scheme of thought which reflected as no other the quality of man's experience in the twentieth century. Barth's ideas expressed a vitally new self-understanding for Western man generally, but particularly for the confessed Christian. These ideas have proven formative in Protestant thought, and they have an increasing influence on Roman Catholic thought.[1] Thus it must be in words as generous as these by John Godsey, the American theologian, that we find adequate expression of the magnitude and quality of Barth's accomplishment:

> When the curtain is rung down on the twentieth century and the annals of its church history are complete, there will surely

be one name that will tower above all others in the field of theology—that of Karl Barth. In him a Church Father has walked among us, a theologian of such creative genius, prodigious productivity, and pervasive influence that his name is already being associated with that elite group of Christian thinkers that includes Athanasius, Augustine, Anselm, Aquinas, and Calvin.[2]

In the first chapter we saw that the theology of Schleiermacher was the most brilliant expression of a type of thinking which had shaped definitively Protestant religious thought in the nineteenth century. This was *anthropocentric* theology, which centered in the view that the road to the knowledge of God has as its starting-point the whole of man's spiritual or creative life, consisting of his intellectual, moral, aesthetic, and religious responses. Thinkers who came after Schleiermacher and were influenced by his writings, such as Albrecht Ritschl, Ernst Troeltsch, and Adolph Harnack, believed that the meaning of God could be found in the various aspects of man's subjectivity. They adopted from Schleiermacher the view that the realm of the infinite and the realm of the finite are united in the human soul; that man expresses his experience of God through the richness of his own culture—in his moral idealism, in the heights and depths of his philosophical envisagements, in his artistic creativeness, as well as in the purity and intensity of his pious devotions.

In his student days, Karl Barth was taught by theologians who were intellectual descendants of the great nineteenth-century thinkers, and for a time he espoused the liberal view that there was a fundamental continuity between the divine and the human. At the age of twenty-five, in 1911, he completed the regular course of theological study in Germany, and returned to his native Switzerland to take a parish of the Reformed (Calvinist) Church at Safenwil, a small mountain village. It was to be the turning-point in the development of his thought.

In the ten years he spent as a pastor in Safenwil, Barth was obliged to preach the Gospel each Sunday, and these questions were constantly before him: What should one preach? What is the Gospel, or the Word of God? How is the Word of God different from man's word? Believing he had to deal with these questions before he could claim a right to preach with the authority of the Gospel, Barth began to reread and study afresh the scriptures, entering seriously for the first time, he confessed, the world of the Bible.[3] The impact of the scriptures on young Barth's thought was profound, complex, and lasting; the immediate result was to persuade him that the anthropocentric standpoint of liberal theology was wrong. The God of whom the Bible is witness is not a "dimension" of man's moral or intellectual or aesthetic or even religious experience; the Bible is witness to a God who announces his own presence in the world by mighty acts. As Barth saw it, liberal theologians from Schleiermacher on had ignored the reality of the person of God in favor of man's own religious proclivities. Historical relativism and psychological subjectivism had been the hallmarks of liberal theology, and both tended to foster uncertainty about the objective reality and meaning of God.

The God of the Bible, Barth wrote, is not the "content" of man's moral experience—some sort of personified goodness with a capital G; nor is he "the divine" about which religious philosophers from Plato to Hegel have written. The God of the Bible is the author of the world, the creator of mankind, the Lord of history who rescued and protected Israel, and who is, most essentially, "the Father of our Lord Jesus Christ." The Bible is witness to a God who is not an inference from man's experience of the world but who has his own identity, an identity made known in and through his divine actions.

Barth's opposition to theological liberalism was not just intellectual, not a mere disagreement about the right idea of God. The outbreak of the First World War sharpened Barth's differences with the teachers and teachings of his youth, and led to a redefinition of his views. In a profoundly theological and historical way, the outbreak of world war marked the end of the nineteenth century and the beginning of the twentieth. Moral idealism, the belief in social progress, the clear evidence of man's reasonableness and good will—the liberal assessment of human history in the closing decades of the nineteenth century, not only in theology but in politics, education, and literature as well—were rudely set aside for the majority of sensitive minds on May 14, 1914, the first day of that "war to end all wars."

Barth shared the disillusionment which most European and some American intellectuals experienced over the Great War. He became disenchanted with the progressivism and idealism of the Christian socialism he had practiced in his early years as a pastor, and abandoned it. Most of Germany's theological professors supported their nation's right to wage war. One of Barth's own teachers, Adolph Harnack, the great liberal historian of Christianity, had helped Kaiser Wilhelm II to draft the declaration of war, and this moral failure on the part of the German theologians symbolized for Barth the failure of their theology. In the eyes of the young Barth, the First World War was, biblically speaking, little else than the evil fruit born of an evil tree. For when men believe that the reality of God is contained somehow in the murky recesses of their own sensibilities, the open door of truth about God and themselves is slammed shut and they are prone to call "God" and justify as right whatever their consciences, their desires, and their loyalties may report to them—with inevitable destructive consequences.

If anything made the task of preaching the Gospel every Sunday more difficult, it was the upheaval of the war. How could one now preach about the beauty of the Christian soul, the meaning of Christian piety and service? The endless list of standard topics for the typical Protestant Sunday service was suddenly dated—and no one was more aware of this than Karl Barth.

It was with this attitude of no longer trusting the moral and religious claims of theological and churchly Christianity that

Barth turned to rediscovering the meaning of scripture. The result of this effort was the publication in 1918 of a book, an extensive commentary on Paul's Letter to the Romans, in which Barth set forth with evangelical zeal his interpretation of Paul's message and, by implication, the message of the whole Bible.[4] So confident was Barth in asserting his views, and so uncompromising was he in opposing liberal theological opinion on Paul, that reaction to his book led to an instant polarization in theological and ecclesiastical circles. Karl Adam, the noted Roman Catholic author, describes the sharpness of the reaction to Barth's commentary when he says that it "landed like a bombshell in the playground of the theologians."[5]

The thesis of Barth's book (stated yet more sharply in the second edition of 1921) was that God should be recognized as God, not to be confused with man's values, actions, and aspirations. Barth based this interpretation of Paul's message in Romans on Paul's theme of the righteousness of God, which condemns by contrast all human pretenses to righteousness.[6] And, like Luther before him, Barth took that contrast to mean the great distance which sin had put between God and man. He reinforced the concept of distance in his preface to the second edition, calling Kierkegaard's notion of the "infinite qualitative distinction between time and eternity" the only correct standpoint for interpreting Paul's message.[7] Barth referred to God as the "Wholly Other";[8] the "righteousness of God" meant for him that God is utterly unlike anything in the world and, further, that none of man's experiences could be utilized as a resource for knowing God.

The sharply stated negative point of Barth's book was that neither man's religion, nor his morality, nor his social, political, and ecclesiastical institutions can give him any knowledge of God—for all these are part of the very unrighteousness against which St. Paul inveighed. This means that the knowledge of God cannot be based, as so many religious thinkers have supposed, on man's spiritual experience. Rather, it must be based on that knowledge *which God has of himself* and reveals unto others. Unless the knowledge of God possesses the very authority of God, it can only be what liberal theology and the watered-down religion of the Christian churches had become: *man's* knowledge of God, which is none other than man's knowledge of his own religious consciousness masquerading as knowledge of God. For Barth, then, the true knowledge of God could be found only in the recognition of those acts whereby God chooses to make himself known *as God.* Knowledge of God is, in short, revelation.

The next question, of course, is, Where is this revelation contained? How does one come to knowledge of the acts of God's self-disclosure? Barth's answer is, the Bible. Not philosophy, not moral and religious experience, but the Bible alone is the medium of God's self-revelation.

Barth was no fundamentalist or scriptural literalist. He found the Word of God in the words of scripture; but he did not equate the two, nor did he lose sight of the fact that the Bible was written by men. His contention was that the men who wrote the Bible were unique in that they, more than other religious thinkers, appeared to be concerned not with their own religious feelings and notions but with God alone.

Barth was willing to acknowledge the validity of the historical-critical study of scriptural texts which had been advanced by the liberal tradition of biblical scholarship—studies which consisted of an analysis of the origins of biblical content by historical, literary, philological, and archaeological techniques. But Barth's interest was theological, and he valued study of the Bible only as it could contribute to an understanding of the revealed Word of God.

The Bible to Barth was not simply a chronicle of history but a message relevant to men at all times. He portrayed Saint Paul, for example, as a passive witness to the divine Word, a man divinely inspired to testify to God's acts—but a man, nonetheless, whose words *contained* the Word of God but were not themselves that Word. A "proper" exegesis of Paul's letters, as one writer on Barth put it, would mean a method "which will succeed in making the wall between the First and Twentieth Centuries transparent, until the man of the Twentieth Century can hear what Paul speaks. . . ." [9]

Barth carried out his exegesis of Paul in the full knowledge that Paul was a first-century Jew of Asia Minor, whose religious notions were deeply influenced by the religio-cultural context of his time. For instance, he knew that Paul shared the commonly held belief in the imminent end of the world, and that this belief undoubtedly influenced Paul's views of marriage, sex, politics, and many other topics he wrote of in his letters. But Barth argued that since God had chosen Paul to witness to his Word, in Paul was to be found the truth about God. And this meant that while the knowledge of God and the actual text of the Bible were not equatable, they were inseparable.

But if they were not equatable, was not a guide needed to discern the Word in the words? To this problem Barth applied an old Reformation principle which was simply an extension of the doctrine of verbal inspiration: [10] He who reads the Bible in faith—and faith itself is not a human achievement but God's gift—will not be misled about the presence of the Word in the words of scripture, for he will have it disclosed to him.[11]

The critics of Barth's *Epistle to the Romans* were provoked not by its theme—the sovereign majesty of God, upon which man can make no claim—for here Barth was bringing to contemporary focus one of the great themes of the Protestant reformers. What offended the critics was the attitude he brought to his interpretations of the biblical text.[12] In such notions as God's "wholly otherness," "the infinite qualitative difference between time and eternity," and the existential crisis of faith, Barth believed that he had discovered the only meanings that were basic to Paul's message, the only meanings, therefore, that would allow God to speak through Paul to men of that day. According to Barth's critics, such notions were alien theological constructions placed upon the scriptural words, and could not be defended as Paul's Gospel. In the eyes of many critics, Barth did not adhere to his stated objective of letting the Bible speak for itself but, worse yet, obstructed its meanings with imported ideas.[13]

The thrust of Barth's book was the absolute need of all men to acknowledge the transcendent sovereignty of God. "Let God be God!" This was the Word which he heard in Paul's letters, the Word which he believed to be relevant for men at all times, everywhere. God is not an idea, not a value, not anything that can be measured according to the things of the world. He is the "Wholly Other." He is the One who lies just beyond the boundary of everything that man understands. "God is in heaven and man is on earth! . . . The relation between such a man and such a God is for me the theme of the Bible and the essence of philosophy." [14]

Paul's Gospel, said Barth, shakes man from his complacency and brings him to that moment of crisis in which he can recognize the stark contrast between himself and God. It is not until man confronts his own inevitable death, the uncertainties of his daily existence, the fallibility of all human institutions, the vanity of all his efforts to find God, not until he stands "naked before God," as Kierkegaard thought, that the awesome truth breaks through to him that God is *God*, the author of his own life and death, and the provider of the meaning of his daily existence.

Barth argued that the knowledge of God which God himself vouchsafes to man in the situation of crisis is dialectical; it is simultaneously positive and negative. What it affirms is that God is God and not man, and that man persists in a destructive illusion when he supposes that he possesses within himself any truth about God. Knowledge of God, then, consists first of the realization that man *has no* knowledge of God—man knows something about Him only when he knows that he knows nothing. It is when man fully appreciates the crisis of his own ignorance of God that he is open to receive God's revelation. The *no* of God's wrath pronounced upon man's illusions must come before the *yes* of his grace, announced in the person of Christ, forgiving and reconciling man to God.

The dialectical meaning of revelation is that God remains hidden even in his revelation of grace, for grace is the living word of God, Jesus Christ, a revelation which can be received only in the posture of penitent faith. The theology which Barth set forth brilliantly and dramatically in the *Epistle to the Romans* came to be called "crisis theology," or "dialectical theology." Barth acknowledged that it was Dostoevsky who opened his eyes to the illusion of man's arrogant self-sufficiency; and in the notion of the dialectical character of revelation in which God is both hidden and revealed, the influence of Kierkegaard is to be seen at every turn.

In 1932, Barth published the first volume of a work whose size alone attests to the singlemindedness, self-confidence, and sheer industry of his theological endeavors. Entitled *Church Dogmatics*, it was a comprehensive statement of the faith of the Christian church. It grew to twelve large volumes of more than eight thousand pages, and was halted only by the death of its author in 1968, at the age of eighty-two.

The appearance of the first volumes of the *Church Dogmatics*, along with a study of Saint Anselm's thought in 1931, marked another major turning-point in Barth's career, setting it off from the early period represented by his *Epistle to the Romans*.[15] In *Romans*, Barth responded vigorously to what he took as aimlessness, uncertainty, and arrogance in theological reflection and in the patterns of men's lives. He accused theologians of adhering not to God's Word but to their own shifting religious moods and attitudes, and he undertook to crush anthropocentrism and theological subjectivism by revitalizing one of the great principles of the Protestant Reformation—that scripture alone guarantees knowledge of the objective reality of God. The malaise experienced by man, given expression by novelists and psychologists as the sense of ultimate meaninglessness in life, and the inevitability of death, were diagnosed by Barth as the inveterate tendency of man to forget that he is not God but man—man, who owes both his life and his death to God. As we have said, Barth saw the message of

God's merciful forgiveness of man's sinful arrogance in the atoning sacrifice of Jesus Christ as a message that can be heard by man only through a personal crisis. The *yes* of God's grace and the *no* of his wrath were dialectically related for Barth, the *yes* appearing only through the *no*, the "yawning abyss" separating God and man bridged only by the miraculous act of grace incarnate in the person of Jesus Christ.

In *Church Dogmatics*, Barth ceased thinking of God's grace dialectically. From about 1930 on, his thinking no longer depended upon an existentialist analysis of the human condition. He rejected the notion, implicit to his commentary on Romans, that man's foolish illusions and disobedience are a sickness for which God's grace and judgment are the cure. He argued that, though grace means the forgiveness of sins, sin is not the cause of God's gracious action in Jesus Christ. In ways known to God alone, the reality and meaning of sin are included—presupposed, as it were—in this fundamental fact of grace. From the first volume of the *Church Dogmatics* onward, Barth's stand was that divine grace enjoys absolute priority; God has accepted man from the outset, an acceptance which sin cannot alter because even sin is somehow comprehended by grace.

Barth assumes from the outset that the only possible way to conceive God's Word is as an utterly unique reality. This means for him that there is no *structure* uniting God's Word and the world of human experience, and therefore no resource in man's experience for the knowledge of God. Yet, Barth claims that God creates in man the capacity for knowing God. Barth's conception of the integrity of God's Word is influenced by the neo-Kantian view that there are two levels of reality which are not united: a phenomenal level, consisting of what we experience through our senses, and a noumenal level, consisting of what things are in themselves, apart from the ways in which we experience them. In his wish to emphasize the autonomy of the Word of God, Barth was disposed to adopt the neo-Kantian notion of noumenal reality—hence his doctrine that the Word is unknowable except to itself. In the period of the

Church Dogmatics, Barth shifted his presupposition from the unknowableness of the Word to the basic Hegelian view of the omnipotence of the Word, the latter becoming the basic framework for his essential understanding of the relation between God and man—namely, that God's grace is the only reality, a basis for all other realities, including man.

Barth came to see that the objective reality and sovereignty of God had a more consistent meaning if the grace of God were regarded not as answering the question posed by the human condition but as itself real and meaningful apart from any question which man poses in the "crisis" experiences of life and death. Barth rejected Kierkegaard's dialectical understanding of the relation between God and man—the "infinite distance" —in favor of Calvin's doctrine of providence or election, in which God's grace is understood to save man, to forgive him and reunite him with God, *even before* man acts sinfully. He now contended that the sovereign and transcendent majesty of God—the backbone of his earlier dialectical theology—could best be conveyed in the doctrine of God's grace which elects, forgives, and reconciles man "from the beginning."

The majesty of God demands that grace be regarded as equally majestic, a grace which is not a divine "response" to man's iniquity but a supreme, providential reality which man's iniquity cannot challenge or qualify. In the period of the *Dogmatics,* Barth was satisfied with nothing less than a theology in which the fundamental notion was the supreme reality of divine grace, that which, as the source and goal of all life, is "all in all."

We can gain a clearer understanding of the importance of grace to Barth's dogmatic theology if we examine what Barth has to say about the method of dogmatic theology, the meaning of creation, the person of Jesus Christ, and the reality of evil.

When Barth began emphasizing in his dogmatic thinking God's gracious condescension in behalf of man, he did not mean to withdraw from his earlier contention that there was no continuity between the realm of God and the realm of man.

He still insisted that there is nothing in man's religious experience, his ethical acts and aspirations, his intellect and philosophies, that gives him any sense of God. If God is to be known, then he can be known only *through grace;* that is to say, by an act of God. The knowledge of God, for Barth, meant that man is made privy to God's self-knowledge.

God has given witness to himself, to his acts, in scripture, and all are bidden to read scripture in order to learn of God. The Barthian theologian has as his task the discernment of God's revelation within the scripture to assess critically the Christian church's proclamations about God. His statement about God, when soundly rooted in the scriptural witness, is "dogma," the authoritative witness to God's Word.[16] But what is the dogmatic theologian's guide to interpreting scripture accurately? Barth's answer was that grace alone is the guide; and grace, for Barth, is God's act to embody his word in Jesus Christ. The Barthian theologian is thus instructed to interpret both the Old and New Testaments, from beginning to end, guided by the norm of God-in-Christ.[17] He must read, study, and restudy the scriptures to see the myriad witness to Christ; he must let his imagination bend to God's will to see this witness in the Old Testament; he must employ philosophical concepts to express the meaning of the biblical witness to God-in-Christ, for the medium of revelation is scripture, and any tool can be used in helping one to hear the scriptures speak for themselves.

Barth recognizes that the stories of creation in the Old Testament were influenced by earlier myths of the religions of the ancient Near East, but there is an important difference. The earlier accounts were concerned with the question of how the world came to be—they were concerned with the moon and stars, the earth, the seas, seasonal changes, the whole panorama of natural "wonders." They sought the origins of all natural phenomena because man's daily existence depended almost wholly on the fortunes that the awesome powers of the physical world could bring. But in the Old Testament's stories of creation, the question of world origins is not primary. The Hebrew writers were concerned primarily with Israel's belief in the unmatched power of God and the goodness of all that he creates. The question answered by the biblical account of the six-day creation is not, "How did the world come to be?" but "Who is the God of Israel, and what is his power and authority as compared with the mighty 'nature gods' of the Mesopotamian religions and cults which tempted the early Israelite communities?" The answer of the Old Testament was clear: The God of Israel is the Lord of the whole natural world, and all things in and of the world are therefore good because of their divine creator; but they cease to be so when the creature's dependence upon the Creator is ignored through acts of disobedience. This disobedience is dramatized by the story of Adam's Fall.

From its inception, the Christian religion affirmed the Hebraic belief in divine creation, and Christian theologians from Saint Paul on sought ways to make intelligible the relation between God's revelation in the world to God's revelation in the person of Jesus Christ. The belief in God's creation of the world had always suggested that the world was unified under a common creator, a world whose goodness rested in experiencing an interdependence based on God. The new religion, which sprang out of Judaism, put forth its belief in Christ as a "new" basis for the world, not replacing the old but bringing it to a new and deeper fulfillment.

Karl Barth's interpretation of creation is an exception in Christian theology to the traditional practice of relating belief in Jesus Christ to the older belief about God's lordship over the world. Basically, for Barth, there really cannot be a *relationship;* for he denies that there is first an act of God called "creation," and later an act called "Jesus Christ," with the second act related to the first.[18] Barth recognized that there are two distinct historical "events"; but there is only one "act," in relation to which all of God's other "acts" are derivative—and this is God's act of grace in becoming man in the person of Jesus Christ which God willed from eternity. Barth believes, with the Nicene Creed, that Jesus Christ was "begotten of his Father before all worlds," that he was "begotten, not made, being of one substance with the Father," and that Jesus was, therefore, at one with the triune God of Christianity from the beginning of time. Not only the creation, but all the other events of which the Bible is witness, are to be interpreted ultimately in terms of the *central* act of God in Christ. What God's decision to become man in Jesus Christ shows is that there is a world, a creaturely human realm in existence. The existence of a world and nothing more is what we learn from the Bible's witness to Jesus Christ.

> Because God has become man, the existence of creation can no longer be doubted. Gazing at Jesus Christ, with whom we live in the same space, there is told us—told as the Word of God—the Word of the Creator and Word of His work and of the most astonishing bit of this work, of man.[19]

The continuous, complicated development of the world, the immensely long evolution of life on the earth, with the staggering variety of species produced, is of no relevance to Barth's claim that the *meaning* of the creation is Jesus Christ.[20]

For Barth, God *means* the act of grace in Jesus Christ, and he interprets the biblical story of the creation with the view that the "world" is a bare existence, a realm whose meaning is derived from the belief that God became man in Jesus Christ.

> . . . We must say that creation itself, God's existence itself, prior to the whole world from eternity, is unthinkable apart from His will as it has been fulfilled and revealed in time. The eternal will of God has this form. From eternity there is no other God than the God whose will was revealed in this act

and in this Word. The Christ message is, let me repeat, not one truth among others; it is *the* truth. In thinking of God, we have from the beginning to think of the name Jesus Christ.[21]

Barth's interpretation, of course, arbitrarily limits the meaning of creation to the human sphere; but it also provides its own rationale for the Bible's rejoicing in the splendor of the natural world. The authors of the opening chapters of Genesis clearly believed that, not only in man but in the very existence of a natural kingdom, there is a forceful witness to divine creation. God, for the ancient Israelite, is a good creator, and the power of his goodness is seen in the beauty and fullness of his creation: the earth, the sky, the variety of animal and vegetable life, and, most of all, man. But when Barth feels compelled to take into his account of creation the place of nature, he does it in bizarre arguments—as when, for example, he claims that the phenomenon of light is a sign or prefiguration of the illumination of God's Word in the person of Christ.[22]

But even if, as Barth claims, God's creation of the world has its meaning in the bare fact or existence of the world, what does it *mean* to say that God has created the world *in Jesus Christ?* How is Christ thus at the beginning of all things, yet appearing in a period of history? Barth does not provide a satisfactory answer to this question. Since he believes that Jesus Christ is the ground and goal of creation, he is compelled to argue that Christ was present at the beginning of the world, and in God's covenant with Israel, as well as in the time of his "birth" in Bethlehem. But what "presence" means here is unclear. The difficulty in meaning is not lost on Barth, for he says somewhat defensively:

By the Word the world exists. A marvelous reversal of our whole thinking! Don't let yourselves be led astray by the difficulty of the time-concept, which might well result from this. The world came into being, it was created and sustained by the little child that was born in Bethlehem, by the Man

73

who died on the Cross of Golgotha, and the third day rose again. *That* is the Word of creation, by which all things were brought into being.[23]

The most serious criticism that can be made of Barth's claim about Christ's relation to creation is that, in arguing his case, he must do so at the expense of the religious integrity of the Old Testament's witness to Israel's history. For Barth cannot claim that Christ is at the beginning of all things without also implying that he is at the basis of Israel's history. Thus Barth's view of the relationship between Jesus Christ and the history of Israel before the appearance of Jesus and the Christian church goes beyond the traditional claim that the Christian revelation is a *fulfillment* of Hebraic prophecy and expectation. For Barth, Jesus Christ is not only fulfillment of Israel's hope, he is the very reason for Israel's existence, the revealed "inner meaning" of its development. The events of Israel's history, including the Exodus, the Sinai Covenant, and the formation of the monarchy are somehow—in ways that Barth is unable to explain —*for the sake* of Jesus Christ.[24] So tenacious is Barth in maintaining the consistency of his position that he suggests, though somewhat eliptically, that Israel was implicitly responding to God's will in rejecting Jesus, for in that way the grace of God in Jesus Christ was made available to the gentile as well as to the Jew.[25]

If, as Barth claims, the author, history, and goal of creation is Jesus Christ, one is finally led to ask what is meant by "Jesus Christ"? The answer is not as easy as it seems. Barth accepted the judgment of the New Testament scholars that the Gospels were not objective histories of the life of Jesus, as earlier Christian traditions had held. The Gospels should be regarded as records of the early church's beliefs about Jesus—beliefs doubtless containing facts about the historical Jesus, but more often recording the impact of Jesus on his followers and reflecting, overall, the climate of religious belief during the beginnings of the Christian religion.

But Barth had a deeper reason for refusing to equate the meaning of Christ with the Gospel portraits of Jesus. Any such equation would mean that whatever is regarded as the religious, ethical, social, and political views of Jesus could be taken as the basis for understanding the divinity of Jesus, that is, his Christhood. As an example, one might argue that Jesus is the Christ, the Messiah, the revealer of God, because the ethical principles with which he identified himself in the Sermon on the Mount are so pure and majestic in their conception as to disclose to all men the goodness of God himself. In Barth's judgment, such arguments amount to a return to the discredited ideas of nineteenth-century liberal theologians. Whenever Jesus' so-called ethical and religious standpoint is used as the clue to his Christhood, this signals the faulty practice of making man's own ethical and religious ideas the standard of what is divine, and hence revelatory of God, in Jesus.

Barth insisted that even the life and teachings of Jesus could not be regarded as the key to the meaning of Jesus as the Christ. But what then could? Barth's answer lies in the very fact of Jesus Christ. The meaning of Jesus as the Christ consists not in what Jesus Christ *did* or *said;* not in his acts of succoring the needy and afflicted, nor in his exhortations to moral purity and neighborly love, nor in his pronouncements against hypocrisy and self-righteousness. The meaning of Jesus as the Christ consists in *who* he is, his identity: the one-in-whom-God-chose-to-become-man.[26] Thus, the Christness of Jesus seems to consist of the expression of divine authority: God's decision to become man. This becomes clearer if one carefully considers how Barth understands Jesus Christ to be the revealer of God.

For Barth, Jesus Christ does not reveal anything *about* God; rather, he reveals *God* pure and simple. When Jesus appears on the historical scene, then, in Barth's judgment, God himself has appeared.[27] This is because Jesus Christ *is* God, without qualification. But what does Barth mean by the word "reveals" in the statement, "Jesus Christ reveals God"? For if we say "X reveals

Y" and mean that X is none other than Y, then we have failed to specify anything that X "reveals." For example, we can say that Moses revealed the ethical will of God, or that Gandhi revealed a divine forbearance in his political relationships. We do not suppose that Moses was God or Gandhi divine; we assume that we know something independently of God's will and divine forbearance to discern it in human beings. But this is not so for Barth; he rejects the view that man can have independent knowledge of God. Therefore, it is not man who can recognize that Jesus Christ reveals God; only God knows this, and man's faith and knowledge await God's act. Hence, it is not Jesus' words and deeds as reported by scripture, and thus as interpreted by man's moral and religious standards, which are the basis of the self-revelation of God in Jesus Christ. Rather, it is God's decision to include man within his own knowledge of his own deed in Jesus Christ. And by "divine decision," Barth means the pure initiative of God: the Word.

But how can Barth as a human being know what the Word is? He cannot. But he can listen patiently for the Word. And where does he listen? The answer is obvious: the Bible. Thus, surprisingly enough, Barth is rescued from theological silence on the meaning of Jesus Christ by the scriptural accounts of Jesus. He, too, is able to say that in the love, suffering, judgment, life, and death of Jesus as presented by the Bible one may hear the Word of God. He is able to say this not because he knows it independently but on the authority of the Bible.

But this does not mean that man knows, through the Bible, how Jesus Christ reveals God. Through the Bible, God has provided the means whereby man may receive God's self-knowledge, but never does this give man *as man* the confidence to say who God is in Christ. This hard conclusion about the human situation vis-à-vis God is implied in the axiom that is at every turn of Barth's theology: Only God can know and reveal God. It is sharply illustrated in the way Barth interprets the simple confession of every Christian that in Jesus Christ the love of God is revealed. He puts it this way:

76

I would not say that God is freedom or that God is love—
even though the second pronouncement is a biblical one. We
do not know what love is and we do not know what freedom
is; but *God* is love and *God* is freedom. What freedom is and
what love is, we have to learn from Him. As predicate to this
subject it may be said that He is the God of free love.[28]

This can only mean that words can be used to talk about
God only if it is acknowledged at the beginning that the
appropriateness of such words rests not on man's empirical
knowledge but exclusively on the mystery and power of God
himself. Thus, we cannot say that in the life of Christ we see the
love of God, if what we mean by this is that we have some
independent, arbitrary notion of what is ideally or supremely
the love of God. For, to repeat, Barth denies strenuously that
we can have any notion of God outside of Christ. Yet the notion
of God we get in and through Christ is not one that we can
dare assume bears any positive relation to any aspect of our
worldly experience.

Barth seemingly contradicts the very witness of scripture
which he is so eager to uphold; for when an apostle like Paul
speaks of Christ's revealing to him the love of God, it is because,
as a Jew of exemplary devotion, he already knows of this
love and finds it confirmed and uniquely enriched in the person of Jesus Christ. The New Testament record suggests—
contrary to Barth's opinion—that Jesus is accepted as the Son
of God because in his life and death there was perceived a
unique embodiment of God's grace and judgment. How else
can we explain the disciples' unique response to the historical
person of Jesus?

Barth's treatment of evil is another example of how his arguments are formulated to help support what one author has
called his "monism of grace." [29] One of the fundamental claims of
Barth's *Church Dogmatics* is that all reality is the work of
God's grace.[30] But if this is so, whence evil? Barth recognizes
the powerful realities of evil in the world. Can evil be reconciled with the view that all reality is due to grace? Must not

Barth deny either the reality of evil or the proposition that grace authored reality? Barth's answer is logical legerdemain, for he wants to say both that evil is nothing and that it is the consequence of grace.

Evil is nothing, Barth states, because everything that is is due to God's gracious goodness. But, he cautions, to say that evil is nothing does not mean that it does not exist or that it is not a powerful force for destruction in the world. To say that evil is "nothing" means that alongside grace, evil has no reality, has been rendered impotent. Evil is what grace has rejected, that to which grace has said *no*. But that is the point; evil, the logical opposite of grace, *exists* only as that which grace has negated. Evil is the negative corollary of grace, existing *by virtue of* grace, but therefore *really* existing in Barth's view:

> . . . this whole realm that we term evil—death, sin, the Devil and hell—is *not* God's creation, but rather what was excluded by God's creation, that to which God has said "No." And if there is a reality of evil, it can only be the reality of this excluded and repudiated thing, the reality behind God's back, which He passed over, when He made the world and made it good. . . . What is not good God did not make; it has no creaturely existence. But if being is to be ascribed to it at all, and we would rather not say that it is non-existent, then it is only the power of the being which arises out of the weight of the divine "No." [31]

It is unfortunate that Barth seems more concerned to square evil with the a priori truths of his theology than to show how the empirical reality of evil as we know it in hatred, oppression, cruelty, destruction, and needless suffering can inform and be informed by the biblical meanings of God, Christ, sin, grace, and creation.

Barth's interpretation of the biblical beliefs about creation, Christ, and evil shows that the fundamental problem of his dogmatic theology stems from his decision to carry over into his later thinking the framework of authority which he had developed in the period of "dialectical theology." When he was contending with the subjectivism and relativism of Schleiermacher and his theological descendants, it seemed appropriate to reintroduce the mighty truth of the sovereignty of God by reminding theologians and churchmen of the object of the Bible's witness. Barth nevertheless moved to a new way of thinking in part because the negativism of the dialectical period, expressed in the notions of God's rejection of man's religiousness and of the "infinite qualitative difference between God and man," was not adequately balanced by the positive truth of God's forgiveness and acceptance of man in Jesus Christ. The keystone of his great arch of dogmatic thought became the reality of divine grace—the continuous act in which God reaches out and grasps erring man. Yet, grace though it may be, Barth's stated concept of it was in precisely the same terms of absolute authority with which he earlier presented his thesis about the meaning of God. The result was that the focus of Barth's interpretation of God's gracious activity in divine creation, the history of Israel and the appearance of Jesus Christ, is not on *what* has occurred but on the *source* of the occurrence; in other words, the focus is not on the deed but on the doer. Grace in the *Church Dogmatics* is invariably reflexive, referring back to its author, underscoring the power, authority, and absoluteness of God. And this is indeed strange, because the word "grace" means "favor," "kindness," or "mercy," in short, "love"—a term which can retain its meaning only when the gift of love and the receiver of the gift are kept in true balance with the giver of the gift.

The consequence for dogmatic theory of Barth's preoccupation with divine authority is a certain abstractness or formalism. The arguments that show creation to be the vehicle of grace, and evil to be the negative implication of grace, are arguments that do not seem to rely upon or relate to real experience. They appear to have meaning only as deductions from the axiomatic principles of Barth's thought—thus they have meaning only if one is initially disposed to accept these principles.

As the primary case in point, consider Barth's notion of the sovereign authority of God. It is a notion founded on the axiom that God is always subject, never an object to anyone or anything. Thus God is never at the disposal of man's knowledge, action, and affection, and never therefore accessible in human experience. God is pure subject; he can be known only by himself, revealed only by himself, and related only to himself. The principle of the inalienable subjectivity of God was advanced in the *Epistle to the Romans* and maintained through all the volumes of the *Church Dogmatics*. More than anything else, this principle accounts for the formalism and abstractness of Barth's later thought. Nowhere is this better seen than in the importance which the doctrine of the Trinity holds for Barth's dogmatic theology.

If the absolute subjectivity of God means that God can never be an object of human knowledge, can one speak of God's revealing himself? We had reason to raise this question before in connection with Barth's doctrine of Christ. Barth's answer to the question was that revelation could not be regarded as empirical, as a datum for human understanding appearing in history, nature, man's conscience, reason, and so forth. It is not man who understands revelation; it is revelation which understands man. Revelation provides man with the means of knowing it in the very act in which it becomes "revelation." Thus Barth has defined revelation in terms consistent with the absolute subjectivity of God. But what is the meaning of such a unique revelation? The answer indicates the importance of the doctrine of the Trinity to Barth's dogmatic theology.[32] For the Trinity is Barth's way of stating how the God who is pure Subject, the "Wholly Other," is also the God who has made himself known to man.

The Trinity signifies that within God himself, there are present the three beings—Father, Son, and Spirit. In Barth's understanding, God is revealed *inwardly* as God, the Father; God, the Son; and God, the Spirit. Thus revelation, God's self-disclosure, is made to be a part of God's inner nature, his subjective self. Barth's utilization of the historic Christian doctrine of the Trinity gives ample evidence of how his theology breaks contact with the concrete world of man's experience. For, from this inner divine revelation, Barth proceeds to deduce his meanings of creation, Christ, and evil. Of course, one feels compelled to accept the soundness of Barth's thinking on these subjects only if one has already accepted the usefulness of the axiom about the divine subjectivity. Deny that axiom by putting in its place—as Paul Tillich and a host of other contemporary theologians have done—the view that God is available to man through the qualitative depths of human experience, and significantly different accounts of the meanings of creation, Christ, and evil become inevitable.

The Trinity is regarded by Barth as the eternal, "inner" life of God, but he never explains how, as a theologian, he deduces from an eternal meaning the meanings of world, evil, and Jesus Christ that are concrete, historical, and temporal. What is the logical basis of this "deduction"? Barth's thinking on this point resembles Hegel's—historical existence is within the meaning of eternity, a dimension of eternity which shows the meaning of eternity in relation to the world and man. Yet it would seem that Barth wishes to deny this, for he is at pains to acknowledge the distinctness of the reality of the world and of man's freedom in it. But to acknowledge is one thing, and to demonstrate by reasoned arguments is another. In fact, Barth's basic view of the nature of God militates against such a freedom for man and the world; and Barth's notion that in Jesus Christ, the second person of the Trinity, God has created and eternally accepted and reconciled himself to man is hardly an argument for man's freedom in relation to God, or for that often affirmed but seldom understood "humanity of God";[33] it is simply one of the many derivations from Barth's theological first principles.

In assessing these principles, one might echo what Kierkegaard said of Hegel's philosophy: the concreteness and distinctness of the world and of man have been overlooked in the system. For Barth's system of grace is not unlike Hegel's system of the Absolute Idea in obliterating all individuality but its own, while claiming that it alone guarantees "true" individuality, "true" freedom, and "true" humanity.

World politics is an important dimension from which to understand and evaluate Barth's theological ideas, for Barth's own political views and decisions had a powerful influence on the attitude and actions of European Protestants. The development of Barth's political consciousness stretches over forty-five years, from his early socialist beliefs before the First World War to his judgments on communism during the Cold War. No analysis of Barth's theology is complete without noting two events on which Barth took a vigorous stand: the early development of Nazism in Germany, and the influence of Russian communism in Eastern Europe after the Second World War.

Barth made clear in his *Epistle to the Romans* and subsequent writings that Christian faith cannot provide the individual with a perspective from which to make political decisions. He contested the Catholic medieval synthesis, with its notions of the Christian State and Christian Society. Just as the Word of God must not be confused with man's words, so God's act in Christ must not be confused with man's political constructions. It is just as foolish to think in the twentieth century that God prefers democracy to monarchism or facism, as it was to believe for countless centuries before that kings ruled by divine right. The realm of God, Barth said, must not be identified with the human realm, particularly in the area of politics, where there is a great temptation to do so.

There is no doubt that as a citizen Barth could have much to think and say about politics. But on the basis of his early writings, as a theologian he could have nothing to think and say—except, of course, to warn against and admonish attempts to confuse God's Word with man's politics. But a change did occur in Barth's thinking in the years of the rise of Nazism in Germany, for he fiercely denounced Nazism—and from the point of view of his theology.

Barth opposed National Socialism in Germany because it violated the prohibition against idolatry in God's First Commandment: "You shall have no other gods before me" (Exodus 20:3). In its blind nationalism, its mystique of blood and soil, in the racialism of its Aryan philosophy, Nazism was, in Barth's judgment, the recrudescence of the ancient pagan religions, seeking to replace by a set of idols the God of Abraham, Isaac, and Jacob—God, "who is our Lord, Jesus Christ." Barth early perceived the encroachment of Nazism on the life of Christianity and warned against it.

In the summer of 1933, the German Church, to which I belonged as a member and a teacher, found itself in the greatest danger concerning its doctrine and order. It threatened to become involved in a new heresy strangely blended of Christianity and Germanism, and to come under the domination of the so-called "German Christians"—a danger prompted by the successes of National Socialism and the suggestive power of its ideas. And it happened further that the representatives of the other theological schools and tendencies in Germany—Liberal, Pietist, Confessional, Biblicist—who had previously, in opposition to me, put so much weight on ethics, sanctification, Christian life, practical decision, and the like, now in part openly affirmed that heresy and in part took up a strangely neutral and tolerant attitude toward it. And it happened further that, when so many fell into line and no one seriously protested, I myself could not very well keep silent but had to undertake to proclaim to the imperiled church what it must do to be saved.[34]

And proclaim Barth did, in word and by deed! At his teaching post at the University of Bonn, in 1935, Barth repeatedly refused to conform to requirements imposed on university professors by the Nazi government, such as rendering the salutation "Heil Hitler!" at the beginning of each class, and was discharged from the University. He returned to Switzerland and to his native city of Basel, where he spent the remainder of his life teaching at its University. He continued his attack on

The Erosion of Faith

Nazism from Switzerland, much to the embarrassment of the "neutralist" Swiss government, and much to the anxiety of his friends, who were afraid that harm would befall the Christian theologian officially listed in Germany as a public enemy. But Barth persisted. In 1938, he wrote:

> . . . Because I could not very well begin my lectures in Bonn with the salutation to Hitler, and because I could not very well swear an unconditioned oath of allegiance to the führer, as I should have to do as the holder of a state office, I lost my position in the service of this state and was forced to quit Germany.
>
> Meanwhile the antichristian and therefore antihuman essence of National Socialism revealed itself more and more distinctly. At the same time its influence over the remainder of Europe alarmingly increased in proportion. The lies and brutality, as well as the stupidity and fear, grew and have long since grown far beyond the frontiers of Germany. And Europe does not understand the danger in which it stands. Why not? Because it does not see that National Socialism means the conscious, radical, and systematic transgression of this First Commandment. Because it does not see that this transgression, because it is sin against God, drags the corruption of the nations in its wake.[35]

Theologians who, like the American Reinhold Niebuhr, expressed admiration for Barth's denunciation of Nazism, were disappointed when, after the Second World War, Barth refused similarly to denounce communism. Barth argued that he had no illusions about the repressive politics of communism and about the harshness of life within the countries controlled by it. But he could not agree that communism and Nazism were equivalent tyrannies. Unlike Nazism, communism was not a paganism in political dress. As far as Barth was concerned, communism did not seek, at least in terms of practical politics, to take the place of God. And that, it appears, is what really mattered to Barth.

In 1948, after a visit to the Reformed Churches in Hungary

in which he commended the forbearance toward the communist rule shown by Hungarian Christians, Barth wrote:

> I am of the opinion that communism can be warded off only by a "better justice" on the part of the Western world, not by the all too cheap denials in which the fear of the West is now expressing itself. And in any case I maintain that the positive way taken by the Hungarian Reformed people is preferable to the glory they might win as standard-bearer for the so-called "Christian West"; rather I think that the locus of Christianity is to be sought above today's conflict between East and West. We shall see who was right in the long run. And if worst comes to worst, I shall be contented to be proved wrong in having refused, this once, to raise a call for immediate battle! [36]

Reinhold Niebuhr claimed to have discerned in Barth's position on communism a reversion to the "other-worldliness" of his early theology, an attitude which, in fostering disengagement with socio-political realities, renders the believer passive before events of political and social injustice. For Niebuhr, Barth's stand on Nazism was not, as Barth claimed, a careful derivation from his theology but a departure in which Barth affirmed practically if not theoretically the ability of man to know the will of God as affecting the total and visible evil of Nazism. But where, as in communism, the evil is less than total and not always visible, Barth finds himself returning to the old theological view of the separation of the divine and human realms. Under this view, Barth cannot single out communism for special condemnation, according to Niebuhr, because it occurs within a realm which itself is under judgment by God. In 1949, Niebuhr wrote:

> . . . Barth's disciples were inclined, before Nazism was revealed in its full demonic dimensions, to see little difference between it and other forms of political evil. In like manner Barth seems inclined today to regard the differences between communism and the so-called democratic world as insignificant when

85

viewed from the ultimate Christian standpoint. But we are men and not God, and the destiny of civilizations depends upon our decisions in the "nicely calculated less and more" of good and evil in political institutions.[37]

For Niebuhr it is Barth's failure to make relative moral discriminations—a failure born of his primary theological ideas—that finally explains what he refers to as "Barth's silence" on the Russian invasion of Hungary. This refers to the absence of any public condemnation of the Russian action on the part of Barth.

In 1958, Barth wrote, partly in tacit response to reactions like Niebuhr's:

> I regard anticommunism as a matter of principle an evil even greater than communism itself. Can one overlook the fact that communism is the unwelcomed yet—in all its belligerence— natural result of Western developments? Has not its total, inhuman compulsion which we complain of so much haunted from remotest times in another form our avowedly free Western societies and states? And was it then something suddenly new and worthy of special horror when communism presented itself as a doctrine of salvation blessing all men and nations and therefore one to be spread over the whole world? Are there not other systems of this kind and tendency? Further, could we really intend to help the peoples governed by communism and the world threatened by it, or even one individual among those suffering under its effects, by proclaiming and seeking to practice toward it a relationship exclusively that of enemies? Have we forgotten that what is at stake in this "absolute enemy" relationship, to which every brave man in the West is now obligated and for which he would give his all, is a typical invention of (and a heritage from) our defunct dictators—and that only the "Hitler in us" can be an anticommunist on principle? [38]

> . . . In my native Switzerland where, remarkably enough, there are many small McCarthys, I have fared badly. Here in 1951 a leading politician, now deceased, started a formal campaign against me; here—especially at the time of the Hun-

garian crisis and then again on the occasion of the odd discussion about a Swiss atomic armament—I have heard in no uncertain terms that I am to be regarded as a dubious citizen and that I have gradually lost the moderate sympathies which were extended me in the time of Hitler. And who was it who accused me because of my silence about Hungary of being an unrepentant man, unlike the repentant Jean-Paul Sartre, and of giving way to resentment toward America, a thing as incomprehensible as unchristian? [It was Niebuhr.] Oh, I already anticipate reading the necrology in which people will one day summarily say of me that I earned certain merits in relation to the renewal of theology and the German church conflict [the opposition to Nazism in German Christianity] but that in political respects I was a doubtful will-o'-the-wisp.[39]

The soundness of Niebuhr's critique of Barth's theology in its relation to politics does not, however, prevent our acknowledging the wisdom of the following summary of Barth's general view of communism in relation to world politics, especially in the light of the war in Vietnam, racial and social conflicts in the United States, resurging political and social vitalities on the continents of Africa and Asia, and the breakdown of the communist monolith.

Communism can never be defeated solely by anti-communist propaganda and military strength. Only if the West works out a positive social order, guaranteeing the freedoms essential for individual and social justice, will it have responded truly to the challenge of communist ideology and strategy. In this respect, the colonial wars of the West are the highest trump cards in the communist deck.

The constant threat of force against communism, the brinkmanship practiced by the West, following in the footsteps of John Foster Dulles and various theologians and theorists of all sorts, is dangerous to the extreme. If pressed too far it will lead to World War III, the catastrophic nature of which cannot be doubted in the atomic age, even if it does not destroy everybody. It is not in this fashion, therefore, that the church ought to act. Both in the East and in the West the church owes it to itself, and owes it to its Lord, to stand between East and West and untiringly to build bridges, establish connecting links and outline steps toward reconciliation, by means of which peace can be established.[40]

The boldness and sweep of Barth's theology, and his tenacious argumentation, make critical scrutiny and evaluation inevitable. Our criticism is by no means to contest or minimize Barth's stature in modern theology, or his unparalleled influence on contemporary religious thought. The present-day crisis in theology cannot be adequately grasped in its depth and complexity without recognizing both the conscious and unconscious influence of his ideas. (And this is true of Jewish as well as Catholic and Protestant thinkers—for in large measure Jewish reaction to, and appropriation of, Christian theological ideas have in fact been reaction to and appropriation of Barth's influence.) In summarizing, let us mention—later to discuss in detail—in what respects Barth is at the root of the contemporary crisis.

The dichotomy of two realms, Godly and worldly, is implicit to all aspects of Barth's thought, at every stage of its development. Contemporary thinkers have found in this dichotomy a basic framework for dealing with the phenomenon of secularization—the erosion of the religious sensibility, in its individual and social expressions, as a result of all the social, political, economic, technological, and scientific forces that define our contemporary existence. They have learned from Barth that since "religion," in the sense of man's personal and institutional expressions of worship and belief, cannot claim a place in God's Kingdom, the dissolution of religion in the human realm need not be lamented. Indeed it is to be celebrated; it means that, perhaps for the first time in man's long history on earth, the world and all its vitalities can now be addressed and affirmed according to their own authenticity—and this without fear or shame. For just as the divine realm has an integrity, so the realm of the secular has its own integrity. Barth has thus taught the contemporary theologian of the secular not only to recognize the authenticity of the secular, but

he has taught him to acknowledge as the basis of this recognition God's own decree that there be an earthly realm
distinct from himself.

A second, parallel feature of Barth's thought indispensable to
understanding the contemporary theological crisis is its understanding of God. Barth's notion that the meaning of God is
not mediated by man's experience but is given as a gift in a
wholly unique act by God himself has meant for many contemporary theologians that no tears need be shed when our
experiences today prove to be strangely silent in witnessing (as
perhaps they once witnessed) to a supreme provider, judge, and
redeemer of human life. This can be regarded as itself a unique
spiritual experience in man's history; but for many theologians
of the secular it confirms the belief that man cannot assume,
as he has historically assumed, all manner of relationship to God.
If there is a God, and if man possesses a relationship to God,
then God himself will make this clear to man in his own good
time and way. In the meantime, man's task is not gaining heaven
but claiming the earth.

The crisis in contemporary religious thought occurs just at
the point that the theologian seeks to make sense of the secular.
The acknowledgment of Barth's "two realms" does not make
clear what criteria, if any, are to be employed for seeking and
affirming the authenticity of the secular. In other words, what
can be meant by *theology* of the secular if there is no fundamental relation between God and man mediated by man's religious, moral, and cultural experiences? In the absence of
defensible criteria, today's theologian seeks to affirm the world
either with very little to say about his affirmation, or by simply
borrowing the language of the secular sciences and social sciences and dubbing it "theology of secularization."

If Barth's is one major voice in the contemporary religious
crisis, that of Paul Tillich is the other. Tillich's thought represents a fundamental alternative to Barth, and hence a different
resource for analyzing and evaluating the process of secularization.

IV

The Theology of Correlation: Paul Tillich

Paul Tillich's greatness as a theologian rests on the success with which he probed the deepest meanings of man's experience in the twentieth century, interpreting it through an elaborate system of ideas drawn both from existentialist philosophy and the theological method of Schleiermacher. Compelled, in a sense, to exist between the old world stabilities of the nineteenth century and the ravages of life in the contemporary world, Tillich took the concept of the "boundary" as the most appropriate symbol for expressing his personal and intellectual development:

> At almost every point, I have had to stand between alternative possibilities of existence, to be completely at home in neither and to take no definitive stand against either. Since thinking presupposes receptiveness to new possibilities, this position is fruitful for thought; but it is difficult and dangerous in life, which again and again demands decisions and thus the exclu-

sion of alternatives. This disposition and its tension have determined both my destiny and my work.[1]

Tillich's entire theological enterprise is marked by the meaning of the boundary, of "standing between," yet seeking the deep, inner ground beneath which—despite the tensions, indeed because of them—religion and culture, church and society, theology and philosophy hold together in creative relationship. Tillich says that the experience and meaning of the boundary began for him in the contrasting temperaments of his parents— a father from eastern Germany, with its stern piety and regard for authority, and a mother from western Germany, a place which has a "zest for life, love of the concrete, mobility, rationality, and democracy." [2]

Like Karl Barth, Tillich fled from Nazi Germany, coming to the United States in 1933. He taught at Union Theological Seminary (New York), Harvard University, and the University of Chicago, until his death at the age of seventy-nine in 1965. He often spoke of the profound psychological, social, and religious impact on one who is compelled to leave his home to take up life in an alien land. Such a man wants to accept the new country, to make it his own, but the living memory of his homeland prevents this. Yet, the departure from the old country against a background of political repression and persecution amounts to a rejection of the homeland. Such a man, Tillich said, is compelled to spend the balance of his life on the boundary, suffering from the experience of his estrangement but somehow deepened by it.

Tillich's theology is as concerned with understanding man's religious feeling and experience as it is with discerning the reality of God. This means that, in contradistinction to Barth, Tillich regards religious experience as a positive resource for disciplined reflection on the meaning of God in his relation to man and the world. Although he agrees with Barth that revelation, not religion, is the *source* of man's knowledge of God, he holds that revelation is mediated by human experience; it is with this *religious* experience that one must begin as a theologian.

One can see here the influence of Schleiermacher, who made the starting-point of his theology the unique content of man's religious experience. For Tillich, like Schleiermacher, religion includes not only formal or traditional practices and ceremonies but also those deeper expressions of man's creative spirit to be found in art, literature, and philosophy.

Tillich argues that if one seeks to understand religion, he must beware of two common but false equations: the equation of religion with a special divine revelation, and the equation of religion with a particular function of man's creative spirit,[3] whether it be his intellect, moral conscience, or capacity for feeling. In the former equation, religion as an utterly unique reality—a particular manifestation or act of the Holy—is cut off from the realm of the human spirit. According to Tillich, this is a mistake because, however unique the phenomenon of religion may be, it is a particular aspect of that complex of feeling, thought, and action which gives man his capacity for creative self-expression.

In the latter equation the opposite error occurs. Religion is identified so completely with one or another function of the human spirit that it loses its uniqueness. When religion becomes identified with morality, as it did with theologians influenced by Immanuel Kant, or when it threatens to become identified with feeling or man's subjective states, as can happen with theologians who follow the method of Schleiermacher, then that which is distinctly *religious* in religion is obscured.

Religion is neither separate from man's creative or spiritual functions, nor is it to be equated with any of these functions. What, then, is religion? Religion, says Tillich, is the dimension of depth in *all* the creative functions of the human spirit. He writes:

What does the metaphor *depth* mean? It means that the religious aspect points to that which is ultimate, infinite, unconditional in man's spiritual life. Religion, in the largest and most basic sense of the word, is ultimate concern. And ultimate concern is manifest in all creative functions of the human spirit.[4]

This is Tillich's fundamental understanding of the role and meaning of religion in human life. He illustrates his point by saying that in the moral sphere, depth is manifested as "the unconditional seriousness of the moral demand." This means that every genuine moral endeavor includes the profound desire to know and to do that which is moral. This is the expression of a moral concern which is ultimate or unconditional, hence, in Tillich's terms, religious. When one takes his moral obligations with ultimate seriousness, one in fact assumes the religious attitude in the very midst of his moral activity. It is not moral reflections or the moral acts in themselves that are religious; rather, it is the *way* in which one engages in them— with "unconditional seriousness," with "ultimate concern," penetrating to and expressing the "depth" of moral feelings, thoughts, and commitments.

Just as Tillich regards moral behavior to have a religious dimension, so he regards other functions of man's spiritual life. "Ultimate concern," he writes, "is manifest in the realm of knowledge as the passionate longing for ultimate reality"; and "Ultimate concern is manifest in the aesthetic function of the human spirit as the infinite desire to express ultimate meaning." [5]

According to Tillich's analysis, when religion is thus understood, no man can escape it, no man can reject it. In the process of rejecting it, in the very act of summoning good moral or intellectual or historical grounds for rejecting religion, one evinces that seriousness, that "ultimate concern" which makes him a religious person. Even the atheist falls within Tillich's definition of religion. In his serious and mature reflection on the problem of God in relation to human life, he shows a sense of ultimacy which in many instances exceeds that of conventional and unreflective religious people.

Here one is compelled to ask Tillich, Is there not a difference between religion as "ultimate concern" and religion as it is traditionally regarded, the religion which is manifestly religious?

It is important to say first that Tillich recognizes the existence of religion in the formal sense. He knows that institutional religion as a discrete realm of experience can be distinguished from other realms such as the intellectual or the moral or the aesthetic. It is also important to note that it is in the patterns of religious traditions that Tillich finds his clue to the presence of the religious dimension in other aspects of man's experience. On this point he informs us that "ultimate concern" is an abstract rendering of the great commandment in the Old Testament that bids every human being to love God with all his heart, with all his soul, and with all his mind.[6] Tillich finds meaning from the converse statement of this injunction: whatever is so loved becomes for the individual a god, and a man's relationship to what he loves is religious whether or not he so recognizes it. The religious factor in human life may be wider and deeper than the beliefs and ceremonies of churches, but the two are related, and in that relationship we find the key to Tillich's whole system of religious thought.

He states that religion in the form of myths, cults, and ecclesiastical institutions has developed "because of the tragic estrangement of man's spiritual life from its own ground and depth." [7] What he means is that, through all history, man has been frustrated in his philosophical and scientific attempts to learn what is ultimately real—not what proves to be real provisionally, or what he experiences as real, or what is regarded in a particular culture as real, but what is real beyond all the relativities of time, history, and human opinion. Man has been similarly frustrated in his efforts to affirm what is of ultimate moral worth, to discover absolute truth, and to give perfect poetic expression to his highest, finest feelings. Man appears to be made for the ultimate, and yet his history is a record of his failures to realize the ultimate. It is precisely in response to this failure that religion has arisen and developed, in the hope that the ultimate will make its own way to man. The hope is that man's uncertainties—cognitive, moral, and aesthetic—will be overcome by a divine revelation which will disclose to him what is ultimately real, thereby giving him insight into the absolute character of truth, goodness, and beauty. To Tillich, religion in the traditional sense is a reaction to a certain failure in human existence. It reflects the discontinuity and brokenness of man's spiritual life, experienced in his failure to achieve ultimate meaning and in his perpetual dissatisfaction with the provisional and partial meanings he discovers.

Religion as ultimate concern, the dimension of depth in man's spiritual life, *and* religion as a reaction to the tragic estrangement of man's spirit from its own ground and depth: for Tillich this seeming contradiction expresses the unique situation of man in relation to religion. Man is both at one with *and* at odds with what is ultimately real. Continuity and discontinuity, harmony and strife characterize his human existence. Man is estranged from his own ground and depth, but he is not divorced from it; he continues to express the ultimate in all his creative experiences, however fragmentedly. We will deal at greater length with the distinct meaning of this estrangement, but, for the moment, we must better understand Tillich's notion of ultimate concern.

An ultimate concern is one which elicits our total, unconditional commitment, as contrasted to a "preliminary" concern, in which our investment is less than complete.[8] Whatever the object of an ultimate concern, one's relation to it is religious because he loves it, as the Bible enjoins, "with all your heart, and with all your soul, and with all your mind, and with all your strength." Implicit to that kind of commitment is the expectation of a commensurate fulfillment: the ultimate aim of a total surrender to the object of ultimate concern is total fulfillment, a fulfillment of heart, soul, and mind. Since ultimate concern is an act of the total personality, the satisfaction of our ultimate concern must occur at every level. It must satisfy our cognitive demand for knowledge of ultimate reality; it must satisfy the demand of our will for action leading to ultimate good; and it must satisfy our emotional demand for a purposeful relationship. Such is the analysis of ultimate concern from the point of view of the subject; but what is the ultimate concern from the point of view of the object?

It is quite clear, says Tillich, that anything in the world could be, and has been, an object of man's ultimate concern. Nation, race, sex, success, and money can be, and are for many, the objects of ultimate concern; each can be a god, an object of total commitment. An ultimate concern is no less religious if its object is one of the objects of the world. What makes an ultimate concern religious is not its object but *the quality of the subject's relationship*—that it is a matter of ultimate or unconditional concern.

But even if anything in the world could conceivably become an object of ultimate concern, it does not follow in Tillich's view that every such concern has meaning and is good; it does not follow that because the attitude toward an object is religious, that particular expression of religion is "creative." It may in fact be the very opposite—demonic or destructive.[9] This, then, raises the question of the status of the object in Tillich's analysis of religion as ultimate concern. Tillich argues that only when the object of ultimate concern is itself truly ultimate is it a *proper*—that is to say, creative, not demonically destructive—object of man's unconditional concern.

Tillich's argument is partly a description of the personality disorder which takes place in human beings when they are neurotically attached to material objects of one kind or another; and it is partly a normative judgment of Tillich's, reflecting his own philosophical-theological judgments as to what is truly ultimate and what is not. To explain the former case, Tillich cites the example of the nation becoming an object of individual or corporate ultimate concern. In extreme patriotism, numerous psycho-neurotic patterns begin to appear, beginning with the unwillingness to tolerate criticism of one's country. "My country can do no wrong," "God has a special love for my country," these are expressions typical of a situation where the nation has transcended the realm of the finite and has become a god for the individual. Here the citizen's patriotic love for homeland has passed into the religion of patriotism. Tillich writes:

> If a national group makes the life and growth of the nation its ultimate concern, it demands that all other concerns, economic well-being, health and life, family, aesthetic and cognitive truth, justice and humanity, be sacrificed. The extreme nationalisms of our century are laboratories for the study of what ultimate concern means in all aspects of human existence, including the smallest concern of one's daily life. Everything is centered in the only god, the nation—a god who certainly proves to be a demon, but who shows clearly the unconditional character of an ultimate concern.[10]

The aim of an ultimate concern is self-fulfillment through an act of the total personality. This fulfillment does not occur when nation, sex, or race become objects of ultimate concern. The basic wholeness of the personality is not preserved and creatively extended; rather, disruption occurs.[11] Obsession with sex satisfies certain specific physical needs but engenders emotional and aesthetic anxieties. Obsession with race satisfies certain basic instincts and loyalties but can engender ethical and intellectual anxieties. In order for the self to be truly fulfilled through its ultimate concern, there must be opportunity for the creative expression of all the faculties of the human spirit: intellectual, moral, and aesthetic. This can only happen, according to Tillich, when that which is truly ultimate replaces that which is finite and conditional as the object of man's ultimate concern.

This introduces the question of the philosophical-theological judgment Tillich feels is implicit to the meaning of religion as ultimate concern. When Tillich talks about the personality disruption that occurs when finite objects are made matters of ultimate loyalty, he is relying heavily on the data of psychoneurosis to which modern clinical psychology points. But for

Tillich these data also parallel, and in a sense confirm, the insight of metaphysical philosophers, such as Plato and Spinoza, who distinguish between the relative and the absolute, between the conditional and the unconditional, and between the finite and the infinite. Although metaphysical philosophers may disagree about what is relative and what is absolute, they have agreed—or at least the more idealistic thinkers, such as Spinoza, Schleiermacher, and Schelling have agreed—that the relative, conditional, and finite refers to the material, temporal world of interdependencies; and the absolute, unconditional, and infinite refers to a transcendent realm of being, value, and meaning which is not material and temporal and is in no way dependent on any higher thing.

The very fact that human beings have ultimate concerns convinces Tillich that they are related to that which metaphysical philosophy has analyzed as the ultimate.[12] It further convinces him that the greatest problem in contemporary existence is man's experience of this relationship as one of estrangement. The experience of ultimate concern, however it occurs, is the experience of the ultimate; it is the experience of that which is finally a matter of life or death, meaning or meaninglessness, good or evil, peace or war in each human being. This is what Tillich means when he states that "our ultimate concern is that which determines our being or not-being." He amplifies his meaning in the following words:

> Nothing can be of ultimate concern for us which does not have the power of threatening and saving our being. The term "being" in this context does not designate existence in time and space. Existence is continuously threatened and saved by things and events which have no ultimate concern for us. But the term "being" means the whole of human reality, the structure, the meaning, and the aim of existence. All this is threatened; it can be lost or saved. Man is ultimately concerned about his being and meaning. "To be or not to be" in *this* sense is a matter of ultimate, unconditional, total, and infinite concern. Man is infinitely concerned about the infinite to

which he belongs, from which he is separated, and for which he is longing. Man is totally concerned about the totality which is his true being and which is disrupted in time and space. Man is unconditionally concerned about that which conditions his being beyond all the conditions in him and around him. Man is ultimately concerned about that which determines his ultimate destiny beyond all preliminary necessities and accidents.[13]

To have an ultimate concern includes perception of the ultimate, but it also includes the risk that one may mistake the finite or conditioned to be the ultimate. This happens in extreme patriotism, in racial ideologies, and in countless other acts of human passion. It is the practice that the Bible calls idolatry, the elevation of a preliminary concern to ultimacy. The ultimate expresses itself through the finite, the material, which is its vehicle; but when the vehicle of the ultimate is mistaken for the ultimate itself, a demonic energy is released.

One can say, in summary, that Tillich uses a method of analysis which aims to disclose the religious dimension or depth in man's cultural experience and expression. Man experiences the ultimate morally, aesthetically, and intellectually, and he gives expression to his experience in moral conceptions and codes, in systems of law, in poetry and art and music, in metaphysical and ethical philosophies, and in scientific accounts of the material universe. Often Tillich speaks of man's ultimate concern as the "dynamic of faith" which can be attributed to all men in their efforts to give meaning to their experience of reality. It is not the intention (nor should it be) of the legislator, the artist, or the scientist to express the ultimate, to speak of his faith as legislator, artist, or scientist; but in performing his chosen task, Tillich thinks, he invariably expresses his faith, showing how the ultimate has been experienced through the unique perceptions of his own special training and knowledge.

Although culture is a vehicle for expressing the ultimate, it is not in itself the ultimate. Culture cannot express perfectly the ultimate; it always falls short. No picture achieves the depth of beauty itself, no law ever presents man with true justice, no scientific hypothesis or philosophical system ever states with perfect cogency the inner nature of reality. The cultural work is material and finite, hence incomplete or imperfect; the depth or ultimacy which it seeks to penetrate is immaterial, infinite, and perfect. One of the great errors in man's thinking about religion is to confuse the cultural work for the object for which it stands; that is, to ignore the *symbolic* character and meaning of man's cultural expressions by interpreting and accepting these expressions literally. The most familiar instance of this occurs when the traditional symbols of religion are accepted literally and treated not as symbolic expressions of the Holy or the ultimate but as the Holy itself. This also happens whenever a particular philosophy, or political system, or moral outlook is deified by making it the exclusive expression of the ultimate. Here again, the symbolic role of culture is forgotten, and a destructive literalism sets in.

Tillich's analysis of religion, having as its aim the discovery of the religious aspects of culture, relies heavily on some rather broad concepts of modern personality psychology and on classical metaphysical philosophy. With these resources, Tillich developed the notions of ultimate concern, estrangement, and the ultimate, and such notions as the courage to be, being, and nonbeing.

The philosophical conceptions of being-itself or the unconditioned gave Tillich insight into the continuity between the expressions of human culture and the ultimate realities to which religion is witness; psychological notions of neurotic behavior gave him insight into the discontinuity of man's existence with those realities. Tillich's overall task was one of correlating the realm of religion to the realm of man's self-understanding and expression. He sought a way to understand man in terms of the continuities and discontinuities of his existence—and to achieve this understanding, he turned as much to man's culture as to the formal ideas and practices of religion. This was necessary for Tillich because of what he considered to be the real, internal connection between religion and culture. Indeed, his whole theological effort has often been characterized as a "theology of culture." [14]

"Whereas religion is the substance of culture, culture is the form of religion." This is the central proposition of Tillich's theological analysis of culture, reflecting his view of the way in which religion is present as the dimension of depth in all man's spiritual experiences and expressions.[15] To say that religion is the substance of culture means that every culture in human history develops from a set of supreme meanings and values, which that culture reflects in the finest acts of its self-expression. Thus, for Tillich, every culture is a culture because of a unifying set of beliefs to which one can refer as the culture's ultimate concern or faith. Every culture expresses its spiritual depth in what we have come to recognize as a culture's unique style— disclosed in its politics, its public and private expressions of worship, its art and literature, and its modes of education, commerce, and recreation.

When Tillich says culture is the form of religion, he means that religion expresses itself most profoundly in and through the style of a culture. Religion is thus incarnate in culture; it takes on flesh in every conceivable work of the human spirit as it responds to what it feels most deeply. In this respect, religion and culture are inseparable. There is no culture which is not at its root religious, and there is no religion which exists apart from culture—even the deliberate "anti-cultural" religion of monastic asceticism.

What is the mark of a theologian of culture? Tillich answers: ". . . in the whole of man's cultural creativity, an ultimate concern is present. Its immediate expression is the style of a culture. He who can read the style of a culture can discover its ultimate concern, its religious substance." [16] A culture's style is expressed symbolically. Each object of cultural meaning is a complex symbol, expressing that meaning which is the ultimate concern of that group which uses it as its symbol. Symbols are the language of religion, and Tillich urges his readers to achieve an exact understanding of the structure and dynamic of the symbol.

Tillich argues that a symbol should be carefully distinguished from a sign; they are alike in that they both point beyond themselves, but only a symbol *participates in the reality to which it points*.[17] This is illustrated by Tillich in the difference between a traffic stop sign and the national flag of a country. The ordinary stop sign has the color red. This color is selected because it is a bright color and can be seen easily at great distances. But, the stop sign could conceivably be another color—any maximally bright color—and continue to perform its assigned task. We have agreed as a matter of convention to make the traffic stop sign red. There is no *necessary* connection, according to Tillich, between this color and the act of stopping at the traffic intersection. In that sense, the stop sign is a genuine "sign," for it does not participate in the reality to which it points.

The American flag, on the other hand, is a true symbol, for it participates in the reality which it symbolizes. The clearest test for this is to imagine for a moment a presidential decree that would substitute for Old Glory another pattern of color. The colors of the flag are identified with important events of America's formative history in a way that the red of the traffic sign is not. The American flag as symbol genuinely participates in the reality to which it points—the unity of the American states—and its own origin is a significant chapter in American history.

Tillich writes: "Every symbol opens up a level of reality for which non-symbolic speaking is inadequate."[18] Artistic symbols, for example, show us levels of reality which the artist has communicated to us, using a medium unique to him.

> You can take that which a landscape of Rubens, for instance, mediates to you. You cannot have this experience in any other way than through this painting made by Rubens. This land-

scape has some heroic character; it has character of balance, of colors, of weights, of values, and so on. All this is very external. What this mediates to you cannot be expressed in any other way than through the painting itself. The same is true also in the relationship of poetry and philosophy.[19]

If the symbol opens up levels of reality, it is because it successfully reaches hidden levels of reality in the human soul, "levels of our interior reality. . . . [the] symbol is two-edged. It opens up reality and it opens up the soul," [20] Tillich tells us. This means that the symbol must not only present its object in a significant way, it must also convey this object effectively to the subject, the human user of the symbol. Tillich's analysis of the "two-edged" character of a symbol is splendidly illustrated by social and political events in the United States that have led to some citizens' disenchantment with the traditional sanctity of the American flag, and have led others to efforts to re-establish the power of the flag in American life. The power of all symbols depends as much on the users' continued experience of the meaning symbolized as on the objective adequacy of the symbol itself.

Culture is replete with political and artistic symbols, religious symbols, cognitive symbols of philosophy and science, and the symbols of law and social relations. But it is in the artistic symbol that Tillich seems to find the most reliable and incisive expression of a people's experience of the depth of reality, disclosing the style of its culture. *Guernica*, Picasso's painting done in 1937, is for Tillich the greatest symbol of the predicament of contemporary man.[21] *Guernica* conveys dramatically the condition of twentieth-century existence: estrangement.

Tillich thinks that the central experience of our time is man's estrangement from a depth of reality and meaning to which he belongs and for which he yearns. Estrangement is the experience of the loss of meaning as exemplified in emptiness, aloneness, destruction, and anxiety. This is the condition of twentieth-century existence, a condition into which all contemporary men are born and from which they cannot flee. It suggests that the style of modern life is a deep, unrelieved insecurity whose results are seen constantly in frantic, obsessive acts and relationships.

Picasso's painting has as its subject the bombing of a small town in Spain by fascist planes during the Spanish Civil War. But it is not the depiction of this event that gives *Guernica* its power; Tillich explains that the power is created by the artistic style employed, and style is what carries the symbolic meaning in a work of art. Picasso's style in *Guernica* most powerfully expresses the quality of man's twentieth-century experience. According to Tillich, style is a function of how the artist sees his subject, and how he is therefore influenced to express the subject. Although style is expressed through lines, shapes, and colors, style has mainly to do with a way of looking at reality, especially the human reality, a way which every artist has and which is profoundly influenced by his emotions, his values, his beliefs, his cumulative experience in the world, and his aspirations. Style is the artist's ultimate concern *as informing his actual labor and as reflected in the objects resulting from his labor.* Tillich writes:

> . . . I would say that every style points to a self-interpretation of man, thus answering the question of the ultimate meaning of life. Whatever the subject matter which an artist chooses, however strong or weak his artistic form, he cannot help but betray by his style his own ultimate concern, as well as that of his group, and his period. He cannot escape religion even if he rejects religion, for religion is the state of being ultimately concerned. And in every style the ultimate concern of a human group or period is manifest.[22]

"Picasso's *Guernica* is a great Protestant painting," Tillich claims. This seems like a strange remark at first, but what he is saying is that *Guernica* expresses symbolically a meaning which can best be interpreted by the religious outlook of Protestantism. Tillich sees in the style of *Guernica*—in the terrifying image presented by the strange shapes, the broken faces, the gaping mouths—the central elements of the Protestant vision of reality: "infinite distance between God and man," "man's finitude," "his subjection to death," "his estrangement from his true being and his bondage to demonic forces—forces of self-destruction." [23]

It is important to add that, though a painting like *Guernica* expresses the estrangement of man's contemporary life, the very existence of works of art, that is, the possibility of artistic creation, is itself a source of healing that closes the gap between man and the depth of reality with which he seeks to reunite. Tillich writes:

. . . The human situation in its conflicts should be expressed courageously. If it is expressed, it is already transcended: He who can bear and express guilt shows that he already knows about "acceptance-in-spite-of." He who can bear and express meaninglessness shows that he experiences meaning within his desert of meaninglessness.[24]

Tillich also finds in *Guernica* a symbolic confirmation of the existential interpretation of contemporary man's existence. Existential philosophers have spoken of the severe dislocation suffered by the human spirit because of the industrialization of society. In man's search for technical mastery over his world, the result, says Tillich, has been the loss of "the dimension of depth in his encounter with reality."

The system of finite interpretations which we call the universe has become self-sufficient. It is calculable and manageable and can be improved from the point of view of man's needs and desires. Since the beginning of the 18th century God has been removed from the power field of man's activities. He has been put alongside the world without permission to interfere with it because every interference would disturb man's technical and business calculations. The result is that God has become superfluous and the universe left to man as its master.[25]

The Erosion of Faith

A second result of the industrialization of society has been the denial of man's sinfulness. For, with the belief that man is the master of the world, comes the accompanying belief that there is no essential perversity in man.

> The conflict between what essentially is and what actually is, [man's] estrangement, or in traditional terms his fallen state, is disregarded. Death and guilt disappear even in the preaching of early industrial society. Their acknowledgment would interfere with man's progressive conquest of nature, outside and inside himself. Man has shortcomings, but there is no sin and certainly no universal sinfulness.[26]

With the belief in man's creative power and the denial of his sinfulness goes the assumption that man's technological, scientific, and social efforts will ameliorate the worst conditions of modern society. Tillich describes two attitudes of the church toward this assumption. The first was conservative in denouncing it and retreating behind the traditionalism as seen in "doctrine, cult, and life." The second was liberal, and involved an accommodation in which Christianity's message, expressed in the belief that Christ came to the world because men were utterly lost in sin, was itself forgotten.

Existential philosophy, Tillich argues, is the only adequate interpretation of the impact of the development of industrial society on the human spirit.

> Existentialism, in the largest sense, is the protest against the spirit of industrial society within the framework of industrial society. The protest is directed against the position of man in the system of production and consumption of our society. Man is supposed to be the master of his world and of himself. But actually he has become a part of the reality he has created, an object among objects, a thing among things, a cog within a universal machine to which he must adapt himself in order not to be smashed by it. But this adaptation makes him a means for ends which are means themselves, and in which an ultimate

end is lacking. Out of this predicament of man in the industrial society the experiences of emptiness and meaninglessness, of dehumanization and estrangement have resulted. Man has ceased to encounter reality as meaningful. Reality in its ordinary forms and structures does not speak to him any longer.[27]

The answer to this predicament is not retreat nor accommodation. The answer, says Tillich, has been provided by divine revelation. Here Tillich explains the relevance of theology to the contemporary predicament of man.

Tillich tells us that theology is the communication of the content of religious faith to man.[28] Since the theologian in this instance is a Christian, his task is to communicate the content of *Christian* faith. The theologian must work between two related poles: (1) articulating the message of Christianity, defining its contents, and (2) communicating the message of Christianity to man. This definition of theology obviously represents an alternative to Barth's. For Barth, the aim of theology is not to communicate the Christian message; rather, it is to reproduce the authentic Word of God dogmatically, to witness to its presence in the authoritative words of the Bible. And man does not so much receive the Word as the Word somehow (by God's own miraculous agency) brings man's faith to knowledge of itself. In contrast to Barth, Tillich recognizes theology as a human enterprise. (Barth also claims this, but his analysis of the theological enterprise makes it impossible for him to defend his claim.) Theology, Tillich asserts, is *logos* about *theos*,[29] human thinking and language about God—language, moreover, that can be effective only if it accurately expresses its subject matter in terms that have meaning for man.

If the theologian is to be successful in communicating the religious message he must know who man is in the sense of his historical-cultural situation. For Tillich, this means implicitly that the terms in which Christian theology communicated its message in the first century or in the thirteenth century or in the nineteenth century are probably not useful terms in the twentieth century. Tillich's theology demands *relevance*. The basis of a relevant theology is its ability to speak within the historical-cultural symbols by which man expresses the meaning of his experience of God, himself, others, and the world at large.

In order for the theologian's work to be relevant, he must use all contemporary modes of inquiry to unravel the symbols of the contemporary historical-cultural situation of man. Through psychology, sociology, philosophy, art, and literature (any discipline, in short, that sheds light on the human situation today), we gain knowledge of contemporary man's understanding of himself.

Every theology which speaks relevantly to the human situation, Tillich says, does so through a correlation—a correlation between the question implied in man's situation and the answer to the question, which theology provides.[30] By "the question" Tillich means man's fundamental questions about himself: "Who am I?" "Where did I come from?" "What is to become of me?" Tillich tells us that men have always asked these questions, but we have come to appreciate them as distinct philosophical questions through the efforts of existential thinkers. Among these basic questions, the larger question, "Who is man?" has come to have special meaning for us now because, through the rapid industrialization of society, there has arisen a challenge to the unique value of the humanity of man. Existentialism, Tillich argues, can be regarded as a philosophical protest against the dehumanization of man which has occurred in the industrial society. Existentialism begins by raising the question of man's humanity and seeks an answer in man's capacity for self-affirmation through his freedom or power of decision. Tillich has been profoundly influenced by the existential analysis of man as it appears in the writings of Kierkegaard and Heidegger, the novels of Kafka, the plays of Sartre, and in modern art, especially in a painting such as Picasso's *Guernica*. These are diverse works, but they share the common perception that the quality of human existence today is shaped by the experiences of meaninglessness, lostness, violence, anxiety, and despair; in a word, "estrangement." Man is estranged from himself and from others; he is dislocated, uprooted, abandoned, without obvious hope of safety or security. The existential situation of modern man as analyzed by the philosophy of existentialism is fundamentally one of alienation. Man is, literally, an alien in his own world; he feels foreign, strange, not-at-home.

We perceive the quality of alienated existence in the stories of Franz Kafka. In "The Metamorphosis," a man wakes one morning to discover that he has been mysteriously transformed into a giant cockroach, forever doomed to remain as a bug—not in a bug-world, to which he might presumably adjust, but in a human world to which he can never adjust.[31] In *The Trial*, a man is suddenly arrested for no apparent reason, and is compelled to spend the rest of his life seeking acquittal from a nameless charge, an acquittal, moreover, which he is told is impossible.[32] These are parables of the modern predicament of man created by the supreme irony that the machines which man has created to liberate himself, have in fact enslaved the creator, making it more and more difficult for man to express himself as an individual. Man, whose brilliant mind invented the machines, is reduced to a faceless, cog-like repairman, who must keep the machines running In losing his sense of individuality, he has lost what the existentialists hold to be the source and seal of his humanity.

Tillich accepts this irony and speaks of man's alienation as a question to which the message of theology is an answer. But if the Christian religion speaks of God, Jesus Christ, grace, sin, and faith, then these must be shown to answer the alienation, the despair, and the meaninglessness of contemporary human existence.

To do this Tillich incorporates into this theology what he identifies as an ontological analysis, that is, an analysis of reality-itself, the structure which underlies all reality, including that of man. If man is estranged, he is estranged from reality; and if Christianity is an answer to estrangement, it is so, in Tillich's view, because it promises a genuine reunion with reality. But what is this reality? And how is reality the basis of the correlation of existential questions and theological answers? Tillich's reply is to be found in his imaginative use of the ancient philosophical notion of being.

The experience of nonbeing, Tillich writes, inevitably raises a question for man: "Why is there something? Why not nothing?" [33] The question of being is unanswerable, argues Tillich, "for every possible answer would be subject to the same question in an infinite regression." [34] Thinking itself presupposes being. Even in the *idea* of nothing, we are attributing the quality of being to nothing. Thus, being is inescapable, but the experience of being threatened by nonbeing continues to be a question in our minds. The question, "Why being?" is unanswerable, but not the question, "What is being?" This, says Tillich, is the fundamental ontological question.

> What is being itself? What is that which is not a special being or a group of beings, not something concrete or something abstract, but rather something which is always thought implicitly and sometimes explicitly if something is said to *be*? [35]

It is the task of ontology to describe being, to articulate the structure of reality present in all things. But ontology cannot answer the question, "What is being itself?" This question, Tillich contends, is answered by theology. God, in the language of the Bible, is affirmed as the being who is above all other beings.

Tillich asserts that all things participate in being, in other words, they are part of reality. But what is the nature of that essential, universal reality which is shared by all existing things? It is the task of ontological philosophy to answer this question. Here Tillich introduces an important point bearing on the relation between ontology and theology. Although the aim of ontology is the analysis of the structure of being as such—the reality which is present in and shared by all things that are—

theology is concerned with being only with respect to man and his existence. Theology wishes to know reality as it has a bearing on human existence, for theology wishes to answer the question of estrangement.

Just as each thing in the world possesses being, so each thing can lose its being. Life, in fact, consists of the alternation between being and nonbeing, a movement in which all things are in the process of either coming-to-be or ceasing-to-be. All things that *are*, are by that very fact threatened by dissolution, threatened by what Tillich calls "the power of nonbeing." [36] But man alone, of all existent beings, is *conscious* of this threat. Man realizes that the world and all things in it, including himself, are in constant change, characterized by impermanence, dissolution, and death. He also realizes, however, that there is a world, a "something" which continues to be despite the acids of change, despite the very power in reality to reduce all to nothing. Theology answers the question of being by saying there is one being which is not *a* being alongside other beings, there is a being which is being-itself, a being which is not threatened by nonbeing but which is the ground of being and the power of being in all things to resist nonbeing; this is God.

Why, then, is there something and not nothing? Why is there reality and not nothingness? The question is unanswerable. But because God *is*—God who is being-itself—there is something and not nothing.

Tillich's definition of God as being-itself reflects his effort to overcome the supernaturalistic theism that has characterized Christian theology. Tillich rejects the concept of God as a being like all other beings, but at a superior level. Were God *a* being, even the most perfect of beings, he would exist subject to the threat of nonbeing, and not, therefore, being-itself with the power to resist nonbeing. This means that Tillich must reject the attempt to prove the existence of God rationally, as such thinkers as Thomas Aquinas and Anselm of Canterbury have assayed to do.[37] Such attempts suppose that God is *a* being, not being-itself. From Tillich's point of view, rational proofs of God's existence are philosophically and theologically meaningless.

One of the important implications of Tillich's notion of God is that all language used to refer to God must be regarded as conveying not literal but symbolic meaning.[38] The language drawn from existence, applicable to man's experience within existence, cannot apply to God in a literal, descriptive fashion. Although God is not part of the world of existence, he is the ground of existence, that upon which existence rests. This means that there is continuity between man's experience, including his religious experience, and the transcending reality of God. So that when man speaks of God, he uses the verbal symbols, "father," "lord," "master," "creator," "God," "justice," "power," "one," and so on. God is not literally the father of mankind, but the religious experience of a common humanity under God renders the phrase "God, the Father" a symbolically appropriate expression of the meaning of man's experience. Tillich's analysis of the power of a symbol shows the inescapability of symbols for expressing the depths of man's experience, including his experience of God. And symbols are not limited to words; any work of man's imagination can be and has been employed symbolically.

The experience of nonbeing is that of estrangement, which itself leads to a profound question: Can man's estrangement be overcome, can his internal division of being and nonbeing be eliminated? This is a question raised by existential philosophy. Christian theology's answer, according to Tillich, is Jesus Christ: he who, living within existence, proved victorious over estrangement, reuniting man with the ground of being. Before we can see precisely how Tillich regards Jesus Christ as a relevant answer to the question of conquering estrangement, it is necessary to see how Tillich understands the origins of man's estrangement.

Tillich claims that of all the creaturely beings of the world, man is unique, for man alone is free.[39] All other creatures are products of their environment. Only man is both subject to environment and shaper of that environment. Only man, because of his freedom, can be regarded as responsible for his actions. Man's freedom bestows on him the unique capacity of self-transcendence; through freedom, man is able to view himself as an individual; and through the creative imagination which is part of freedom, to develop as a person.

But, says Tillich, man possesses his freedom only within the limiting conditions of his creaturely existence.[40] Man may be unique among creatures, but he, too, is a creature, therefore his freedom is limited by the same force that operates on all beings in existence: the threat of nonbeing. Man is free but he is *finitely* free, Tillich states, and the measure of his finitude is his subjection to the power of nonbeing. In his insecurity about life, in his desperate efforts to preserve the present moment, in his fear of the future, we see man's reaction to the awesome mystery of death. The impermanence of all living beings creates in us a great insecurity about our relationships, especially with other human beings.

The power of nonbeing is also seen in the quality of contemporary man's experience of the loss of place. Through the rapid industrialization of society, man no longer has his "place"; he is uprooted, cast into space without the security of a home.[41] To be sure, man is aware of these forces of nonbeing and seeks to cope with them. In this respect, man again shows his uniqueness, for he alone is capable of reflection and able to develop an idea about the power of nonbeing. In this lies man's freedom, and though it is "finite freedom," it is *freedom;* it is the possibility of creative meaning and living and, through the freedom of choice, the possibility of self-destruction as well. Despite his finitude, man possesses "infinity," the capacity for constantly envisaging and realizing new possibilities of meaning and value.

Man is free, yet he is finite; he is subject to the threat of nonbeing; he is capable of self-transcendence, of appreciating the uniqueness of his creatureliness, yet like every creature, he comes into life facing the destiny of death. This is man's existential predicament: between possibilities and limitations, be-

The Erosion of Faith

experience of man in this predicament is that of anxiety. Pos-
and alienness, man cannot but be anxious about the meaning of
his existence, the worth of his labors, the shape of the future,
and the real meaning of his life. It is in this anxiety, a condition
produced by finite freedom, that man submits to the threat of
to reckon with death. We see man's surrender in the psycho-
which seeks to meet the threat of death; in obsessive personal
which seek to compensate for the loss of a sense of place.
Psycho-neurotic actions like these are, for Tillich, the empirical
ground of his being when, declining the courage to affirm being
(in spite of the threat of nonbeing), he submits to nonbeing in

It is important to recognize that in Tillich's view the threat
despairing actions. If this were so there would be absolutely no
hope for man to overcome the threat of nonbeing, there would
be no basis for that courage by which man affirms being in

Tillich contends that, though man's estrangement is not ne-
cessitated by his finitude, it is made inevitable. There is a fine,
tability. He claims that the biblical story of the Fall is a dramatic

have interpreted it—as an event that happened "once upon a time"—it should be understood as a myth or complex symbol, depicting not a set of individual sins but a universal human condition. Adam's Fall points to the condition of estrangement in which all men exist. Biblical symbolism and modern existential psychology reinforce each other by demonstrating that estrangement is an inevitable outcome of the anxiety of which finitude is the source.

As we indicated earlier, Tillich's argument is that theology alone can answer the question of human existence, and it has done so in communicating the meaning of Christianity's proclamation about Jesus Christ—the one who proved victorious over estrangement, and made that victory available to man. We can now see how Christ figures in Tillich's thought.

Is it possible for man to overcome his estrangement and reunite himself with the ground of being? If he cannot, he is doomed to an empty, meaningless life. But how can this condition be overcome? Tillich rejects the humanist solution that man, through his own powers, can overcome his estrangement. If man could truly help himself, Tillich argues, he would not be in the condition of estrangement. Tillich also rejects that traditional religious solution based on the belief in divine intervention in which God acts to "lift" man out of his estrangement, miraculously restoring him to unity with the divine ground. This solution is inadequate because it ignores the human, "receiving" side of salvation. If man is to be truly saved, then salvation must be available to him, but man must be able to receive it as his own, otherwise it could not be effective.

According to Tillich's existential-ontological analysis, estrangement can only be overcome by a source other than man, but in a way in which man himself can form a personal relationship to that which saves him. It is in the *person* of Jesus Christ that Tillich finds the answer to the question posed by man's estrangement.[43]

Tillich tells us that there are two intimately related aspects to the person of Jesus Christ: his genuine humanity, in which he is kindred to all mankind; and his oneness with God, utterly unique, which makes him the Christ. Jesus Christ is the man Jesus of Nazareth, born of human parents, who lived, preached, suffered, and died. It is not his actions that make Jesus the Christ, Tillich contends, but it is through his humanity, as we know it from the Gospel writers, that the qualities of the Christ are made manifest.

What makes Jesus the Christ is the presence in him of what Tillich calls the power of the New Being: the manifestation of the grace of God, a grace that redeems men from their self-destruction and gives them a new beginning, a new life, or what Saint Paul calls a "new creation." The New Being is the reassertion of the divine ground of being, reconciling estranged man in and through the person of Jesus.

The New Testament is itself evidence of the power of the New Being "shaking and transforming" those who came into contact with Jesus. The moral deeds, the sermons, the acts of healing, the willingness to undergo suffering and to be put to death are all, in Tillich's judgment, events which show the power of the New Being in Jesus. But they show something else, too: that Jesus is not a mere conductor or passive receptacle of the redemptive energy of God. Jesus may be the Christ because of the presence in him of the power of the New Being, but he also *became* the Christ because, at every point of his earthly career, he remained one with the will of God. Jesus was willing to sacrifice everything human in himself to everything divine—in other words, he was willing to make his humanity a perfectly obedient servant of the power of God. The stories in the New Testament of Christ's temptations in the desert symbolize Jesus' profound temptation which confronts all men: to arrogate to themselves the powers of God. According to Tillich, Jesus alone among men resisted this temptation by steadfastly offering his humanity as a willing servant to the divine will.

Jesus, as the Christ, is the answer to the question of existential estrangement, because he participated fully in human life but, through the power of the New Being in him, proved victorious over its estrangement. Therefore, says Tillich, only through him is the power of the New Being a possibility for other men, only through him can there be a new basis for a reunion of God and man, a healing of the breach in existence. But how is this victory of Jesus Christ brought to men? This is a question which Tillich must answer if he is to succeed in showing that Jesus Christ is a relevant answer to the question of estrangement.

Tillich says two things about the conquest of estrangement by Jesus Christ. First, the reunion of God and man accomplished by Jesus is a reality that cannot be undone by anything man does or does not do in regard to it. In traditional theological language, this reunion is the reconciliation of man and God through vicarious atonement wrought by Christ through his sufferings. Second, this reality can be beneficial to man only if man accepts it, and this requires a personal appropriation, "making it one's own." Man, Tillich states, must have the faith to acknowledge the fact that he has been accepted if he is to become a "new creature." That, says Tillich, is the hardest thing of all for the contemporary, guilt-ridden man: the courage to accept the fact that he is accepted, knowing very well that he is "unacceptable." [44]

The existential aspect of man's relationship to the New Being in Jesus Christ, requiring as it does the decision of faith, raises a crucial question for Tillich's theology of correlation. If, as Tillich asserts, Christ is the answer to man's estrangement, does this mean that "the answer" is nothing more than an apologia for the Christian religion or the Christian church—that man's only hope of reunion with the ground of being lies in his acceptance of Jesus as his Christ, as the New Being? Tillich strenuously shuns this conclusion. The beliefs and practices of the historic, institutional churches of Christianity are often unfaithful to the New Being, he tells us. In fact, man participates in the New Being without depending on confessed Christian faith whenever he has the courage to affirm being in spite of the threat of nonbeing.[45] Which is merely to say that when man courageously affirms and creates meanings in the midst of meaninglessness, when he struggles morally and intellectually against estrangement, then he is in fact responding to the New Being, to the renewing power of God himself, though he may not know or acknowledge this power in the person of Christ.

Despite Tillich's argument, however, it would be a mistake to think that one could regard Christ as the answer to the question of human existence without making the Christian religion a significant feature of this answer. Christ is not easily abstracted from the history of the Christian church, no matter how resolutely the *meaning* of Christ is construed as a universal meaning. Thus it is difficult to see how estrangement, a universal human condition, is "answered" by a religious event so closely identified with Western cultural history.

A comparison of the theological schemes of Paul Tillich and Karl Barth will show that what appears at first to be a difference in emphasis is ultimately a fundamental difference in philosophical presupposition and understanding. At first glance, Barth's thought represents an emphasis of the freedom or integrity of the Word of God, which is distinguishable from but not in conflict with the emphasis of Tillich's theology—the effective communication to man of the Word of God made manifest. Barth acknowledges the importance of communication, and believes that his dogmatic theology effectively communicates God's Word to man; Tillich acknowledges the integrity of the Christian message, and sees no compromise of this message in his theology of correlation. Where the fundamental difference occurs in the two theologies is at the level of presupposition.

Tillich seeks to emphasize the relevance of the Word of God as manifested in the Christian message, but he believes that the only intelligible way to state this relevance is by assuming from the beginning a structure common to both God and man. The integrity of the Word leads Barth to deny such a structure on the strength of a type of neo-Kantian presupposition of noumenal reality. The relevance of the Word leads Tillich to affirm such a structure, which he calls the structure of being. Tillich has continued the general outlook of German Romantic philosophy since Kant, that man's unity with God is fundamental to the human makeup and is given expression through the distinctly human qualities of imagination, feeling, freedom, and reason. Schleiermacher located the seat of this unity in man's affective states of feeling; Tillich locates it in man's experience of ultimate concern, an experience which is intellectual, moral, or practical, as well as affective. Tillich, like Schleiermacher, regards man as having a fundamental religious disposition which makes it possible for man to receive God's action. Without this disposition, God's Word, the Christian message, might as well be addressed to a stone wall. In this regard, Tillich looks on Barth's idea that the Word of God *creates* its hearer in the moment of its disclosure as a piece of supernaturalism which his theology of correlation can only reject. For one pole, the human pole of this correlation, consists of the criterion of intelligibility, and Barth's idea plainly defies this criterion. Tillich views theology as a distinctly human enterprise in which the human forms for receiving or understanding God's Word enjoy as much integrity or freedom as the Word itself.

It is important to recognize that Barth's critique of the tendency of Schleiermacher's theology and of liberal Protestant thought to domesticate the Word of God by equating it with the moral, religious, or "spiritual" experiences of man cannot be applied to Tillich. Tillich (and Barth) learned from Kierkegaard to appreciate "the infinite qualitative difference between God and man." Where Tillich saw the relevance of this statement was in the contemporary predicament of man as analyzed by existentialist philosophers and writers. Thus, when speaking of man's estrangement, Tillich does not mean total separation. Even in estrangement man can know God; he knows him in the form of the "question" which his experience of estrangement raises, a "question" which demands, and in part anticipates, the "answer" of God. In a remarkable fashion, Tillich avoids the religious optimism and idealism that beset liberal religious thinkers by facing directly the "tragic" dimension of human history as manifested in man's imperfect relationships to himself, to other men, and to God.

In the preceding chapter on Karl Barth's thought, we indicated the extent and character of Barth's influence on contemporary theology, especially in dealing with the problem of secularization. On the basis of Barth's critique of religion, many contemporary theologians welcome the displacement of religion by secular values and meanings as a recognition of the authenticity of the worldly realm hitherto denied by theology.

Paul Tillich, however, represents an alternative to Barth apropos the meaning of secularization. Tillich is no advocate of conventional religion, but he does regard religion, as "ultimate concern," as a dimension of the human psyche, manifested in virtually every human act. Religion, as ultimate concern, is inescapable. Secularization is the displacement of what is conventionally religious, not of what is *essentially* religious. Precisely in that way, the forces of secularization make a tremendous contribution to the discovery of what is truly religious in modern life. Indeed, in the very processes of secularization, in modern politics, economics, science, and technology, are to be found, according to Tillich, vivid expression of ultimate concern, and, hence, genuine witness to the ultimate, even though this witness may be negative and demonic.

Tillich must reject a theology of secularization that rests on the separation of the worldly and God, and whose aim is to affirm the worldly values. For Tillich, there can be no separation of the worldly and God; if religion in its essence means ultimate concern, then the worldly and God are joined in the depths of the human spirit. The task of the theologian of the secular cannot be the authentication of the worldly but rather the illumination of the authentic (or relevant) relationship between the worldly and God.

Younger theologians of the secular have now begun to argue

that what is at stake in the dissolution of the traditional style of religious life is the very notion itself of an ultimate. In such recent works as Harvey Cox's *The Secular City*, and the radical or death-of-God theologies of Thomas J. J. Altizer and William Hamilton, young authors have come to ask whether the central realization of modern man is not in fact the *loss* of ultimacy. Is man in the position, as one writer puts it, of "waiting for a new epiphany," in the meantime affirming, in a modestly human and not very religious way, persons and things closest to him? This question, as well as the writings of the young contemporary theologians, will be investigated at greater length in the closing chapters.

V

Theocentric Humanism: The Thomistic Philosophy of Jacques Maritain

The three men whose thought we now confront in succeeding chapters—Jacques Maritain, Nicolas Berdyaev, and Martin Buber—represent an important departure from the vision of God's relationship to the world and man, a vision which Barth and Tillich basically share. Barth and Tillich assume the perspective of a fundamental discontinuity between the divine and the human, though Tillich, unlike Barth, wishes to argue that despite this discontinuity man possesses knowledge of God. Maritain, Berdyaev, and Buber, on the other hand, proceed from an opposite point of departure: a fundamental *continuity* between the divine and the human. At its root this difference is explained by the different religious traditions that personally molded, as well as intellectually informed, each man. Maritain, Berdyaev, and Buber, like their Protestant counterparts Barth and Tillich, were influenced by the writings of Kierkegaard, and, with small exception, all of them continue in the style of Schleiermacher to regard theology as the task of understanding God and man's faith in God in the light of modern knowledge and the challenge of secularization. But Maritain was a convert to Roman Catholicism; Berdyaev was an Eastern Orthodox Christian exiled from his native Russia; and Buber was a Jew who, though educated in the traditions of European philosophy and letters, was decisively influenced by the mystical spirit and thought of Hasidism. Each of these thinkers draws from a religious tradition which emphasizes the relationship between God and man as symbolized by the biblical story of creation, a relationship that is not destroyed by secularization. Each of these thinkers tries to understand this relationship in the light of his own tradition.

The closing decades of the nineteenth century and the opening decades of the twentieth were an exciting period in European intellectual life. It was a time shaped by Nietzsche's critique of Christian culture, the application by Julian Huxley and Herbert Spencer of the new theory of evolution to social problems, and the writings of Marx and Engels. The intellectual style was skepticism on matters religious; a vigorous anti-clericalism prevailed. Science and the scientific method were hailed as the source of progress and the way to truth. The intellectual life was thought to be incompatible with religious belief and practice; ethical humanism, not theism, was the spiritual commitment of the intellectual. Jacques Maritain, regarded by many as the foremost Roman Catholic philosopher-theologian of the twentieth century, was born into this milieu in Paris in 1882, and educated at a time in which skepticism and scientism were at their zenith.

Maritain began his advanced study at the Sorbonne in biology, a field which at the time was deeply influenced by notions of the mechanistic character of reality, and of the progress of society through scientific and technological advances. At the Sorbonne, Maritain formed three associations which were to have a deep and lasting influence on his life and the development of his mind. The first was his marriage to Raissa Oumansoff, a fellow Sorbonne student. In a remarkable way his wife became Maritain's spiritual-intellectual *confrère*, beginning with their joint conversion to Roman Catholicism shortly after they were married. Maritain's appreciation of the role of religion in the human spirit, and of the relevance of the Christian religion and Catholicism to modern life, owes much to Raissa's sensibility, which she expressed in her own poetry, essays, and autobiography.[1]

The second association that Maritain formed during his Sorbonne days was with Henri Bergson, the great French philosopher who was then lecturing at the neighboring Collège de France. Bergson had become famous through his two earliest books, *Time and Free Will* (1888) and *Matter and Memory* (1896). Through him, Maritain came to see an alternative to the mechanistic and materialistic concepts of reality prevailing in scientific circles. Refuting materialism, Bergson claimed that there was an inner unity present in each thing. It could not be measured nor described; it could be grasped only by the intuitive capacities of the mind. He rejected the view of reality as a machine which functions "automatically" without purpose; instead, he "saw a 'creative evolution' that was grasping, blindly perhaps but yet steadily and irresistibly, toward some goal beyond even its own ken." [2] In reaction to the cosmic determinism fostered by the mechanistic philosophy of science, Bergson upheld the essential freedom of the individual human being in the world. His ideas persuaded Maritain that the basis of reality was spiritual, not material, and made it possible for Maritain not only to avoid the trends of the scientific philosophy of the day but also eventually to accept the philosophy of Thomas Aquinas.

The third association which Maritain formed at the Sorbonne led directly to his conversion to Roman Catholicism. Maritain was the son of a Protestant mother and a nominally Catholic father, and Raissa the daughter of orthodox Jewish parents who had immigrated to France from Russia. Early in their marriage the two became acquainted with Leon Bloy, an author, social critic, and devout Catholic. Once described as a "French

Catholic H. L. Mencken," [3] Bloy attracted followers through his fierce denunciations of "the political, social, and moral evils" of contemporary French life. It was he who persuaded the Maritains that the life of the intellect and Christian belief could be united to their mutual enrichment. He became their spiritual godfather when they embraced Catholic Christianity in 1906.

Some three years after Maritain's conversion, following the lead of his wife, he began reading Saint Thomas Aquinas. Quickly convinced of the supreme wisdom of Thomism, Maritain devoted himself to showing the relevance of this wisdom for the modern world, a sixty-year effort which led to a veritable Mount Everest of writings. In what follows, we have sought to grasp the essentials of the religious philosophy which Maritain constructed from the thought of Aquinas, and which he entrusted to modern men.

Despite the many differences of background, perspective, and method among Schleiermacher, Kierkegaard, Barth, and Tillich, there is a single question sounded in the theological reflection of them all. This is the question of the relation between two realms: a divine realm, which consists of the authority of God, the events of God's action attested by the faith of the writers of the Bible, the unique person of Jesus Christ for Christian faith, and, in a sense, the act of faith itself; and a human realm, which consists of the history of human events and the creations of the imagination which comprise man's culture. Our authors divide into two camps on this question: Kierkegaard and Barth tend to see the two realms as separate, the human realm in no way contributing meaning to the realm of God. Schleiermacher and Tillich view these realms as basically united in the depths of the human spirit, interpenetrating so that neither is complete without the other.

In introducing Jacques Maritain's contribution to contemporary theology, we can begin by saying that he belongs very much to the latter camp: Maritain has sought to articulate the claim that God is accessible to man through all the resources of

meaning present in history and culture. Maritain, like Schleiermacher and Tillich, believes that if these lines of the Bible mean
anything—". . . God said, Let us make man in our image, after
our likeness" (Genesis 1:26, RSV)—they mean that man, who
is the work of God, precisely as *God's* creature cannot be
without knowledge of his creator. Like his Protestant counterparts, Maritain seeks to formulate a system of ideas which can
illumine that spiritual dimension of existence in relation to which
man comes to know and express his "likeness" to God.

Maritain is no less a theologian than other authors in this
study; but, following the distinction between theology and
philosophy drawn by Aquinas, Maritain prefers to identify his
work as largely philosophical. Aquinas argued that there were
two sources of the knowledge of God: reason and faith.[4] Though
many truths of God can be known through *both* reason and
faith, by and large the knowledge of God discovered through
reason is different from the knowledge of God vouchsafed to
the faithful. Through rational reflection on his experience of
the world, man can discover particular truths about God, for
example, that God is the Creator and that God is one. This
knowledge is limited, however, in that it is not about God *per se*
but rather about God's agency in the world as known through
its effects. Other truths consist of what God himself has revealed
to the faithful for their salvation, for example, that God is one-
in-three and that God became man in Jesus Christ. Accordingly,
the philosopher can be distinguished in his methods from the
theologian. Whereas the philosopher relies on reason alone, that
is, rational reflection on the meaning of man's experience of the
world, the theologian uses reason for the "higher end" of interpreting and presenting those beliefs, based on scripture and
acknowledged by the church, that are necessary for salvation.
Following Aquinas in this restricted definition of theology,
Maritain, as we said, wishes to be regarded as a philosopher.
Let us rather avoid both words, however, and call Maritain's
thought "theocentric humanism," a term drawn from his own
essays. It conveys vividly the import and spirit of Maritain's

outlook.[5] For if Maritain's thought is a philosophy, it is in the main a philosophy of man in which the informing or controlling vision is religious, that is, the biblical affirmation of the divine roots of man.

The following passage in Saint Paul's Letter to the Romans is essential to the meaning of Maritain's theocentric humanism. Writing sometime between 54 and 58 A.D., and referring to those followers of Christ who were not fellow Jews, Paul says:

> . . . The wrath of God is revealed from heaven against all ungodliness and wickedness of men who by their wickedness suppress the truth. For what can be known about God is plain to them, because God has shown it to them. Ever since the creation of the world his invisible nature, namely, his eternal power and deity, has been clearly perceived in the things that have been made. So they are without excuse. . . (Romans 1:18–20, RSV).

Paul's point is that, though the gentiles were not born to the law of Moses which imparts knowledge of God and what God expects from man, still they are "without excuse," for the truth of God is written on the face of the earth; it is empirical, a truth contained in the common experiences of men in the world, the knowledge of which requires only the opening of one's eyes. This knowledge of God is more rudimentary than the law revealed through Moses, for it is man's *natural* knowledge of God, a knowledge shared by all men by virtue of their being living human beings.

Jacques Maritain's theocentric humanism is based on the belief that all creatures possess knowledge of God as a part of their creaturely nature. The creature knows the creator who brought it into being, and sustains it in being. And since the creature exists in direct dependence on the creator, to forget or ignore the creator for even one moment is to commit an act of self-destruction, for it is to deny the very power of one's being. In the case of the creature man, Maritain holds that man can be fully human, fully creative in exercising all his powers as a human being, only when he chooses to live in a responsive relationship to the knowledge of God which he already possesses. Thus, for Maritain, as for Schleiermacher and Tillich, God is part of the meaning of the creaturely world. To defy God is, in fact, to rend the moral order of the world. This was seen by Paul in the words that conclude his statement:

> . . . For although they know God they did not honor him as God or give thanks to him, but they became futile in their thinking and their senseless minds were darkened. Claiming to be wise, they became fools and exchanged the glory of the immortal God for images resembling mortal men or birds or animals or reptiles.
>
> Therefore God gave them up to the lusts of their hearts, to impurity, to the dishonoring of their bodies among themselves, because they exchanged the truth about God for a lie and worshipped and served the creature rather than the Creator, who is blessed for ever! Amen (Romans 1:21–25, RSV).

We have seen what meaning God's presence in the world holds for Schleiermacher and Tillich. What meaning does it hold for Maritain? Our answer can only be found by looking first to the system of Thomas Aquinas, and particularly to his concept of being, which Maritain adopted as the cornerstone of his own thought.

We have encountered the term "being" before, in the chapters on Kierkegaard and Tillich. "Being" is an English translation of the ancient Greek word *to hon*, which bears the general meaning of the ultimate or essential character of reality as contrasted with what is considered secondary or incidental. "Being" refers to the "really real," but it should be noted that philosophers use the word with different concepts about *what* is really real. Hegel identified the really real as the dialectic. Tillich makes much of the term "being," and his view closely resembles the position of Aquinas and Maritain. Tillich refers to God as "being-itself" or "the ground of being," and he claims that all reality participates in the ground of being. For Tillich, knowledge of God could be possible only if God is structurally related to the world of reality, in other words, if being unites both God and the world—which is exactly the position of Aquinas and Maritain. However, Tillich was at pains to argue that God is not *a* being but the *ground* of being; that is to say, not one reality or even a superior reality among others, but the very *source* of all reality, and he accused the theological tradition rooted in Aquinas' thought of forgetting this.

Aquinas' notions of God and world are rooted in certain Greek philosophical ideas which we must first understand. Plato contended that no knowledge of the sensible world was possible because of the great disagreements that occur over man's sense impressions and the opinions he derives from them.[6] Plato saw the world as a dualism: a stable, intelligible realm of ideas, and an unstable, unintelligible realm of sense impressions. It was a dualism that influenced succeeding generations of Western thinkers to regard man's body as not only inferior to his mind but as a real obstacle to his knowledge of God and ultimately to his personal salvation. This dualism entered Christian thought through the neo-Platonic thinker Plotinus, and led to that disparagement of the material and bodily aspects of human life that one finds in Augustine, and in all the neo-Platonic-Augustinian Christian thinkers who followed.

Aquinas rejected the Platonic idealistic philosophy in favor of the greater realism to be found in Aristotle's philosophy. Aristotle argued that reality could not consist of Plato's abstract or pure ideas; for if these ideas bear no positive relation to the world of sensible experience, then man, who is a sensory as well as an intellectual creature, cannot achieve full knowledge of the world.[7] That which is real, according to Aristotle, must consist of *both* the concrete-sensible *and* the rational-intelligible. More specifically, what it means to be something consists of the presence of an idea, an intelligible structure, *dwelling in* the concrete, sensible, individual thing. Aristotle analyzed the unique union of the rational and sensible which makes a thing "to be" as the dynamic of actualizing potentiality: things come to be because of actualizing their potentiality.[8]

For example, the process of a boy growing into a man can be understood as an actualization of potentiality for manhood resident in the boy. The actualization of potentiality is the power of maturation which defines each living thing in the world, showing how things come to be what they actually are. This process is not limited to living things; it defines all things in existence, including artificial objects which are the products of ingenuity or artistry. For example, in the hands of the artist a statue which can come from an uncut block of wood does so only because the wood contains the statue "potentiality." Aristotle understood reality to be movement, things-coming-to-be—this movement being that of the actualization of potentiality.

Mere movement, however, was not for Aristotle the key to reality. The movement in existing objects is growth, and growth is movement toward an end. Growth is purposeful movement. The movement in each thing from potentiality to actuality is a movement which has a rationally discernible end. Thus, reality, as Aristotle understood it, is the concrete, sensible world, the world alive with movement, but a world in which random movement, movement without end or aim, is excluded.

If each thing in the world comes to be by virtue of the movement-toward-an-end, then, asked Aristotle, what is that end toward which the world *as a whole* moves? What is that end which serves to propel all the potentialities in the world into the state of actualization? Aristotle believed there was such an end, and that it was distinct and different from the objects of the world. He spoke of the propelling aim of the world's vitalities as the "unmoved mover," a being which initiates and sustains the world in its life but is itself not a part of the world.[9] In the actualization of potentialities, Aristotle argued that an external agent is required which itself must be actual not potential. The world of individual objects can be understood as a vast, unending movement of things coming-to-be by virtue of an equal number of external actual agents. But that agency which causes the world's movement as a whole, the supreme mover, itself must be *unmoved* lest it, too, be the "result" of another's agency, and therefore no longer supreme as the cause of the life of the entire universe.

Thomas Aquinas adopted the "unmoved mover" as a general idea for giving intellectual flesh to the biblical belief in God, the "maker of heaven and earth." But Aristotle, though he ascribed divine properties to the "unmoved mover," did not look on it as a god-person with anthropomorphic characteristics, such as the ability to enter into personal relations with human beings. He viewed the unmoved mover rather as the supreme force of the world, not a separate deity but a distinct, divine being which is known not religiously through prayer but philosophically, as a logical requirement of a system of concepts for elucidating the character of reality.[10] Aquinas regarded Aristotle's view of reality as the most adequate framework for interpreting the meanings of the biblically based Christian religion. This becomes particularly evident in his treatment of God and of God's relation to the world.

Aquinas adopted Aristotle's principle of the "unmoved mover" as a way of conveying the biblical affirmation of the singular majesty and power of God. God, who is the effective cause of all that exists, is himself "uncaused"—which means, in effect, that he is self-caused.[11] Christian theological tradition has spoken of God's creating the world "out of nothing," a miraculous act in which the divine word brings something to be where there was nothing before. The world thus has an absolute beginning in time, but the same does not hold true for God, the world's creator. God always was, is, and will be. As the self-caused cause of the world, God is eternal. The existence of the world and each thing in it has *contingent* existence—that is, existence which depends upon a cause outside itself; God's existence, by contrast, is *necessary*, dependent on no one or nothing outside itself.[12] Further, God's necessary existence means that the movement from potentiality to actuality which applies to everything in the world cannot apply to God. There is no potentiality in God, for if there were, the conversion from potentiality to actuality would require an external agency, which would clearly be inconsistent with the self-caused nature of God. God, Aquinas stated, following Aristotle, is "pure act," the perfectly actual being, the only being which always *is*. Whereas each thing in the world comes into existence as a result of the growth process and by means of external agents, God alone exists by virtue of who he is. To be God is to exist necessarily. God's essence is his existence; [13] it is the very nature of God *as God* to exist. Thus, God's existence cannot be something he must strive to possess, with the risk that he might fail to possess it, as so often happens to objects in the natural world.

In the opening passages of the book of Exodus, after God has commanded Moses to inform the people of Israel that he will deliver them from their Egyptian captors, Moses asks God his name, and God answers, "I AM WHO I AM. . . . Say this to the people of Israel, I AM has sent me to you" (Exodus 3:14, RSV). Aquinas wedded this mysterious confession of the divine identity to Aristotle's notion of pure act to produce the view that the fundamental truth about God is the fact that God *is*. What man knows of God basically is that God is the "self-subsisting Act of being." Moreover, the world exists only because of the prior existence of God. And knowledge of the world is itself knowledge derived from the fundamental truth of God's necessary existence.

As the self-subsistent cause of the world, God is dependent for his existence on no one; he is infinite being. But worldly beings, by contrast, depend on each other and ultimately on God for their existence; therefore, they are finite beings. Aquinas argued that the relationship between God and the world can best be envisaged as a hierarchy, a "chain of being" in which God, the infinite cause of being, is at the summit of a vast array of finite beings. This hierarchy is a hierarchy of *being*, of all existent reality. For Aquinas, the gradation among finite beings was a function of rational intelligibility: every being consists of an idea, a pure concept wedded to sensible, concrete matter, but some beings partake of the conceptual more than others.[14] By virtue of his reason, man resembles God; therefore, man's place is at the summit of finite being. Between God and man, Aquinas located the angels—pure spiritual beings who, unlike man, lack body.

The chain of being, with angels, man, animals, plants, and physical elements ranged in descending order, is in fact the order of creation as executed by God. It is an essential structure showing that each existent thing has its place; it is a structure of value and therefore of meaning for each object in existence. For example, man, by virtue of the reason in which he resembles God, is the lord of the created world; he should look on all things as subject to his rational will. In so doing he is obeying the will of God as it is shown to man's reason. Conversely, when man subjects himself to the material world, abandoning his reason before the natural vitalities, including the mindless passions of his body, he defies the will of God, with the result that he subverts the order of creation and the order within himself as an individual created being.

The belief that each thing has a place in the scheme of reality means that each is under a law that stipulates the behavior most appropriate to that thing. Thus, man is required to behave rationally to be human and not animal. The law which governs the activities of all objects in the world is, according to Aquinas, a law of God which states that each natural object has an aim. The aim of man is happiness or well-being, and the means before man for achieving this aim is his reason. Consequently, man is acting naturally in a life of reason, but perversely or unnaturally in unreasonable or irrational acts.

But Aquinas also held that man has a supernatural end for which his reason is inadequate as a means. This supernatural end he spoke of as union with God, in which is found the experience of one's vision of God. Faith alone can give this experience, and only God in his grace can impart faith to man. But the church, in its role of dispensing sacraments instituted by God, mediates grace to man. Thus did Aquinas draw a clear distinction between God's natural relation to the world, shown to man through his reason and manifested in every aspect of man's worldly or cultural activities, and the supernatural relationship between God and man, which presupposes the church and the religious life of the church as contained in the dispensation of sacraments, the priestly hierarchy, and in the theological truths necessary to man's salvation.

Jacques Maritain is a neo-Thomist, which means that the aim of his thought is to defend the validity of Aquinas' system by showing that its chief principles can be applied to contemporary problems. This does not mean that Maritain's thought is a "carbon copy" of Aquinas'. The originality of Maritain's mind is demonstrated when he is able to show how Aquinas offers a more compelling analysis of human life than rival schools of thought.

For Maritain, the basic validity of Aquinas' thought is that Aquinas was able to synthesize a sound philosophy of existence with the central affirmations of the Christian faith. Aquinas showed, as no one before, a creative relationship between human existence and reason, on one side, and God's life and activity in the world on the other. It is the organic character of Aquinas' thought that convinces Maritain. It is not a system of existence based on the self-sufficiency of reason, as one finds in modern, skeptical philosophies, nor is it a system of religious truth exclusive of reason, characteristic of Protestant theologies (particularly Barth's). It is a system in which what is true of God and of man is regarded as an interdependent truth, showing the coherence of rationality and divinity.[15]

Nothing illustrates this coherence more than Aquinas' use of the Greek notion of being. For Aquinas, everything that exists does so by virtue of God's creative will, and everything that exists is possessed of a certain rational capacity and purpose as a part of its divinely created nature. Being, then—or reality—is this coherence of divinity, rationality, and material existence. It has been Maritain's task not only to defend the general validity of this notion of being but, more particularly, to show the relevance of this notion in such areas of human endeavor as politics, art, and morality. The grave concern sounded throughout Maritain's writings is that the social and political disruptions that have marked modern life since the Reformation, and especially since the French Revolution, will prove to be man's final destroyer. This is so precisely because man, having abandoned an organic vision of reality, is easy prey to these forces. Relinquishing the vision of reality's unity, he cannot but fall victim to the forces of disunity. Maritain's writings are exhortations toward the renewal of a unified vision of life, exhortations in the hope that they will stave off, if not overcome, the modern upheaval.

Maritain sees the coherence of divinity, rationality, and concrete existence most sharply in man. Man's inner unity is based on God, his creator, and man experiences and expresses this unity only in intelligently guided acts. This means that unless man's will is informed and guided by reason, man will lose his being, his internal unity. Maritain makes this clear in an essay "Christian Humanism," which expresses the essential character of his thought.

The contemporary image of man as autonomous, Maritain writes, had its beginning not in some atheistic or skeptical philosophy of the past but in those secularized Christian views of man that one finds in Descartes, John Locke, and Jean-Jacques Rousseau, whom Maritain regards as architects of the modern age.

> . . . The man of Cartesian Rationalism was a pure mind conceived after an angelistic pattern. [John Locke's] man of Natural Religion was a Christian gentleman who did not need grace, miracle, or revelation, and was made virtuous and just by his own good nature. The man of Jean-Jacques Rousseau was, in a much more profound and significant manner, the very man of St. Paul transferred to the plane of pure nature—

innocent as Adam before the fall, longing for a state of divine freedom and bliss, corrupted by social life and civilization as the sons of Adam by the original sin.[16]

Maritain's point is that, though each of these thinkers affirms that man's grandeur and creativity consist of his resemblance to God, in the thought of each the accent falls not on the resemblance but on man. In Descartes it falls on man's pure reason; in Locke on man's goodness and native piety; and in Rousseau on man's natural innocence.

What these thinkers bequeathed to their modern successors was not only a secularized version of the old Christian-biblical image of man but, along with it, a highly optimistic faith about man's capacity, through reason, goodness, and innocence, to solve his social, economic, and political problems, and to eliminate in himself the pride, greed, ignorance, and willful destructiveness that the old theology called man's "sinfulness."

This liberal, rationalistic faith in man proved, however, to have the opposite result. What came of it, Maritain claims, was not an amelioration of the human situation but another condition for its deterioration. This can be seen in the development of recent intellectual and socio-political history. The liberal faith produced Darwinism, Freudianism, and Marxism, modern intellectual movements in which was taken the final step toward the complete secularization of man. In his freedom, rationality, and individuality, man no longer resembles God; he is now to be understood according to the scale of the animals with whom he forms a common ancestral tree, his own appearance on this tree being one of the many chance occurrences in evolutionary history; or he is to be understood through his bodily instincts and unconscious drives; or in the light of vast, relentless, impersonal movements of social history. Maritain recognizes the singular intellectual achievements of Darwin, Freud, and Marx, but he rejects the ideologies that grew out of their achievements—the work, for the most part, of these masters' earliest,

Maritain: Theocentric Humanism

most passionate, and most uncritical followers. These are ideologies which carry the refrain that man is "nothing but" his
animal ancestry, or "nothing but" his sexual impulses, or "nothing but" a mere strand in the vast fabric of social history.
Maritain rejects the practice of taking the rich and complicated
psycho-physical organism that is man and equating him with
only an aspect of his constitution and development, thereby
ignoring his capacities for freedom, imagination, reason, feeling,
and faith—all the faculties identified as spiritual and which comprise, in Maritain's judgment, the experiential resources through
which man expresses his relation to God.

Maritain does not seek to blame these intellectual movements
for the emergence of such forces as communism and Nazism,
nor for the brutalization of life in modern industrial society.
But he does believe that the atheistic bent of these movements
has led to a depreciation of the sanctity of the human individual
which has played into the hands of contemporary tyrannies.
The optimism of the early secularized, Christian view of man,
and the error committed in its adoption by the modern philosophers of society, are nowhere shown more clearly than in
the havoc loosed upon the earth in the past fifty years by communism, Nazism, and the bourgeois industrial state. Those humanistic philosophies from Descartes to John Dewey which
sought their basis in man separate from God have proved,
ironically, to be most ignorant of man, most self-deluded in
their idealism.

> . . . The development of which I am speaking has its real
> sources in something . . . which began to reveal itself from
> the second half of the last century on: anguish and despair, as
> exemplified in Dostoevsky's *Possessed*. A deeper abyss than
> animality appears in the unmasking of man. Having given up
> God so as to be self-sufficient, man has lost track of his soul.
> He looks in vain for himself; he turns the universe upside
> down trying to find himself; he finds masks, and, behind the
> masks, death.[17]

Maritain calls for the rejection of that *anthropocentric* humanism which has proved so destructive to man in modern life, and its replacement with a *theocentric* humanism. This does not mean the return to the religious orientation of human life typified by the medieval centuries; it means the reconciliation of two realities presently regarded by many people as irreconcilible: the secular and the sacred. The key to the reconciliation is to understand the nature and range of reason. Modern man has divested reason of its metaphysical foundation and thrust, to apply it exclusively to the limited end of developing techniques to carry on the tasks and to achieve the goals that industrialization has put before man. The result, says Maritain, is the beheading of reason. Reason has lost its sense for being. It no longer has an ultimate purpose; it serves only itself and is thus robbed of all but the narrowest meaning.

> Human reason lost its grasp of Being, and became available only for the mathematical reading of sensory phenomena, and for the building up of corresponding material techniques— a field in which any absolute reality, any absolute truth, and any absolute value is of course forbidden.[18]

Reason turned in on itself, converted to purely technical ends, is reason without critical and moral responsibility; it is a reason that is helpless and compliant before the power of modern social and political tyrannies. Maritain urges the restoration of ultimate purpose in reason:

> After the great disillusionment of "anthropocentric humanism" and the atrocious experience of the anti-humanism of our day, what the world needs is a new humanism, a "theocentric" or integral humanism which would consider man in all his natural grandeur and weakness, in the entirety of his wounded being inhabited by God, in the full reality of nature, sin, and sainthood. Such a humanism would recognize all that is irrational in man, in order to tame it to reason, and all that is suprarational, in order to have reason vivified by it and to open man

to the descent of the divine into him. Its main work would be to cause the Gospel leaven and inspiration to penetrate the secular structures of life—a work of sanctification of the temporal order.[19]

Maritain speaks of the humanization of society as a "humanism of the Incarnation," in which man seeks to discern and express creatively the divine in the world by transforming this world of nature and history in the light of supernatural grace.

This "humanism of the Incarnation" would care for the masses, for their right to a temporal condition worthy of man and to spiritual life, and for the movement which carries labor toward the social responsibility of its coming of age. It would tend to substitute for materialistic-individualistic civilization, and for an economic system based on the fecundity of money, not a collectivistic economy but a "Christian-personalistic" democracy.[20]

. . . We need an awakening of liberty and of its creative forces, of which man does not become capable by the grace of the state or any party pedagogy, but by that love which fixes the center of his life infinitely above the world and temporal history. In particular, the general paganization of our civilization has resulted in man's placing his hope in force alone and in the efficacy of hate, whereas in the eyes of an integral humanism a political ideal of justice and civic friendship, requiring political strength and technical equipment, but inspired by love, is alone able to direct the work of social regeneration.[21]

The aim of reason, for Maritain, is the disclosure of the deep, internal relation between world and God, the natural and the supernatural. This is the uncovering of being, that divine order in existence through which each thing possesses purpose, meaning, and value. Any endeavor that results in the disclosure of being is thus inherently rational.

Maritain claims that in the work of the artist we are given a unique disclosure of being, and thus a knowledge of existence we could not otherwise have. The aim of the practice of art is the production of the art work itself, the concrete object.[22] Everything that comprises art and that is directed toward the product—the material medium, the artistic technique and concepts, the genre and tradition in which the artist works, the practical tools of artistic work, whether they be words or paints —have as their exclusive goal the work of art. The aim of art is not moral, its purpose is not to transform man's will toward the good, nor is its goal political, so familiar to civic art or official state art. The aim of art is itself.

But Maritain does not agree with the formalist school of "art for art's sake." It is true that the aim of art is art, but this does not mean that the art work consists of nothing but those technical efforts and considerations by which the artist produced the art object. Art is more than artistry, it goes beyond all that we regard as the technical means within the artist's talent. The artist is also a human being, and Maritain suggests that if the artist succeeds in creating art, he does so as much by infusing his art with humanity as by applying technical means. He states:

> . . . If art is not human in the end that it pursues, it is human, essentially human, in its mode of operating. It is a work of man that has to be made; it must have in it the mark of man: *animal rationale*.[23]

Maritain's view is that the artist's humanity is far more than just another of the skills he must master in order to accomplish his task; his humanity is a value that guides his technique and is manifested in every aspect of the completed work. The achievement of art really depends on both: the artist's technical skill and his humanity. If both occur, according to Maritain, the work cannot but be beautiful.

Art is truly art, that is to say, "beautiful," when the artist succeeds in impressing a form upon matter, not simply shaping materials haphazardly, but giving the materials *intelligible* shape, giving them meaning; and meaning is always rational meaning for Maritain. This rational, intelligible shaping reflects the artist's humanity—his self-understanding, his understanding of the world about him, his appreciation of his fellow human beings, his spiritual beliefs and commitments. This intelligible shaping or rational pursuit of artistry is what Maritain means by imprinting an idea on matter when he says:

> Art . . . is of the intellectual order, its action consists in imprinting an idea on some matter: it is therefore in the intelligence of the artifex that it resides, or, as is said, this intelligence is the subject in which it inheres. It is a certain quality of this intelligence.[24]

Art's immediate appeal is, of course, to the senses, but its ultimate aim is the mind. The art work is beautiful when it successfully engages the mind *through the senses*, when it engages man's intellect, enlightens him, and thereby ennobles him through the unique genius that is that particular work of art.[25]

But if beauty is intellectual, as Maritain states, then the art work which has beauty as its end must communicate some truth about man and the world. This is exactly Maritain's point. The metaphysics of art is that genuine art discloses to man dimensions of reality, it shows him an aspect of the inner meaning, power, and value of reality; it shows him an aspect of being. But art—at least genuine art—does not do this in a propagandistic way. Art cannot be translated into prose statements about what is true and not true; it makes no statement beyond itself. Art is its own statement. The truth about being that art discloses is a truth contained only within the formal limits of the art work and manifested only through its unique, material particularity, for art is not translatable.

Art which has beauty as its proper end has, in fact, God as its end; for God, Maritain says, following Aquinas, is Beauty. The art work that succeeds in making "a form shine on matter," really succeeds at pointing to the power of God. The art work is a microcosm of the world of God's creation, in which the artist is like the Creator-God. The artist puts the stamp of his humanity on his work, and thereby infuses his work with the meaning of the Creator whence the artist comes, and whence he draws his powers of intelligibility and creative accomplishment. Beautiful art is art in the image of man, which means that because man himself is in the image of God, man's art is in God's image as well.

> [God] is beauty itself, because He gives beauty to all created beings, according to the particular nature of each, and because He is the cause of all consonance and all brightness. Every form indeed, that is to say, every light, is "a certain irradiation proceeding from the first brightness," "a participation in the divine brightness." . . . "The beauty of anything created is nothing else than a similitude of divine beauty participated in by things." [26]

Maritain's aesthetic is a carefully formulated application of the principles of his theocentric humanism to art, and in the last analysis his aesthetic stands or falls on the adequacy of these principles. It is hard to see how this theory of art could be effectively employed as a principle or criterion of practical art criticism and evaluation. Maritain seems to acknowledge this, asserting that his function is not that of the critic but of the philosopher who is obliged to understand art in relation to reality-itself.[27] Nevertheless, a good many works that have as their objectives moral edification, or religious observance, or political affirmation would be excluded from the realm of art by Maritain's analysis. Similarly, purely experimental exercises would most probably encounter Maritain's stricture that unless a significant form (a human, rational meaning) can "shine on the matter," art has not been achieved. Artistic beauty, for Maritain, is the unique embodiment in matter of technical skill and rational meaning. Through this embodiment the work of art has "significance"; it has a meaning beyond the object.

In the actual appreciation of a work of art, however, this

criterion could degenerate into a tendency to accept realistic art as "significant" and reject abstract art as "insignificant." This possibly governed Maritain's acceptance of Cézanne and Chagall and his rejection of the cubist paintings of Picasso. Of Cézanne, he says, "If he is great, and if he exercises such a dominant influence on contemporary art, it is because he brought [to his own art] a conception or a vision of a superior quality. . . ." [28] But of Picasso:

> Picasso's art, in its present character, is the true art of atheism; I mean of that thorough defacement of contemporary man, which is mirrored in atheism. We are no more persons than the distorted imbecile faces of those ferocious females are true human faces.[29]

This statement comes very close to capitulating to the distorted view of the aim of art as propaganda which Maritain deplores. The problem does not lie in the criterion of a rational intelligibility; rather, it lies in Maritain's restricted and somewhat parochial concept of the rational, the significant, and the meaningful. Moreover, if Tillich's criterion of ultimate concern were applied, one could argue that the paintings of Picasso's cubist period are profoundly significant and intensely human.

Maritain's view of man as a rational, moral being is derived from his acceptance of Aquinas' doctrine that the world is the work of God's creative wisdom, and reflects this wisdom in every aspect of its being, most essentially at the level of man. If one conceives of God as a Creative Wisdom, as Maritain does, there is no escaping the conclusion that to deny the inherent intelligibility of the world of God's making is in effect to deny the reality of God's presence in it. A philosophy of life founded on the category of the irrational would, then, necessarily be atheistic in Maritain's judgment. In this regard it is useful to our analysis of Maritain's thought to examine the critique he has made of contemporary existential philosophy, a philosophy, as we have seen, which affirms the primacy of the irrational.

Maritain identifies two distinct but historically related schools of existentialist philosophy.[30] There is the *religious* existentialism of Pascal, Kierkegaard, Dostoevsky, and Kafka, and the *atheistic* existentialism, which counts such luminaries as Sartre and Heidegger. Maritain's general position is to acknowledge what he considers to be the genuine insight of religious existentialism, but to reject atheistic existentialism wholly as a perversion of the former.

The insight of religious existentialism is the view that man's deeply personal sense of himself consists of guilt: the realization that alone before God one stands under terrifying judgment. This is the experience of dereliction that many have seen in Christ's "dark" moments in Gethsemane and on the cross. It is an acute, personal sense of anxiety before the dreaded judgment that one has been abandoned to one's sinfulness. Sin has made man nothing before the Almighty, and it is this burden of "nothingness" which one must carry all his days until, by God's grace alone, one is given the faith that erases his guilt and replaces sin with love, dereliction with acceptance. This is the insight that has come into existential philosophy by way of Saint Augustine's profound analysis of the religious psyche in the fifth century. Maritain accepts this insight as a genuine dimension of man's highly subjective religious experience, an experience for which the prototype is the great mystical tradition in Christianity. Existentialism, then, has the appearance of a contemporary reaffirmation of the anxiety and glory of the mystic's experience of being alone in the presence of God.

Atheistic existentialism, in Maritain's view, has distorted the religious insight of the earlier existentialism by taking the highly personal sense of nothingness and universalizing it as a philosophical category, claiming that human existence is defined by the quality of nothingness—that at the center of life are not rational value and meaning (reflecting the creative and sustaining wisdom of the God-Creator of the Bible) but a void, an absurd, irrational condition for living which defeats all value and meaning. Contrasting the two schools of existentialism, Maritain writes:

Everything that was essentially linked with the supreme combat for the salvation of the self, or the imprecatory tension and posture of faith, has inevitably disappeared. The soul has been evacuated. The cry sent up to God, the frenzy or the despair born of excess of hope, the expectancy of miracle, the sense of sacrifice and the sense of sin, the spiritual agony, the eternal dignity of the existent, the grandeur of its liberty raised up on the ruins of its nature, all have necessarily been evacuated. Job has been evacuated: only the dunghill has been kept. The nothingness *in* the existent has been replaced by the nothingness *of* the existent.[31]

Maritain's rejection of atheistic existentialism is little else than the rejection of the atheistic implications of the irrational on the basis of his belief in a divinely ordered universe. What Maritain fails to appreciate is that the existentialism represented, for example, by Jean-Paul Sartre involves a universalization of meanings treated in limited fashion by Kierkegaard. When Kierkegaard speaks of the subjective meaning of Christianity, Sartre recognizes that what is being affirmed is the value of individuality as such, a condition for responsible action and personal meaning placed on human beings everywhere and at all times.[32] Similarly, the believer's sense of anxiety as a sinner before the heavenly High Judge contains the seed of Heidegger's claim that fundamental to man's daily existence is his anxiety before the dark, forbidding, unknown, and unknowable death he cannot escape.[33] There is a continuity between the religious psychology of Augustine, Pascal, and Kierkegaard and the analysis of contemporary human existence by Sartre and Heidegger. The continuity is especially vivid when the problem of man's religious subjectivity as dealt with by the former is broadened by the latter to include human subjectivity in itself: the individual whose value and meaning precisely *as an individual* is undermined by all that threatens it in modern industrial society.

Sartre, in his widely read essay "Existentialism Is a Humanism,"[34] argues that man cannot be truly free, truly a human being, unless he begins to understand that he does not possess a "nature" in the sense of an indelible image placed upon him by a creator-god, which obliges him to adhere to a code of conduct appropriate to this nature. Such a view, according to Sartre, is the very opposite of freedom because it compels man to conform to an extraneous norm, forcing him to become what he may not in fact be. Man really becomes free as man only in the recognition that he is responsible to no one but himself. This means that man has no "nature," no external rule of behavior to obey; man is what he becomes by action of his will, by his decisions. Man is what he *becomes*, his freedom consists in the *exercise* of his freedom. Sartre believes that each man is offered innumerable opportunities to exercise his freedom. If he fails, he loses this freedom and becomes less than man. Sartre repeats Kierkegaard's precept that man's value as an individual consists in choosing and in the personal relationship he establishes to what he chooses; *what* he chooses, the content, is secondary. Thus a man may choose to marry or not marry, join a political party or not join it, elect to go to war or decide not to—the value of this decision consists in its being *his* decision, for then the real decision is the self's decision for itself, the self's affirmation of itself.

To Maritain, however, Sartre's brand of humanism is really an atheism that represents the height of immoralism. In declaring that man has no nature and thus serves no transcendent ideal, Sartre has declared man to be God, and thereby bestowed a blessing on all of man's actions. There is nothing that man does— so long as it is *his* action—that is not right. This, for Maritain, is immorality, following inevitably from Sartre's irrational, totally subjectivist philosophy. The immorality of Sartre's philosophy is, moreover, self-destructive. For when man is informed that no higher rule of reason guides him in life, he is placed at the mercy of the powerful and unstable forces of his sensuous, instinctual nature, eventually to be victimized and torn asunder by his chaotic appetites. Freedom without reason, choice without a controlling wisdom governing *what* is chosen are, for Maritain, a freedom and a choice that are demonic and enslaving.

This fundamental disagreement between Maritain and Sartre over what constitutes man's freedom reveals contrasting metaphysical convictions. In saying that man's selfhood consists in the act of freedom alone, Sartre assumes an ultimate value— "the self"—which transcends all those conditions for human living that comprise man's rational culture: education, family, religion, the state, and so forth. Somehow, for Sartre, the value of selfhood which the act of freedom imparts is a value independent of and often opposed to social, cultural, and religious meanings.

Sartre's autonomous self is precisely what Maritain rejects. For Maritain, the self is constituted by God in the act of divine creation which brings and continues to bring the world into being, and is expressed through the structures of living—church, society, family, state, and so forth—that are the source of the rationality of man's existence, the reflection on earth of the divine creative wisdom.

But the difference between Maritain and Sartre goes deeper than conflicting metaphysical concepts of the self. At its root, the argument consists of a different vision of the moral structure of man's life in history. Despite Sartre's atheism, his philosophy of freedom comes out of the theological tradition which finds in the biblical myth of the Fall the most dramatically truthful portrait of the human condition. Sartre's notion of man abandoned in the world is a secularized version of the world *after* the Fall, as envisaged by a number of Jewish and Christian theologians.

It is this view of man's basic insecurity, his abandonment in the world, or what Tillich calls man's "estrangement," that Maritain cannot accept. He cannot accept it because his vision of the world is controlled not by the myth of the Fall but by another—the myth of creation. Although perhaps an oversimplification, it is basically correct to say that, in contrast to the image of moral disorder and disunity conveyed by the myth of the Fall, Maritain develops his philosophy after the image of moral order and unity conveyed by the story of the creation. In this regard it is important to realize that Aquinas' and Maritain's philosophies emphasize not action or the will—not what is immediate and concrete in human existence—rather, they emphasize reflection and reason—what is ideal in human nature as this nature was originally conceived by God. The tendency of their thought, therefore, is to judge man's actual, historical existence by what man is according to God's original creation of him. And, because the doctrine of the Fall must occupy a secondary position in their systems, the assumption of these two thinkers must be that despite the wretched character of man's moral history, man *can* be what he *ought* to be, that is to say, what God intends for him to be. The root of this assumption is plain enough. Neither for Aquinas nor Maritain is the world completely fallen, utterly corrupt as it appeared to Augustine, the Protestant reformers, and the existentialists. Man's reason is not corrupted; indeed, it cannot be corrupted so long as man exists and so long as there is a world in which he can exist. To believe that God, the Creative Wisdom, is the author of the world, means for Maritain that the mere fact of the world is enough to guarantee that God exists and that the wisdom of God continues to be reflected in the world, even in the moral tragedies of human history. If there is doubt of this, Maritain is prepared to defend the continued relevance of the famous five proofs of God's existence which Aquinas constructed out of what he regarded as the inherent intelligibility of the world of man's daily experience.[35] For Maritain, then, man's reason is ultimately incorruptible. And if man will but follow his reason, that is, allow his will to be guided by the divine light which shines through his reason, he will exchange evil for good.

What, then, does Maritain make of evil? What meaning does evil hold for him, given his tendency to view man and moral history from the viewpoint of the ideal? In answer to this question it is not surprising to discover that Maritain's account of evil bears a close resemblance to Karl Barth's, and for roughly the same reasons. Barth's view is that evil exists by virtue of God's rejection of it. Following Aquinas, Maritain's position is that evil is not real but is the opposite of goodness, the negation of reality.[36] Since God is the ultimate author of all reality—a reality that is good for that very reason—evil, too, exists by virtue of God. The expression "by virtue of" is crucial to both accounts of evil, since Barth and Maritain wish to declare at one and the same time that evil is the absolute antithesis of the work of God's creative goodness, *and* that evil is not an independent reality, a powerful being alongside God in the world, rivaling his creative goodness.

In our analysis of Barth's thought we argued that Barth's view of evil was derived from the basic proposition of his thinking— that God is the author of all reality. The intellectual problem evil occasioned for Barth was to reconcile the empirical exis- tence of evil with the dogmatic axiom about God's reality and authority. The same kind of problem apparently faces Maritain. Maritain has sought a way to reconcile intellectually the con- crete reality of evil with the axiomatic truth of his system that God is the author of all being. The result for Maritain's thought is exactly what we found it to be in Barth's: that in seeking a way to render evil intellectually compatible within a system of reality, Maritain ignores the truth contained in the sheer power of evil as it is empirically known. For it is not only the *fact* of evil to which existentialist thinkers have been pointing, it is also the *power* of evil, the way in which evil, not goodness, seems to lie at the heart of modern man's existence. As Dostoevsky's tales show, it is a power in light of which no man can rest easily if evil has a "place" within the universe of God's making, or if it is comprehended by God's grace. Existentialists are not saying that evil is beyond study, or that no meaning can be given to it; the Absurd is, after all, a category of meaning, as is Tillich's notion of "meaninglessness." What they say is that evil is not reducible to the meanings that man has constructed out of his experience of evil; in fact, there is a fathomless mystery to evil which matches the mystery of God, precisely because evil and God in the modern context of experience appear to be inseparable realities.

In an essay in which he likens the persecution of innocent peoples during the Second World War to the persecution of Jesus Christ, Maritain asks what is surely one of the most essential, if not *the* essential question, about the relation of God to evil and the tragedy of human history:

> Where lay the consolation of these persecuted innocents? And how many others died completely forsaken? They did not give their lives, their lives were taken from them, and under the shadow of horror. They suffered without having wanted to suffer. They did not know why they died. Those who know why they die are greatly privileged people.[37]

The weakness of the answer which Maritain offers to the powerful question he raises in this statement is signaled by his use of the word "consolation." He states the issue of the suffering of innocents in asking how consolation is possible for them. But one would now wish to ask, Is there consolation for such suffering, a real restoration of palpable losses, a healing of the wounds of body and mind? For what can console the *memory* of the experience of persecution itself?—and memory cannot be undone, even by God. Yet it is in terms of "consolation" that Maritain wishes to answer the question. He tells us that the persecuted imitate Christ's dereliction on the cross.[38] Like Christ, they are helpless before the violence done to them. Through this recognition and identification with Christ, the victim can be lifted up to sit with the Father in glory. To some extent this is consolation, something with which the "faithful" may assuage their memories, but—and the existentialists recognize this—it is not an *answer* to the question of the suffering of innocents. It is a theological apologia, a "defense."

When Aquinas adopted the Aristotelian framework for expressing the meaning of Christian faith, the vibrant, poetic

imagery through which the Bible expresses the relation between
God and the world was exchanged for the coldly abstract if
more precise concepts of Greek philosophy. The result of this
exchange was an unbiblical preference for the static conditions
of reason, order, and eternal essences over the dynamic forces
of movement, change, and growth. It may be possible to claim
that rational order and worldly change—the eternal and the
temporal—were organically related in Aristotle's philosophy,
but it would be harder to make that claim for Aquinas. Aquinas'
preference for a static concept of God and his relation to man
and the world can be seen in his fundamental dichotomy between nature and the supernatural: nature is clearly understood
to be lower in value and meaning than the supernatural, and
the most valued elements in nature are the unchanging essences
embodied in it, one of the most important of which is man's
rationality.

Aquinas' bias toward the unchanging and eternal is seen in
Maritain's own system of thought, which is the chief source of
the weakness of that system. Maritain's vigorous defense of
rational intelligibility and moral humanism, his critique of the
irrationalism in existential philosophy and of the atheism and
anti-humanism in modern intellectual movements such as Freudianism and Marxism, are based on a concept of the reality of
man consisting of a rational-moral essence to which he must
adhere if he is not to court self-destruction. Such a concept
might be more valid if Maritain did not equate man's rational-
moral essence with certain traditional and highly conventional
styles of behavior. For what it is to be rationally moral in
Maritain's terms is, in all matters nonreligious, to assume that a
careful application of mind and will unveils the solution to the
problem; and in matters religious, to conform mind and will to
the sacred teachings of the Holy Church.

Consider Maritain's rejection of such modern movements as
existentialism, Freudianism, Marxism, and abstract art. Maritain
is persuaded on the basis of his "theocentric humanism" to reject
the irrationalism and subjectivism in existentialism. But he

ignores completely the possibility that irrationalism may dramatically describe contemporary existence, that the subjective self may now have greater value for the individual than some sort of objective social order—or, in these times, that the self may be more trustworthy than society, the state, the church, and other institutions of objective order. In a similar vein, Maritain rejects Marxism and Freudianism; their atheism contradicts his notion of the divinely rooted rational-moral essence in man. But Maritain's rejection comes at a high price, for he must ignore hard empirical facts about social transition, economic necessity, and man's instinctual drives which lie at the center of these intellectual movements. Also, Maritain's apparent rejection of nonrepresentational art bespeaks a certain conventionalism in taste and judgment that must surely spring from his concept of human nature. The rational-moral man, according to tradition, is the man who looks and acts like *man*, and Picasso's cubist portrayals of human beings are a long way from men who "look" and "act" like men. According to Maritain, those "distorted imbecile faces" are not "true human faces."

We have said that the root of Maritain's concept of man is Aquinas' preference for the changeless and the eternal over change and the temporal. Because of this preference, a follower of Aquinas such as Maritain must reject insights born of experiences which fundamentally contradict the notion of an eternal, fixed concept of human nature.

One of Maritain's most sensitive perceptions as a philosopher-theologian is the "givenness" of human life, through which man grasps the meaning of life as shared. He writes:

> . . . When a man has been really awakened to the sense of being or existence, and grasps intuitively the obscure, living depth of the self and subjectivity, he discovers by the same token the basic generosity of existence and realizes, by virtue of the inner dynamism of this intuition, that love is not a passing pleasure or emotion, but the very meaning of his being alive.[39]

Yet it is precisely in Maritain's grasp of the "generosity of existence" that one discerns again the major weakness of his thought. Life is "given"; it is a generous gift of the Creator. Maritain is a Thomist who wishes to understand this gift according to the "sense of being," which means that he wishes to understand life in the light of certain universal or essential meanings, "truths" which God has set forth eternally about man's existence in the world. Thus, in spite of his claim that Thomism is a philosophy of realism, Maritain's thought suffers from a priorism, the practice of assigning meaning to experience basically in the light of first principles.

What Maritain overlooks or minimizes through his emphasis on natural order and intellectual structure is the *particularity* of existence, the natural world as an unfolding scene of indescribably varied life at every level—mineral, vegetable, animal, and human. One supposes that Maritain can demonstrate the "sense of being" in any given aspect of nature's growth; but the cardinal scientific truth about the vast movements of nature is that they are not orderly, predictable, and creative in the sense of suggesting rational, moral progress. If God is the author of nature as Maritain and Aquinas claim, then surely God must be involved in the conditions of nature as we know them. Maritain's anthropocentric humanism tends to view nature according to idealized or abstract principles that ignore or reject all that is disorderly or nonrational in existence.

The strongest thrust of Maritain's thought has been his effort to define that spirituality pervading the world, without which human life would lack depth and direction and be not worth having. Maritain seems to regard modern culture in its philosophic, artistic, and moral expressions as destroying this depth and direction. Only through the principles of Aquinas' philosophy, he tells us, can a new total vision be achieved through which all cultural expressions can reflect, each in its own way, God's presence in the world of His creation, and man's reality as God's greatest creature.

VI

The Theology of Godmanhood: Nicolas Berdyaev

Nicolas Berdyaev's achievements as a philosopher-theologian lead one to regard him as the Eastern Orthodox counterpart of Jacques Maritain, the Roman Catholic: a thinker who sought to relate the vision of life expressed by Russian Christianity to modern intellectual developments and the experience of man in the twentieth century. The turbulent quality of his writing reflects the struggle of his early life in Russia and his experiences in Western Europe after he was exiled from Russia by the Bolsheviks.

Born in 1874 in Kiev, of an aristocratic family, Berdyaev studied at the University of Kiev, where he came under the influence of Marx's writings and joined the Social Democratic party, as the Marxists then called themselves. Their concern for social justice won the young Berdyaev over to the Marxist camp. In 1900, he was arrested by the tsarist government for revolutionary activity and exiled to the northern city of Vologda for three years. It was during this period of imprisonment that

Berdyaev and other Marxists began to seek a way to synthesize Marx's social philosophy with German idealism, especially the critical idealism of Kant, whose analysis of truth and freedom they were coming to accept. Berdyaev eventually saw this synthesis as an impossibility, because in dialectical materialism the spiritual dimension to existence is denied, and Berdyaev claimed that there could be no freedom without spirit.

Matthew Spinka, the contemporary American scholar of Russian religious thought, says that Berdyaev finally broke with Marxism because he regarded its political outgrowth in communism to be a rigidly orthodox, literalist, authoritarian sort of religion.[1] The Marxists had no reverence for personality, and Berdyaev was coming to regard personality as the clue to the meaning of man's reality. Despite his rejection of Marxism and communism, he fully accepted Marx's claim that the evolution of society toward the modern industrial state was made possible only by the exploitation of human beings.

Berdyaev began to consider himself a Christian well before his exile from Russia in 1922; but his Christianity was not that of the church in Russia, which he considered as corrupt as the pre-revolutionary government. He identified himself with a spiritual Christianity, whose focus was the hero of freedom, the universal Christ portrayed in Dostoevsky's story of the Grand Inquisitor.[2] The characteristic posture of Berdyaev by temperament and by conviction was that of independence: a Christian but not of the Russian church, a revolutionary but not identifying with the Bolsheviks, a socialist but repudiating Marx. This independence became a part of his theological vision, incorporated into that freedom of spirit, that "Godmanhood" which is the keynote of his thought.

Berdyaev took no active part in the revolution of 1917, but he did serve for a brief time in the first Soviet government. He recorded a clear impression of Lenin, the hero of the revolution: "Philosophically and culturally Lenin was a reactionary, a man terribly behind the times; he did not reach the heights of Marx's dialectic." [3] Berdyaev's attitude was typical of Russian intellectuals who, though sympathetic to the revolution, found its activist leaders uncultured bores, having little imagination and unable to grasp the philosophical subtleties of Marx's writings. For a time, Berdyaev was tolerated by the Bolsheviks and was allowed to lecture in Moscow. He enjoyed the confidence of some of the early revolutionary leaders. But power eventually passed to a new younger group, whose leader was soon to be Joseph Stalin. By the late summer of 1922, persecutions of religious believers had begun; Berdyaev was arrested and finally banished from Russia in 1922.

Berdyaev went first to Berlin, where he resided for two years. In Berlin he lectured at the Russian Institute of Sciences, which the German government had established. He generally avoided political activity and refused to share the monarchist sentiments of most Russian émigrés. He also lost all sympathy with the new wave of Bolshevik leaders, and saw little good in the continuation of the revolution.

In his last years in Russia and his first few months in Western Europe, Berdyaev began turning his attention to wider themes of religious philosophy. His book *The Meaning of History*, published in 1923, signaled this change. Here Berdyaev reveals himself as a thinker capable of metaphysical speculation on history, after the fashion of Saint Augustine and Oswald Spengler. He pursued the ultimate meanings of man's historical existence, as they had done. The historian *qua* historian, Berdyaev said, does not raise ultimate questions regarding the meaning of history—the whence, whither, and why of human life.

> These "damned questions," as Dostoevsky used to refer to them, cannot be answered merely from the point of view of recorded history, although the historical span must be considered as integral. Essentially such questions are cosmic and metaphysical; they deal with beginnings and ends of history, of which historical science knows nothing and can know nothing. And yet they are absolutely essential. For without an answer to them history as such is meaningless.[4]

In 1924, Berdyaev journeyed to Paris, there to remain until his death in 1948. It was during these years in Paris that Berdyaev became closely associated with French intellectuals, in many cases French Roman Catholics, the most notable being Jacques Maritain and Fr. Gillet, who eventually became general of the Dominican Order. They and their colleagues frequently met at each others' residences to present papers dealing with various problems of religious philosophy. Some of Berdyaev's own attitudes toward his French contemporaries, particularly Maritain, can be found in his autobiography, *Dream and Reality*. He regarded the group on the whole as traditional and conservative:

> Western Christians, Catholics as well as Protestants, are in the grip of religious reaction, although in distinction from the Russian Orthodox, a reaction of a highly cultured form: they feel the need of a return to the past and seek firm authority and tradition. I perceived with sorrow that the Russian religious movements are foreign or little known to Western Christians, although the same must be said of the present generation of Russians.[5]

Berdyaev's religious views differed greatly from the official position of the Eastern Orthodox Church; moreover, Berdyaev repeatedly admitted that he felt himself to be a "leftist" or "modernist" even in comparison with liberal Catholics and Protestants. "I felt it keenly at international meetings at which Protestants predominated; but these Protestants were much more conservative, traditional, and authoritarian than I who represented Orthodoxy. In the end I felt isolated and suffered by reason of either not being understood or by being misunderstood."[6]

Berdyaev's theology of Godmanhood is based on the notion of divine-human mutuality, the view that God and man need each other so that God cannot be completely God without man, nor man truly man without God.[7] Many, perhaps most, theologians would regard this as a startling and patently indefensible claim; certainly it signals a radically different orientation in religious thought than we have thus far encountered in Schleiermacher, Kierkegaard, Barth, Tillich, or Maritain. All our theologians would agree that man depends upon God, but none—with the possible exception of Martin Buber—would turn that sentence around to say that God depends upon man. After all, how can God save man, who is lost in sin, if in some way God depends upon man? Is not the truth of reconciling grace— God doing for man what he cannot do for himself—brought into question by the suggestion of mutuality? Are not God's majestic power and glory denied by the thought that God needs man?

Nothing illustrates the distinctive aspect of Berdyaev's theology more than his assertion that the relationship between God and man includes the meaning of redemptive grace but that the relationship is not exhausted by it. Indeed, grace is to be viewed as a moment or act within a deeper relationship—and that relationship, for Berdyaev, is a common, shared life. The essence of the relationship between God and man is mutuality, because this relationship consists of a living which man makes possible for God and God makes possible for man. Berdyaev saw grace, the act by which God forgives man his sinfulness and seeks to reconcile with him, as finding its true aim in generating a new, deeper, better quality of the life which God and man share.[8]

It was Berdyaev's judgment that freedom alone makes it possible for man and God to have life together.[9] God is free to act for man, to give him life, to sustain, judge, and redeem him. But man is also free, and the meaning of man's freedom is that whatever man does, either creatively or destructively, in love or enmity, has the power to alter the quality of existence, hence, to influence the quality of God's own life in the world. Thus, freedom confers on man a power equal to God; indeed, when we recall that God's freedom is freedom-for-good alone, whereas man's freedom is freedom-for-evil as well as for good, man is in a sense more powerful than God.

The thrust of the theology of Godmanhood is that God seeks from man a response to his own yearning for life. Berdyaev speaks of God's yearning for a "partner" in creation, for an answer to his call for love, for encounter and union with his "other self." Berdyaev is prepared to interpret the whole of world history in light of his fundamental principle of mutuality: whether or not, and to what degree, man has responded to God's need of him and has used his freedom to enrich the life of God in the world.[10]

Man was born to be a partner of God in the creation of a world, but his history on earth shows him to be a failure. It is a distinctly human failure, for man was summoned to cooperate with God through the very substance of his humanity—in freedom, creativeness, and love; when man refused to act out of freedom, spurned the adventure of creativeness, and declined to love and be loved, he failed God because he failed himself. History, as Berdyaev interprets it, is the story of man's de-humanization, the story of how man came to lose that spirit that makes him uniquely man. It is a story which involves three great epochs in the development of man's spirit.[11]

The first epoch is the pre-Christian pagan epoch during which man is immersed in nature, regarding it not as something external to him but as something to which he has an intimate relation. Man's sense of unity with his physical environment is expressed in his development of animistic beliefs about the world, assumptions that spiritual beings and powers inhabit and give conscious life and feeling to all the objects of the world. The second epoch begins with the advent of Christianity, and reaches its high point in the Middle Ages. In this epoch, man looks on nature with hostility, as a source of sinful temptation. Nature, including man's body, is pitted against his spirit. Man seeks to flee from nature, to transcend the world, to purify and liberate his spirit. The third epoch is identified by Berdyaev as the age of the machine. In this epoch—which Berdyaev believes to be the *last* historical epoch—the human spirit is neither one with nature nor aiming to transcend nature;

its goal is the conquest of nature. In the time of the machine, man seeks to subjugate nature, to bend nature completely to his will. It would appear that in this epoch the human spirit has come to fulfillment, that man has succeeded in his uniqueness as man, that he has triumphed in placing the unique stamp of his creativeness on the whole of the world. But, as Berdyaev sees it, just the opposite has happened. In seeking to conquer nature, man has been conquered by himself. Instead of instilling the world with the spiritual qualities of freedom, creativeness, and love, he has lost his spirit by allowing himself to become separated from nature. In creating the machine, man has put the machine between nature and himself. Now he has no relation to the world except through the machine, so that the machine has in fact become his world. He is enslaved by his own creation.[12]

Ordinarily one regards a machine as a tool created by man for a specific purpose, usually to ameliorate the conditions of life and thus enhance the value of living. The machine has no more value than the use to which it is put. But Berdyaev sees an inherent danger in the machine. Man invents machines with the aim of improving life, and in the process he makes himself dependent on an inanimate object, with the result that the quality of human life is diminished—and by "quality," Berdyaev meant freedom, creativity, and love.[13] Man invents the machine to enrich his life, but the machine drives the spirit out of his life and diminishes his freedom, feeling, and imagination. Man's life is marked by mechanization, routinization, and unceasing boredom.

A powerful example of Berdyaev's thesis about modern existence is the scene of the gigantic bank office in Kafka's *The Trial*. In a cavernous room are rows upon endless rows of clerk's desks, all arranged in perfect order, each desk exactly like the other, the whole scene giving a sense of order, precision, efficiency, and production, the perfect image of the modern industrial society. Visualizing this scene, one has an overwhelming sense that in this world the human spirit perishes. There simply is no provision for the individual, no provision for the freedom, creativeness, and love that make his life possible. Berdyaev saw in the mechanization of life exactly what Kafka saw: greater capacities for mindless evil than could ever have been imagined or accomplished earlier in human history. Indeed, from Berdyaev's point of view, the political and social history of the epoch of the machine is the fulfillment of the potential for evil in this age.[14]

The industrial state is produced by the social and political forces of modern life: capitalism, socialism, democracy, fascism, communism, nationalism, racism, and even the romantic ideology of individualism. Through these forces a society has emerged which cannot tolerate the individual human spirit, a society whose every effort is to group, collectivize, manipulate, exploit, seduce, and deceive man, to achieve ends that are ideological and abstract, such as the "classless society," the "master race," "self-determination," or "private enterprise." According to Berdyaev, these socio-political forces have "objectified" man because they cannot function in the world without robbing man of his freedom as a private, personal human being, and rendering him a lifeless object. These are basically socializing forces because they seek to take the individual and produce through him a style of life that will realize certain ends "higher" than the ends of the individual. For Berdyaev, every such force finds man in his individuality inimical, and it must oppose that power of freedom in man by which he retains and expresses his individuality or personality. Thus, the self and society are finally in fundamental conflict by virtue of the powers which constitute each of them, and by virtue of their opposing and irreconcilible goals.

There has never been, in Berdyaev's view, a society that has not acted to objectify man, from the tribal societies of primitive peoples, to the great empires of the East and West, to the theocracies of Egypt, Israel, and medieval Europe. Even the revolutions very quickly turn into the oppressive societies it was their aim to destroy. The cry for the rights of man sounded in the French Revolution soon became an empty ideology used to rationalize the tyrannies of Napoleon Bonaparte. The panorama of world history which Berdyaev surveys is a series of tragedies in which man hopes for freedom and discovers at every point forces which enslave his spirit. Objectification, the conversion of man into a disposable object, is not *a* process in history, it is *the* process of history, it is history's "achievement."

The tragedy of history has profound ontological and theological implications. For if man's efforts at moral and spiritual fulfillment have failed, so has his freedom. By failing to achieve freedom, man has fallen into bondage, which means that God, of whom man is a partner in creation, is also a victim of tragedy.[15] God's yearning for a divine-human unity of spirit remains unsatisfied. Tragedy is the right description for the situation of man in the world—tragedy exactly in the Greek sense. For by his own free decisions, man has fallen from his greatness in freedom, suggesting thereby that perhaps freedom is too great a burden for man to bear. This suggestion haunted Berdyaev all his life—that the threats to man's freedom may really serve the interests of man by destroying that freedom whose power is too great for man to accept in his life.[16]

His reflections on God, man, and the moral tragedy of history eventually evoked from Berdyaev a kind of philosophical mythology about freedom. The critical question was this: Does freedom have its source in God, or is there some other source? That God is the author of freedom as of everything else in creation is generally held in Western theology, Jewish and Christian. Man used the freedom which God granted him at the time of creation to disobey God, with the result that man was enslaved by sin, a condition that could be overcome only by God's grace. But then the question arose, If God is the author of man's freedom, is God not *ultimately* the cause of sin?

The problem of God's relation to evil is one that every theologian has had to confront. Many have concluded that evil, as contrasted with good, possesses no ultimate reality; and, a corollary of this, that God "permits" evil in order to preserve the integrity of freedom, which is essentially good. Furthermore, whatever evil has occurred in God's creation will be compensated, "made right," by Christ's Second Coming and the manifestation of God's Kingdom.

These doctrines are present in theologies as divergent as Barth's and Maritain's. But Berdyaev considered the notion of God's authorship of freedom the sure road to atheism.[17] He could not accept a God who is in any way responsible for evil. The doctrine of the nonreality of evil, Berdyaev looked on as plain nonsense; evil is one of the indisputable realities of human history. And the doctrine of God's permission of evil he regarded as attributing immorality to God. A God who does not battle evil constantly is quite unworthy of man's trust, love, and belief. Berdyaev's judgment is that the only way in which one can truly acknowledge the reality of evil, and still affirm the morality of God, is to abandon the orthodox theological belief that God is the author of freedom. After all, that view was held not out of a desire to understand freedom but out of the conviction that nothing should stand outside God, in any way qualifying or limiting his power. The belief that God is the author of freedom is another way of attesting to the supreme power of God. It is exactly this view, in Berdyaev's opinion, which leads to charging God with immorality.

But if God is not the author of freedom, who or what is? Berdyaev's response is that no rational answer can be given to this question.[18] One can point to decision and responsibility as the evidence of freedom, but there is no comparable evidence for the *source* of freedom. The source of freedom is truly mysterious, Berdyaev said. We know there is a source of freedom independent of God, but we cannot fathom its meaning. Freedom finally transcends all the rational-empirical categories of meaning at our disposal. In declaring freedom to be a mystery, Berdyaev turned to the mystical ideas of the great sixteenth-century thinker Jacob Boehme, whose ideas influenced Berdyaev's philosophical-mythological account of freedom.[19] Boehme made it possible for Berdyaev to understand how the tragedy of history can occur in a world of God's creation. The answer lay in the kind of dualistic cosmology that Boehme had developed.

Boehme spoke of a primordial level of divine reality which consists of irrational energy. This reality is not "God" in the biblical sense of the Creator, nor is it something that God has created. Boehme regarded it as a primordial source of everything that is, and he identified it as the *Ungrund*, the divine ground, suggesting a fathomless depth or abyss, a Nothing from which everything comes. Deeper than God, the *Ungrund* is the source out of which God creates the world. The *Ungrund*, then, is not a reality alongside God; rather, it is a depth of divinity from which God himself emerges. Although there are not two realities, *Ungrund and* God, there are two aspects to everything that exists: the createdness due to God, and irrational energy, the *Ungrund*. These two aspects are present in everything precisely because it is the Creator who draws from the *Ungrund* in his acts of creation. Boehme spoke of the *Ungrund* as the "dark side of God." In his theosophy, the world is governed by two principles, a principle of light representing the creative effort of God, and a principle of darkness representing the abiding power of the erratic energy of the *Ungrund*.

Berdyaev reinterpreted the *Ungrund* as the irrational and independent reality of freedom. God did not author freedom; but freedom is divine and in some sense "precedes" the event of creation. God acted from freedom to create the world, and the world must be free if it is to fulfill its aim of answering God's call for a life-partner. But—and this was the crucial point for Berdyaev—freedom, like the *Ungrund*, is independent of the creator of the world. Following Boehme very closely, Berdyaev sometimes says that God himself emerges from divine freedom as the creator of the world. The world, then, is the product of both God and freedom. God creates from freedom, and the world of his creation is free. To suppose that God is the author of freedom, as traditional theologies have done, is, according to Berdyaev, inherently contradictory. For this means that God governs freedom in the world, which in fact must mean that there is no freedom in the world, or that God is responsible for everything that happens, including that which we regard as evil. The only basis of the morality or "humanity" of God is the recognition that freedom is independent of God, a reality surely as powerful as God, a reality whose source is a profound mystery.

The tragedy of freedom is the tragedy which is shared by God and man; when God created the world out of freedom, the inherent irrationalism of freedom was loosed on the earth. Freedom is freedom for good and evil, creativeness and de- structiveness. The myth of the Fall symbolizes the essential moral fact of history, that freedom has never been used con- sistently for the creative good leading to the liberation of man; rather, it has been used consistently for evil destructiveness leading to the enslavement of man. The purpose of creation was to enjoy life, hence God needed his "other self" who in freedom and love would give him "life." But just the opposite happened. Out of its freedom, God's "other self" acts against God. The result is the frustration of the divine aim in the world, and the destruction of the quality of life which man can enjoy with God, the conversion of life from divine-human community to destructive isolation.

What, then, is the nature of God's life on earth? Berdyaev answers in a word: suffering! The life of God on earth is a life of a yearning for love that has not been and cannot be satisfied. Berdyaev rejects in the strongest terms the prevailing Western Christian concept of God as an omnipotent, self- sufficient, immobile deity. He opposed this concept with the claim that God is not self-sufficient but has concrete needs; that he is not immobile but rather enjoys a real life of movement through his experience of man and the world; and that he is not omnipotent because he is not powerful over freedom. Berdyaev's concept of God becomes clearer if we consider it in its relation to the reality of evil, the sacrifice of Jesus Christ, and the meaning of creativeness.

Berdyaev argues that the traditional notion of God as absolute in power and goodness simply cannot be reconciled with the travail that evil causes in the world. A God, absolute in power and goodness, could banish evil by fiat. If man is to go on believing in God, it must be in a God who is absolute not in power but in goodness, a goodness attested by his combat of evil even to the extent of suffering evil. By the example of his sacrificial love, good may come out of evil.

Moreover, to suppose that God has absolute power over evil is also to suppose that God is powerful over freedom, for freedom is the root of evil and of good. If God can banish neither freedom nor evil, what he *can* do is seek ways to persuade man in his freedom to act creatively rather than destructively. Persuasion then, and not acts of absolute power, is the character of God's grace—chiefly, persuasion by example, as evidenced by the story of Christ's life and death.

The belief that God does not undergo qualitative change, that he is eternally himself as befits the ancient notion of divine perfection, is shattered in the event of Christ's cross. In the crucifixion God himself experiences a profound sorrow and pain.[20] God knows the suffering of Christ as the Father knows the Son. The cross is not a gratuitous act on God's part, it does not happen by accident; it is in fact God's own answer to evil: the redeeming of the world through the force of sacrificial love. The whole life of Christ as biblically portrayed is, for Berdyaev, one continuous symbol of the inner life of God, a life containing the meanings of love, need, goodness, sacrifice, suffering, tragedy, and judgment.

Berdyaev rejects the traditional notion of God's self-sufficiency, for the creativeness of God suggests that he does have needs. God's yearning for his "other self" is at the heart of his creativeness. God creates in order to enter into a richer existence than he could have alone. This means, too, that God is continually creative, that he constantly seeks through his own love to inspire the responsive love of his creatures, his "other self." Berdyaev sees genuine movement in God, for where there is creativeness there are possibilities for realization. In the failure of creative realization, as well as in its success, God enjoys a qualitative experience or "movement."

Indispensable to the realization of the divine life is the reality of freedom in the world, for the world cannot respond in love to God's yearning for his "other self" except in freedom. Coerced love is not love. The tragedy that befalls God is that history shows freedom to be a great burden for man. Man will not accept his freedom, but weakens and willingly falls prey to social and political forces of enslavement. This tragedy is freedom's tragedy as well, in that God and man are never able to unite in and through their common freedom. The internal contradiction of freedom is never healed.

Although the character of man's historical existence is tragic, Berdyaev regarded the positive use of freedom to be manifested in divine-human creativeness. Creativeness represents in Berdyaev's view the way toward the union of God and man in a common life of love.[21] Creativeness is evidence that man is in two worlds: the fallen world of history, in which the spirit has gone out of things, and a transcendent world of creativeness where the spirit in things is constantly replenished by freedom, feeling, and imagination. When man acts creatively, he introduces for that brief moment the realm of spirit into the realm of history, and for that length of time the fallen world is uplifted, renewed, and transfigured. But, Berdyaev believes, all too soon the fires of creativeness cool, and the hand of routine is again laid over our lives.

In contrast to Maritain, who thinks man's humanity consists in reason, and in contrast to Barth, who finds the essence of man to be man's conformity by faith to Christ, Berdyaev locates the distinctness of man in his creativeness, more particularly in the imagination which is the key to his creativeness. In creativeness man is truly man, for in creativeness he imprints his personality on the unformed and undifferentiated character of the material world; through the imagination he brings something out of nothing. By creativeness man introduces spirit into a lifeless world. Through his imagination he makes the world come alive with meaning, thus giving new value to the world. Creativeness frees man from the oppressive power of purely materialistic and necessary existence.

Berdyaev claimed that in his creativeness man is most like God. The "image" of God that he bears is of a creator who is able by virtue of his freedom of imagination to create something genuinely new. God's yearning for his "other self" is satisfied only when man responds to God by creative acts of his own, for then man is introducing into reality that quality of meaning through which God enjoys life. Thus man, like God, creates life through his own powers of creativeness. Whatever life is created by God and man respectively is life shared by both.

Berdyaev referred to this co-creativity as the "divine-human spirit." It is a double movement and is partial and fragmentary because it takes place in the fallen world. No matter how great the effort on the side of God or man, their spiritual union through creativeness is never complete. And because it is not complete, creation has yet to be achieved.

Berdyaev did not equate creativeness with artistic creation, nevertheless he was greatly influenced by art. The achievement of the artist is that he brings something radically new into the world. His work would not be a creation of art if it were not something "new." The "newness," however, does not have its source in the material object or product but in what goes into it as inspiration and imagination. What makes art a radically new quality is the subjective factor, the artist's endeavor. It is thus possible to discern creativeness in human activities that are not, in the technical sense of the word, artistic. Whenever there is use of the imagination, giving qualitative meaning to a material world, giving life to what is lifeless, there is the creative. The creative can be seen in art, but it can also be seen in moral decisions, in politics, in social and family relations, in the religious life, in work and in play, literally in any act of man's self-expression.

When measured by the yardstick of history, Berdyaev

acknowledged, man's creativeness has to be judged a failure. The imagination, the feeling, the inspiration and freedom that are the well-springs of political, religious, and artistic creations, cease at the moment of accomplishment; from that moment on, these creations become objects consigned to the deadening, objectified culture of political systems, religious movements, and the museums of world art. Berdyaev discerned the breach between the creative and the created that evinces the tragic character of history.

Tillich's notion of estrangement is a close parallel, the estrangement between what man ideally *is* and what he has actually *become*. Like Tillich, Berdyaev views Jesus Christ as an answer to the question or problem of estrangement. But where Tillich regards Christ as a purely redemptive answer to estrangement, reconciling God and man by atoning for man's sinfulness, Berdyaev finds Christ's redemptive act as meaningful only in relation to a deeper purpose, that of God's continual yearning for life in and through man and the world. The appearance of Jesus Christ represents a new spirituality, a new resource for both God and man to come together in freedom and creativeness. Berdyaev writes:

> Not human nature alone, but the whole world, the whole of cosmic life, was changed after the Coming of Christ. When a drop of blood, shed by Christ on Golgotha, fell upon the earth, the earth became something other, something new.[22]

In Christ, God meets man as one who forgives man his failure to respond to his call for love, for a creative partner in life; and in Christ, man meets God as one who is willing to accept the cross of his freedom and respond to God in his uniqueness as a man. What Christ represents for Berdyaev is a double movement: a redemptive movement of God toward man, and an "anthropological" movement of man toward God. The appearance of Christ is thus due not only to an act of God but also, in some sense, to an act of man.

If Christ is not only God, but man as well, then not only God's nature is active in redemption, but man's nature also, heavenly, spiritual, human nature. . . . The human nature in Christ participates in the work of redemption. Sacrifice is the law of spiritual upsurge. In the Christian race, in the new spiritual race, a new period in the life of creation is opening. . . .[23]

And so, Christ provides a new spiritual ethos for the world, an ethos in which man is finally free to respond to God with all his creativeness, love, and freedom, and in which God finally will enjoy that richness of life in the world which was his original aim in creation. Berdyaev voices this new Christ-centered hope for the world when he speaks of the "third revelation," the revelation of the Spirit. There was the revelation of the Father before Christ, then the appearance of Christ the Son, and as a result of these two previous appearances, the way has been prepared for the Spirit:

The third creative revelation in the Spirit will have no holy scripture; it will be no voice from on high; it will be accomplished in man and in humanity—it is an anthropological revelation, an unveiling of the Christology of man. God awaits the anthropological revelation from man, and man cannot expect to have it from God. And one cannot merely wait for the third revelation; man must accomplish it himself, living in the Spirit; accomplish it by a free, creative act. In this act everything transcendent will become immanent. The third anthropological revelation, in which the creative mystery of man will be revealed, is man's final freedom.[24]

Christ is an answer to the estrangement of existence, but Christ has become distorted in the form of the Christian religion and its history. Can the new hope that Christ brings for man be realized in history? This is a question which Berdyaev could not easily or clearly answer. His response inevitably became eschatological, that is, it entailed the viewing of history from the extra-historical point of its fulfillment. Berdyaev was certain that creativeness possessed eschatological meaning. The creation of something out of nothing, the achievement of what is genuinely new, suggests a realm of meaning greater than history. He writes:

> Creative activity does not consist merely in the bestowal of a more perfect form upon this world; it is also liberation from the burden and bondage of this world.[25]

> . . . If one looks more deeply into creative activity we can say that there is a prophetic element in it. It speaks prophetically of a different world, of another, a transformed state of the world. But that means that the creative act is eschatological. In it the impossibility of resting content with this given world is proclaimed, in it this world comes to an end, and another world begins.[26]

The failure of human creative power is due to the objectification of all the products of that power. But the actual creative power itself moves out beyond the limits of objectification and is directed towards a new life, towards the Kingdom of God. The products of great creative minds prepare the way for the Kingdom of God, and enter into it. Greek tragedy, the pictures of Leonardo, Rembrandt, Botticelli; Michaelangelo's sculpture and Shakespeare's dramas; the symphonies of Beethoven and the novels of Tolstoy; the philosophical thought of Plato, Kant, and Hegel; the creative suffering of Pascal, Dostoevsky, and Nietzsche; the quest for freedom and for what is true and right in the life of society—all enter into the Kingdom of God.[27]

Creativeness contains glimmerings of "another world." Thus, despite the cooling of creative fire in the works that become part of objectified culture, the world is transformed, indeed replaced, by this other world, whose way is prepared by creativity. The Christ is rejected on earth, but the creativity of his life and death makes ready the Second Coming. Berdyaev's answer to the tragedy of history, then, is the dissolution of history. Here, of course, Berdyaev was relying upon the New Testament's prophecy of the Kingdom of God. The divine-human spirit, receiving new spirit in Christ, prepares the way for the Kingdom. Finally the Kingdom must and will come if man is to be saved from the tragedy of his own existence, and if man and God together are to achieve that quality of their common life which was the original purpose of existence. Consistent with his theme of divine-human mutuality, Berdyaev identifies the Kingdom of God as a Kingdom of "God-humanity."

It is in his eschatological "solution" to the problem of history that a most important element of Berdyaev's theology is underscored. When speaking of the Kingdom of God-humanity, Berdyaev means *all* humanity, all men everywhere and at all times, the living and the dead. This is a social note in his thought that helps to balance the subjectivism of his main ideas. Salvation ultimately becomes universal salvation; no one is truly saved unless and until all are saved. Certainly Berdyaev here reflects one of the motifs in the spirituality and theology of the Eastern Christian church. Berdyaev's vision of the final union of God and man, this realm of spirit which would replace the realm of historical necessity and objectification, he called *sobornost*, a Russian word which is best translated as "all-togetherness." [28]

Berdyaev stands with those religious thinkers—Schleiermacher, Tillich, Maritain, and Buber—who, in contradistinction to Kierkegaard and Barth, are convinced that there is a fundamental relation between God and the world, experienced as a spiritual depth of meaning in man's life and culture. God is inseparable in meaning from the deepest meanings of the human spirit: freedom, creativeness, love, sacrifice, guilt, judgment, suffering, death, and tragedy. God is Spirit encountered and known at the depths of the human spirit.

But though Berdyaev agrees with Tillich and Maritain about *how* God is known, he differs radically in his understanding of the character of the God so known. Berdyaev boldly claims that God's self-meaning as God includes his experience of the world and of man. This is what Berdyaev meant by theogenesis or the birth of God. The reality of God is his life, and the only recognizable meaning of "life" is life in relation to the world. In Berdyaev's judgment, it is precisely God's frustration with life in the world that is the source of his personal tragedy and the occasion for the eschatological overcoming of tragedy in the manifestation of the Kingdom, the new eon which will end history as God and man have known it.

Berdyaev employs a highly anthropomorphic way of speaking about God that is only slightly mitigated by his claim that all man's talk of God is symbolic—a claim which Tillich also makes. But the question is not whether one speaks symbolically or literally about God, but what kind of symbols are used. And here Berdyaev is prepared to defend human ways of speaking about God—God's "suffering," "need," "life," "pain," "joy," "tragedy"—as the most adequate means of doing justice to the witness of God presented by the life and death of Jesus Christ. If God is revealed in any measure by the Bible's portrait of Jesus, then surely what is revealed is not a lordly absolute. What is revealed is a rare quality of love that is willing to suffer and die for men, reclaiming them from their own powers of self-destruction; a compassionate, wise, courageous, and steadfast love for human beings; an acceptance of man and a realistic recognition of the price to be paid for accepting man in freedom —the picture of a God whose life is a life in, with, and for the world.

The reason the concept of a divine absolute figures so prominently in the thought of Kierkegaard, Barth, and Tillich is that the exclusive relationship between God and the world is understood by all these thinkers to be man's redemption from sin by God's grace. For Berdyaev, however, and to some extent for Schleiermacher and Buber, too, the meaning of redemption comes from the wider and deeper perspective of God's original commitment to the world. The reality of redemptive grace to which the Christian myth points is, of course, included in this commitment; but the myth that comes closer to symbolizing the truth of God's life in the world is the myth of creation in the Bible. Berdyaev is right to interpret the meaning of Jesus Christ not as some exclusive revelation of God, supplanting all other revelations, but as a new, fresh spirit of the divine-humanity which began with creation and has been struggling for expression throughout history. What this means for Berdyaev is that Christ illumines that deep relationship of freedom, creativeness, and love which God had with the world and with man long before the birth of Christianity. Although Berdyaev did not make this implication clear, that truth which Christ reveals of God is open to new encounters between the divine spirit and the human spirit since the birth of Christianity, wherever they appear: in the Christian religion, in religions other than Christianity, in events of life that are outside organized religion, in any act of man's imagination, feeling, thought, and will. For the basic concept of Berdyaev's theology—God-humanity—is a concept of universality, a freedom of spirit found wherever and whenever God and man meet through the realities of freedom, creativeness, and love.

Freedom is what makes the life of God a reality and makes the world necessary to the life of God. For life is meaningless without growth and newness, and these are possible only through freedom. Berdyaev argues that God can have life only in relation to the "other," and "world" is another name for the "other." Berdyaev made clear that God's relationship to the world is not exhausted by his relationship to man, though because of man's greater capacities for spirit, this is God's "highest" relationship. Like Pierre Teilhard de Chardin and Alfred North Whitehead, Berdyaev was prepared to recognize that God's relationship to the world reaches down to the animal kingdom and to every facet of the organic and inorganic world—for there is nothing which is devoid of meaning and nothing which is without that spirit through which God experiences community and life.

But the tragedy of life is that that freedom which makes life possible also makes its destruction possible. And this tragedy, Berdyaev claimed, is as much God's as the world's. Berdyaev answered this tragedy, as we saw, with the eschatological message of the New Testament: the Kingdom of God and the Second Coming of Christ. So far as we can see, in offering this answer Berdyaev capitulated to that tendency toward romantic idealism that was always present in his ideas. Berdyaev always saw things dualistically, in terms of antitheses between the ideal and the actual. Thus he celebrates the creative but laments the created; he rejoices in spirit but bemoans matter, which he thinks does not so much actualize spirit as imprison it and extinguish its fire.

Berdyaev's view that freedom is a force independent of God is a defensible one in light of the scriptural understanding of God. Berdyaev reasoned that God cannot be the author of freedom, for if he were, he must then be regarded as the ultimate source of man's evil or sinfulness. But in attempting then to provide an explanation for freedom, to assign freedom an ultimate source or cause, Berdyaev bound himself to a dualism which may represent a critical flaw in his thought.

There appear in Berdyaev's thought not one divine principle but two: there is God who is the Creator, and there is freedom which is "irrational" and a source either for creative good or for destructive evil, though God himself always acts freely for the good. This means that the "tragedy" of history is not merely the result of man's decisions; it is that, to be sure, but more profoundly it is the result of a divided freedom that not even God in his act of creation can effectively heal. Here is a primordial conflict: the continual struggle between God's creative wisdom and freedom's irrationalism, a conflict that precedes history and therefore appears at every stage of man's life on earth. It is Boehme's dualistic or gnostic vision of the world as the scene of contention between two gods or divine forces, a dualism which Berdyaev accepted uncritically.

This dualism exerted an enormous influence on Berdyaev's ideas, particularly on his idea of creativity. It led, as we have said, to his assigning the highest value and meaning to what is ideal in the creative act, and the least value to what is actual or concrete. He subordinates the material objects of creation to the unique feelings and thoughts that go before them. For Berdyaev, the highest freedom, the most genuine creativity, lie in the expression of man's heart and mind, not in what is consigned to the world of historical objects once the creative process has resulted in actual accomplishment. Here Berdyaev echoes Nietzsche's sentiments in *Thus Spake Zarathustra*, where it is the God of spirit who makes man free, not the god of matter, who represents freedom turned against itself. Berdyaev failed to see that our knowledge of what is creative, as contrasted to what is routine and ordinary, comes not from "ideas" or the imagination *per se*; rather, it comes from actual creations.

Berdyaev's dualistic conception of the historical conflict between God and the negative side of freedom means that the answer to history's tragedy lies "above" history: it lies in the New Testament's announcement of the coming Kingdom of God. Berdyaev interpreted this eschatological event as a symbol of a new, transfigured existence for man in perfect communion with God, a life transcending the material, historical conditions of man's "past" and "fallen" life. But the question we must raise is, What meaning can there be in a "life" that is not temporal and thereby inescapably part of history, a "life" earthly and not material? To suppose that there could be such a life suggests precisely that "other-worldliness" or supernaturalism which is so clearly rejected by everything else that Berdyaev has said about God, freedom, and creativity.

If Berdyaev had recognized that he need not assign a "source" for freedom, he would not have been led to believe that the solution to the problem of history lies "above" history. For freedom is one of the a priori meanings of reality, a meaning which requires no ultimate explanation—certainly not one that requires a myth of origin.[29] Just as there need be no "reason" for creativity or "reason" for reason, there need be no "reason" for freedom. Freedom, creativity, reason, and—for many thinkers—God, are fundamental structures of reality which we know of through the intuitions of our experience. The task of the philosopher is to elucidate them, not to "account" for them. In relation to God, freedom is a kind of "limit"; freedom makes life possible for God, but only because there is before God the life and freedom of the "other." For God to "take over" freedom would mean that he would have nothing truly opposite him, apart from him, an "other" to which he can be related. The taking over of freedom would mean, then, the destruction of life. But, as Berdyaev believed, God does not take over freedom; rather, he lives and works through it, as he lives and works through the "other." And if the Bible is to be believed, God suffers for freedom so as to preserve its power to give life to man and to himself.

VII

The Theology of Dialogue: Martin Buber

Two great cultural traditions shaped the emotional and intellectual development of Martin Buber, considered the greatest Jewish religious thinker of the twentieth century. One of these was the literary, philosophical, and artistic culture of late nineteenth-century Western Europe. When the nineteen-year-old Buber went to study at the University of Vienna in 1896, romanticism and idealism reigned in German letters and thought, and no city embodied this spirit more than Vienna. Kant, Hegel, Schleiermacher, Feuerbach, Rilke, and Hugo von Hofmannsthal were the acknowledged masters.

The "high" culture of Europe was fused in Buber's development with another tradition: the ethnic and religious culture of Eastern European Jewry. Born in Vienna in 1878, at the age of three Buber went to live with his grandparents in Galicia, a region that became part of southern Poland after the First World War. Solomon Buber, his grandfather, was a fine rabbinic scholar who had an enormous influence on young Martin.

He not only exposed his grandson to the riches of learning but imparted to him a lasting sense of the religious genius of Judaism. From Solomon Buber the young grandson learned of the Haskalah, the impact of the Enlightenment on Judaism, and under his grandfather's guidance he began to study the Bible in the original Hebrew. It was during these early years with his grandparents in Galicia that Buber came into contact with Hasidic Jews practicing a form of piety which, in contrast to the rigidities of organized, synagogal worship, emphasized a personal sense of spiritual freedom. Hasidism had an enormous impact on Buber's later development, and was to be a turning-point for his own religious thought.

One must speak of a *fusion* of these two traditions in Buber's thought. Buber is the cultured European who finds in the Haskalah a "faith" perfectly consistent with his university education and his development as a scholar; but he is also the Jew who began the road to religious self-consciousness in his grandfather's house reading the Bible, and who was exposed early in life to the spiritual fervor of the Hasidim. In all of Buber's writings, most particularly in his best-known work, *I and Thou*, one finds both traditions reflected.

At the close of his formal education, Buber met Theodor Herzl, leader of the Zionist movement, and thereafter worked actively in Europe for the advancement of Zionist causes. Initially it was through Zionism that Buber began to give expression to those roots in him which were distinctly Jewish. He edited Zionist journals and later, after moving from Vienna to Berlin, founded a publishing house whose aim was the dissemination of materials that could nourish the Jewish spirit throughout Europe. Buber's activities embodied his own understanding of the Zionist goal, which he took to be the preservation and enrichment of Jewish culture wherever it existed. In later years he found himself at odds with many fellow Zionists, including Herzl, who began to equate the Zionist ideal with the establishment of a Jewish national state.

It was during this period of his work as a Zionist that Buber made the fateful decision to withdraw into an uninterrupted study of the literature of Hasidism. For five years, from 1904 to 1909, Buber read the stories of the Hasidic sages, and reflected at length on the vision of God, man, and world expressed in these stories. In Hasidism, he says, "I recognized the idea of the complete man. At the same time I became conscious of the call to make this known to the world." [1]

Maurice Friedman, one of Buber's best interpreters and translators in the English language, writes of the relation between Buber's thought and Hasidism.

> . . . It is to Hasidism, more than to any other single source, that [Buber] has gone for his image of what modern man can and ought to become. For Hasidism, as for Buber's philosophy of dialogue, one cannot love God unless one loves his fellow man, and for his love to be real it must be love of each particular man in his created uniqueness and it must take place for its own sake and not for the sake of any reward, even the salvation or perfection of one's soul.[2]

According to Friedman, Hasidism "hallows community and everyday life" while rejecting asceticism and the denial of the life of the senses. The Hasid looks on an individual's attitude as the great source of his bearing in the world: whether he is a whole man or whether he is divided in himself so that not good but evil comes from him. A man will continue to sin if he yields in despair of his sinfulness; but he will overcome sin if he puts his thoughts on God's love of him and God's need of him in spite of his sinfulness. Contained in the Hasidic wisdom is an ethical and psychological doctrine of the supreme value of the individual. The greatest error any man can commit is to compare himself with others. Hasidism teaches that each man has his own genius. A man is perfected if he but fulfill his own potentialities whatever they be, whether they steer him toward a life of religious devotion, scholarly reflection, the simplest domestic duties, commerce and the world of affairs—whatever. God loves each man in himself and not because he has succeeded in patterning his life after some "great" man. To this effect Buber retells some of the old Hasidic stories:

> The wise Rabbi Bunam once said in old age, when he had already grown blind: "I shall not live to change places with our father Abraham! What good would it do God if Abraham became like blind Bunam, and blind Bunam became Abraham? Rather than have this happen, I think I shall try to become a little more myself."
> The same idea was expressed with even greater pregnancy by Rabbi Zusya when he said, a short while before his death: "In the world to come I shall not be asked: 'Why were you not Moses?,' I shall be asked: 'Why were you not Zusya?'" [3]

What Buber sees in these and other Hasidic stories is that man serves God not in achieving acts of moral heroism but rather in the modest and all-too-human efforts of expressing one's own particularity, as one comes to discover it, in his daily life. This is the secret to "hallowing the everyday" by which alone, according to the Hasidic outlook, God brings the world to perfection. Religious and ethical ideas are to be adhered to, and heroes will indeed emerge from time to time who will help us to see the great heights and depths of God's life with man; but the task assigned to each man is to live out each one of his days not imitating the hero but inspired by him to discover his own life with God.

This Hasidic affirmation of the mutuality between God and man is virtually identical to Berdyaev's conviction that God is himself given life in the life of man on earth. Commenting on the Hasidic tradition in Judaism, Buber writes:

> God's grace consists precisely in this, that he wants to let himself be won by man, that he places himself, so to speak, into man's hands. God wants to come to his world, but he wants to come to it through man. This is the mystery of our existence, the superhuman chance of mankind.
> "Where is the dwelling of God?"

This was the question with which the Rabbi of Kotzk sur-
prised a number of learned men who happened to be visiting
him.
They laughed at him: "What a thing to ask! Is not the
whole world full of his glory?"
Then he answered his own question:
"God dwells wherever man lets him in."
This is the ultimate purpose: to let God in. But we can let
him in only where we really stand, where we live, where we
live a true life. If we maintain holy intercourse with the little
world entrusted to us, if we help the holy spiritual substance
to accomplish itself in that section of Creation in which we are
living, then we are establishing, in this our place, a dwelling
for the Divine Presence.[4]

As these comments of Buber's suggest, there is a trinity in
Hasidic thought: God, man, and the world. When man affirms
the world for the sake of God, nothing is debased, and whatever is already debased can be transformed in this affirmation;
for God lives in the world through man's sanctification of his
own life in the world. But when man affirms the world for its
own sake, or affirms God apart from the world in the posture
of religious idealism, then the essential trinity is broken and both
man and his world become debased. Politics, family relations,
sexuality, art, leisure, eating—every aspect of living maintains
its integrity for man, its wholeness, only when man affirms it
for the sake of God. The attitude of the Hasid is that life in
the world is not good in itself but good because, through man,
it serves God. Life in the world cannot become debased if man
keeps sight of the transcendent or eternal element in each
earthly thing, just as he must not lose sight of the earthly
presence of the transcendent God. This theme becomes dominant in Buber's thought, and, as we shall see, enters into the
essence of his theology of dialogue.
In the early twenties Buber made the acquaintance of Franz
Rosenzweig, the leader of the Free Jewish Academy in Frank-
fort-am-Main, and the two decided to collaborate on a modern

German translation of the Hebrew Bible. Their aim, like that of Martin Luther centuries before them, was to make the scriptures accessible to people who had lost contact with them through ignorance of the original language. Rosenzweig died in 1929 before the project was completed, but Buber continued to labor alone until he finished the translation late in his life. The publication of the initial volumes of the work achieved instantly the desired result. German-speaking Jews everywhere were led back to the religious traditions of their forefathers. In Jewish communities all over German lands, a new awareness of the meaning of Jewishness arose. This scholarly work on the Bible placed a lasting stamp on Buber's own thought. Buber went on to write commentaries on various biblical themes, and to seek the creative nexus of the scriptural tradition, of German idealistic philosophy, and of the ethical and psychological wisdom of Hasidism, a nexus which bore fruit in his notion of the I-Thou.

In 1923, Buber accepted an appointment as Professor of Jewish History of Religion and Ethics in a newly created post at Frankfurt University. Ten years later, upon the ascendancy of the Nazi party in Germany, he was deprived of his position. From 1933 until 1938 Buber remained in Germany, working actively with Jewish communities throughout Germany to preserve and defend the quality of Jewish life. By 1938, however, there were ample portents of the future of German Jewry. In that year Buber migrated to Palestine to accept a position as Professor of Sociology at the newly created Hebrew University of Jerusalem.

Buber continued to study and write for the remainder of his life in Jerusalem. As a lifelong Zionist, he took a keen interest in the politics of Palestine. He continually urged political leaders to make every effort to secure "a peaceful coexistence" between Jews and Arabs. When Buber died in 1965, at the age of eighty-seven, he was one of the most famous citizens of a nation, Israel, which in his own way he did much to create, but which, as a modern political state heavily dependent on the military for survival, he could never fully approve in his heart.

Martin Buber's theology of dialogue is based on the recognition of a profound dimension in man's life which he calls the relation of "I-Thou." The I-Thou contains clues to the meaning of man's humanity, his significance in the universe, and his destiny as God's creature. Buber describes the I-Thou as an event, a "meeting" wherein man personally addresses and is personally addressed by the other. The character of such meeting is dialogue, the communion of an "I" with a "Thou," and a "Thou" with an "I." [5]

Though man's relation to God, world, other men, and himself is essentially constituted by the dimension of dialogue in his life, Buber is at pains to show that the meaning of human life is not exhausted by dialogue. There is a second, equally significant relation, in which man addresses and is addressed by the other, not as his "thou" but rather as an "object of experience." Buber calls this relation the "I-It." In it, man's I is not I-for-the-Thou but an I which is the experiencing subject. Through the relation of I-It there occur all man's experiences of feeling, thinking, and doing, experiences in which the subject always has an object facing it. These experiences are characterized by independence and the absence of mutuality. Let us take, for example, a farmer who tills the soil, contemplates the newest agricultural techniques, and has strong feelings about the expected harvest. In every respect the land is an object of the farmer's experience, but we cannot say that the land experiences the farmer. The farmer's relation to the land is the relation of I-It. For, insofar as his purpose is "farming," his relation to the land will be that of "disposing" of the land through feeling, thought, and action. But a farmer is also a man, and if the value and meaning of his humanity as a man are not realized through I-Thou relationships as well, he will be reduced to the sterility of a purely utilitarian existence. Buber regards both dimensions essential to life; man cannot live from day-to-day without It, but a life of It alone is sterile.

By contrast with I-It, I-Thou is characterized by mutuality. If the farmer's relation to the land is I-Thou as well as I-It, the land can be said to "experience" him. The I-Thou is mutual appreciation, the communion of being with being, the opposite of I-It's necessary exploitiveness. There is no subject-object structure in the relation of I-Thou, it is subject-subject. The essence of I-Thou is dialogue between subjects. The land claims the farmer, but it claims his humanity; it admits him to a level of value and meaning which does not negate the functional but which transcends it. When the farmer acknowledges the land as a being which confronts his own being, drawing from him the purest respect for its integrity, then he has encountered the land, the land has "experienced" him. The farmer does not cease to have the land as his It, but now also as a man he lives in relation to its "thou-ness."

The event of I-Thou resembles mysticism, but that resemblance is only an apparent one, for there is no dissolution of the I in the Thou, as in classical expressions of mysticism. The meeting of I and Thou is not union but communion, dialogue wherein the I retains its identity as I in the encounter with the Thou. Yet Buber's notion of I-Thou is easily confused with mysticism, and easily misunderstood in any event. A sharper sense of it is imparted by two stories recounted by Buber about his own life.

The first story concerns the young Buber and a horse whom he loved.

When I was eleven years of age, spending the summer on my grandparents' estate, I used, as often as I could do it unobserved, to sneak into the stable and gently stroke the neck of my darling, a broad dapple-grey horse. It was not a casual delight but a great, certainly friendly, but also deeply stirring happening. If I am to explain it now, beginning from the still very fresh memory of my hand, I must say that what I experienced in touch with the animal was the Other, the immense otherness of the Other, which, however, did not remain strange like the otherness of the ox and the ram, but rather let me draw near and touch it. When I stroked the mighty mane, sometimes marvellously smooth-combed, at other times just as astonishingly wild, and felt the life beneath my hand, it was as though the element of vitality itself bordered on my skin, something that was not I, was certainly not akin to me, palpably the other, not just another, really the Other itself; and yet it let me approach, confided itself to me, placed itself elementally in the relation of *Thou* and *Thou* with me. The horse, even when I had not begun by pouring oats for him into the manger, very gently raised his massive head, ears flicking, then snorted quietly, as a conspirator gives a signal meant to be recognizable only by his fellow-conspirator; and I was approved.[6]

The second story concerns Buber in later life, when he would receive students at his home.

What happened was no more than that one forenoon, after a morning of "religious" enthusiasm, I had a visit from an unknown young man, without being there in spirit. I certainly did not fail to let the meeting be friendly, I did not treat him any more remissly than all his contemporaries who were in the habit of seeking me out about this time of day as an oracle that is ready to listen to reason. I conversed openly and attentively with him—only I omitted to guess the questions which he did not put. Later, not long after, I learned from one of his friends—he himself was no longer alive—the essential content of these questions; I learned that he had come not casually, but borne by destiny, not for a chat but for a decision. He had come to me, he had come in this hour. What do we expect when we are in despair and yet go to a man? Surely a presence by means of which we are told that nevertheless there is meaning.

Since then I have given up the "religious" which is nothing but the exception, extraction, exaltation, ecstasy; or it has given me up. I possess nothing but the everyday of which I am never taken. The mystery is no longer disclosed, it has escaped or it has made its dwelling here, where everything happens as it happens. I know no fulness but each mortal hour's fulness of claim and responsibility. . . .[7]

These stories suggest that I-Thou is the living of a deep, internal relationship, a true mutuality. Mutuality is not mutual dependence, for the "other" cannot properly become a Thou-for-an-I if it is in some way dependent on or part of an I. In this respect the mutuality of the I-Thou relationship preserves the integrity of the parties of the relationship; indeed, the meeting of I and Thou would not be possible without the integrity of the respective parties.

The two stories are meant to show that the possibilities of deeply personal meaning between man and animal, teacher and student, are realized only in the event of meeting, in what Buber sometimes calls the "betweenness." The reality of I-Thou is, then, the reality of dialogue, consisting not of an "experience" but of a *lived relationship* mediated to us by feeling, thought, and action.

Though the interhuman seems to give the greatest access to the I-Thou, the story of the horse shows that mutuality is not limited to the dialogue between man and man. There are three gates to the reality of the I-Thou: nature, man, and God. The following comment of Buber's makes this clear, and helps to point up the meaning of our analogy about the farmer and his land.

I CONSIDER A TREE.

I can look on it as a picture: stiff column in a shock of light, or splash of green shot with the delicate blue and silver of the background.

I can perceive it as movement: flowing veins on clinging, pressing pith, suck of the roots, breathing of the leaves, ceaseless commerce with earth and air—and the obscure growth itself.

I can classify it in a species and study it as a type in its structure and mode of life.

I can subdue its actual presence and form so sternly that I recognize it only as an expression of law—of the laws in accordance with which a constant opposition of forces is continually adjusted, or of those in accordance with which the component substances mingle and separate.

I can dissipate it and perpetuate it in number, in pure numerical relation.

In all this the tree remains my object, occupies space and time, and has its nature and constitution.

It can, however, also come about, if I have both will and grace, that in considering the tree I become bound up in relation to it. The tree is now no longer *It*. I have been seized by the power of exclusiveness.

To effect this it is not necessary for me to give up any of the ways in which I consider the tree. There is nothing from which I would have to turn my eyes away in order to see, and no knowledge that I would have to forget. Rather is everything, picture and movement, species and type, law and number, indivisibly united in this event.

Everything belonging to the tree is in this: its form and structure, its colors and chemical composition, its intercourse with the elements and with the stars, are all present in a single whole.

The tree is no impression, no play of my imagination, no value depending on my mood; but it is bodied over against me and has to do with me, as I with it—only in a different way.

Let no attempt be made to sap the strength from the meaning of the relation: relation is mutual.

The tree will have a consciousness, then, similar to our own? Of that I have no experience. But do you wish, through seeming to succeed in it with yourself, once again to disintegrate that which cannot be disintegrated? I encounter no soul or dryad of the tree, but the tree itself. [8]

Buber's "confession" in these three tales is of the experience of a distinct quality of life, the perception of a meaning which rises out of relationship alone, a meaning which is at once personal, unifying, and redemptive or healing. This is the meaning of the I-Thou. The melancholy truth about man is that the I-Thou is not and cannot be sustained in our lives. All too quickly, that deep, personal relationship between I and Thou passes back into the essential subject-object structure of experience—the I-It—whence it came. But insofar as the I-Thou is a profound dimension of reality, it is a possibility for man in his life with the world of nature, with his fellow man, and with God.

The I-Thou is a matter of relationship in which the accent falls on *how* one is related—the quality of relationship—and not on *what* one is related to—the object. This being so, the I-Thou includes but does not consist only of knowledge, utility, or "experience." The I-Thou is rather a way of standing in relation to life, a way of "being." Thus the *It* of one's wife and children, friends, work, political party, and religion can also become the *Thou* when the attitude of knowing, living with, and expressing oneself through them passes into the attitude of "meeting," the mutuality inherent to dialogue.

If relation is of the essence of the meeting of I and Thou, then, in Buber's judgment, there must be a fundamental basis of relationship. There is a supreme Thou which makes possible the meeting of I and Thou everywhere else. This supreme Thou—the ultimate basis of all relation—is Buber's way of speaking of God. God is the "eternal Thou," but this is not so much a notion of God as it is a notion of man's *experienced relationship* to God. Man encounters God as the "eternal Thou" in all the Thou's with which his I is related. ". . . Through contact with every Thou, we are stirred with a breath of the Thou, that is of eternal life." [9]

Buber has given psychological and ontological meaning to the powerful biblical theme of God, the Creator. In the notions of dialogue and the eternal Thou he has shown how men—all men, believers or not—experience the power of the Creator through their experiences of the world. Each man may perceive a supreme unity which underlies but exceeds those other "unities" of family, friendship, and vocation. There is no one place in which man encounters God, no special area or type of experience which affords a "better" relationship to God. Religion is no better for experiencing the living God than morality, and morality no better than art or sex or politics. What matters is not *what* is experienced, but how—that the experience be not just the experience of an object but the experience of a relationship.

In contrast to the tradition rooted in Schleiermacher and exemplified by Tillich, Buber does not regard the essence of life as a religious experience, such as the "feeling of absolute dependence" or "ultimate concern." The encounter of I and Thou can indeed occur within an identifiable religious context, but the I-Thou does not consist of religion, because it does not consist of any particular experience. The distinctions between secular and sacred, God and world, are distinctions within the realm of I-It, not of I-Thou. Buber writes:

> . . . To step into pure relation is not to disregard everything but to see everything in the Thou, not to renounce the world but to establish it on its true basis. . . . "Here world, there God" is the language of It; "God in the world" is another language of It; but to eliminate or leave behind nothing at all, to include the whole world in the Thou, to give the world its due and its truth, to include nothing beside God but everything in him—this is full and complete relation.[10]

> . . . There is no such thing as seeking God, for there is nothing in which He could not be found. Every relational event is a stage that affords him a glimpse into the consummating event.[11]

It is possible to confuse Buber's notion of the I-Thou with various forms of mysticism: freedom from the ego in the attainment of eternal bliss or Nirvana, or realization of the true self by union with God in the world soul. The critical difference for Buber is that I and Thou is a philosophy of "meeting," where the integrity of meeting is preserved by the acknowledgment of two different but integral beings. Were the I absorbed by the Thou, there would cease to be a Thou, for there would be no *relation*; dialogue between I and Thou is afforded by relation alone. As Buber sees it, the problem with the mystical tradition is that it does away with relation, thereby negating concreteness and particularity. The meeting of I and Thou is the recognition of meaning within the world of concrete particulars; this is the opposite of mysticism's judgment that meaning comes only from the overcoming of differences in a nonconcrete or transcendental unity. Buber's affirmation of the concreteness and diversity of the world seems peculiarly biblical and Hebraic. This can be seen, for example, in Buber's "reverence" for the earthly, and his repugnance at "winning heaven" at the cost of the world. He asks:

> What does it help my soul that it can be withdrawn anew from this world here into unity, when this world itself has of necessity no part in the unity—what does all "enjoyment of God" profit a life that is rent in two? If that abundantly rich heavenly moment has nothing to do with my poor earthly moment—what has it then to do with me, who have still to live, in all seriousness still to live, on earth? Thus are the masters to be understood who have renounced the raptures of ecstatic "union." [12]

Buber's doctrine of the I-Thou is a kind of realism which opposes all the idealisms which either dissolve the subject into the object or which subordinate the object to the subject. For Buber, the self cannot truly be a self without relation to the world. Thus a doctrine of the true self must be a doctrine of relation; the self which would have knowledge of God has it only in *relation* to the world. Man discovers God as well as himself only in relation to the world. Without the world, the self discovers not God but its own thoughts, its own imaginings —abstractions that move further and further from the living nexus of a person's existence. This is what Buber means when he says:

> . . . He who merely "experiences" his attitude, merely consummates it in the soul, however thoughtfully, is without the

world—and all the tricks, arts, ecstasies, enthusiasms, and mysteries that are in him do not even ripple the skin of the world. So long as a man is set free only in his Self he can do the world neither weal nor woe; he does not concern the world. Only he who believes in the world is given power to enter into dealings with it, and if he gives himself to this he cannot remain godless.[13]

In light of his theology of dialogue, Buber must reject a conception of faith such as Kierkegaard's, which exchanges relation and mutuality for heroic individualism and solitude. In Buber's view, solitude or the deliberate renunciation of the interhuman is not the ground of faith but precisely its denial. ". . . If solitude means absence of relation, then he who has been forsaken by the beings to which he spoke the true *Thou* will be raised up by God, but not he who himself forsook the beings." [14] Buber proposes a distinction between true solitude, which is necessary to man as a "purifying" of his spirit that he may more fully enter into relation, and that false solitude which is a self-imposed isolation, wherein a man cuts himself off from the possibility of relation by supposing that God is religiously apart from the world. The latter falsely supposes that one can possess God. This, Buber says, is the degeneration of spirit into spirituality or religiosity:

> . . . Man can advance to the last abyss, where in his self-delusion he imagines he has God in himself and is speaking with Him. But truly though God surrounds us and dwells in us, we never have Him in us. And we speak with Him only when speech dies within us.[15]

For Buber, a faith which leads to sacrifice of the human and worldly is as idolatrous as a faith that has as its object some finite thing such as wealth or success. A man may have an idolatrous relation to God, just as he may have an idolatrous relation to some object of the world of It. The keynote of idolatry is not the object but the relation, where the subject seeks to possess and therefore to subjugate the object. To convert a man from idolatry to "true faith" is to convert him from possessiveness to the recognition of the "solidarity of relation."

> The man who is possessed is saved by being wakened and educated to solidarity of relation, not by being led in his state of possession towards God. If a man remains in this state what does it mean when he calls no longer on the name of a demon or of a being demonically distorted for him, but on the name of God? It means that from now on he blasphemes. It is blasphemy when a man wishes, after the idol has crashed behind the altar, to pile up an unholy sacrifice to God on the desecrated place.[16]

Although Buber shares with Barth the rejection of the "religious" route to God, Buber's notion of the deep relation that unites God and man is an implicit repudiation of Barth's theology of the wholly other, which separates God and world. It is not idolatry to perceive God in the world, says Buber; it is idolatry to *identify* God with the world, or to separate God from the world. Since reality for Buber is "mutuality," that which denies relation by supposing two completely separate realms, the divine and human, is most destructive of reality. Such a denial strikes fundamentally against the biblical affirmation that as Creator, God is not without witness in the world of his creation.

> Life cannot be divided between a real relation with God and an unreal relation of *I* and *It* with the world—you cannot both truly pray to God and profit by the world. He who knows the world as something by which he is to profit knows God also in the same way. His prayer is a procedure of exoneration heard by the ear of the void. He—not the "atheist," who addresses the Nameless out of the night and yearning of his garret-window—is the godless man.[17]

We said that Buber does not have a notion of God but rather of man's *experienced relation* to God. Consistent with this, Buber's notion of God's self-revelation is not that of a particular content—some special truth about God, a special person of God, such as the Son of God—but rather the accessibility to man of a supreme presence and power. Thus, in contrast to all the other theologians we have explained, Buber views revelation as relational. Revelation, he states, is threefold.[18] First, man receives an acceptance, the awareness that he has been put into a living relation. Buber speaks of this as "the whole fullness of real mutual action, of the being raised and bound up in relation." Second, this "real mutual action" bestows meaning on man's life, after which "Nothing can any longer be meaningless." Third, what is given to us by the revelation is the recognition that the meaning bestowed on our lives is not of "another life," not some "Yonder," but "that of this life of ours," and "of this world of ours," a meaning which "desires its confirmation in this life and in relation with this world." This is not a meaning in which one learns the meaning of something or someone; it is a meaning in relation to which one daily lives his life.

Buber's rejection of "special revelation" is part of his rejection of religious parochialism, whether in the form of Christianity's claim about the uniqueness of Jesus Christ as Savior, or in the form of Judaism's claim about the exclusiveness of its own community of faith. The deep bond between God and the world, and therefore between God and all men, Jew and gentile, believer and nonbeliever, makes it impossible to restrict God to any one person or group, to any "one" revelation. The meaning of God's revelation is presence and power. Buber writes:

> I do not believe in a self-naming of God, a self-definition of God before men. The Word of revelation is *I am that I am.* That which reveals is that which reveals. That which is *is,* and nothing more. The eternal source of strength streams, the eternal contact persists, the eternal voice sounds forth, and nothing more.[19]

The mystery of God is preserved in revelation. Man experiences God's presence and power, but in no way is God "shown" or "displayed." Man knows God, but he knows him in his mystery. Thus Buber writes:

> We have come near to God, but not nearer to unveiling being or solving its riddle. We have felt release, but not discovered a "solution." We cannot approach others with what we have received, and say "You must know this, you must do this." We can only go, and confirm its truth. And this, too, is no "ought," but we can, we *must*.[20]

Buber is not opposed to religion as such. He recognizes that the meeting of I and Thou can occur through the various cultic, symbolic, and dogmatic forms of religion. But, like Tillich and Berdyaev, Buber rejects religious forms when they have lost their living relationship to the deep meanings that God shares with man and the world. Religious symbols lose their meanings when, as Tillich noted, man worships the symbol instead of *through* the symbol. The fault here is man's, not God's.

> God is near His forms if man does not remove them from Him. But when the expanding movement of religion suppresses the movement of turning and removes the form from God, the countenance of the form is obliterated, its lips are dead, its hands hang down, and God knows it no more, and the universal dwelling-place that is built about its altar, the spiritually apprehended cosmos, tumbles in. And the fact that man, in the disturbance of his truth, no longer sees what is then taking place, is a part of what has then taken place.[21]

By the "expanding movement of religion" Buber is referring to the communal growth of religion. This growth can be seen time and again in history. Buber's argument is that this growth may in fact be an obstacle to the life of spirit which God and man can share through "meeting." When this is so, then the spirit itself bids man to forswear the temple for the open spaces. Buber sees this conflict between the person and the religious community throughout history. But he also sees that when religion is most oppressive to the divine-human spirit, new possibilities of redemption emerge, a new "turning" takes place, a different manifestation of the Kingdom "in our midst":

> History is a mysterious approach. Every spiral of its way leads us both into profounder perversion and more fundamental turning. But the event that from the side of the world is called turning is called from God's side redemption.[22]

The great turning-points in man's history—the junctures of culture—occur precisely at those points when:

> . . . the true element of the human spirit, suppressed and buried, comes to hidden readiness so urgent and so tense that it awaits only a touch from Him who touches in order to burst forth. The revelation that then makes its appearance seizes in the totality of its constitution the whole elemental stuff that is thus prepared, melts it down, and produces in it a form that is a new form of God in the world.
>
> Thus in the course of history, in the transforming of elemental human stuff, ever new provinces of the world and spirit are raised to form, summoned to divine form. Ever new spheres become regions of a theophany. It is not man's own power that works here, nor is it God's pure effective passage, but is a mixture of the divine and the human.

And Buber concludes:

> Although we earthly beings never look at God without the world, but only look at the world in God, yet as we look we shape eternally the form of God.[23]

Buber's theology of I and Thou contains a critique of the quality of human existence in our modern technologically oriented society. Though the gap between "spirit" and "matter" is not as great in his view as it was for Berdyaev, he observed, as did Berdyaev, the dehumanization of life that has come about as a result of technology. But where Berdyaev saw the solution to modern man's problem in narrowly religious or eschatological terms—a decisive revelation of God, the Kingdom Come, the return of Christ—Buber, consistent with the inner meaning of I-Thou, finds the basis of his hope in man himself; that is to say, in the capacities of man to reintroduce and maintain the spirit or quality of human life in the midst of, and despite, technology. This is not some sort of humanistic idealism rooted in a vain optimism about the future of man. Buber is careful to avoid predicting any future improvement in man's moral and spiritual condition. But he sees hope for man in his link with God, a link which cannot be broken by what happens in history. What this means is that man *always* has the possibility of spirit, quality, and meaning in his existence, because the capacity within him—his real freedom for dialogue—cannot be destroyed. God is eternally accessible to man in the world. One need not be tempted, as Berdyaev was tempted, to find the solution to the problem of man outside the world of man, if one believes, as Buber believes, that God stands in unseverable relation to the world. It is precisely because of this belief that Buber points to the possibilities of dialogue for man, even within the daily acts of his social existence. The life of dialogue is "not an affair of spiritual luxury and spiritual luxuriousness." This life is for all men, any man, no matter how ordinary his task, it is for "him in the factory, in the ship, in the office, in the mine, on the tractor, at the printing press. . . ." [24]

The "hallowing of the everyday" can take a slightly romantic turn in Buber's mind, as when he extols the possibility of dialogue with one's work.

No factory and no office is so abandoned by creation that a creative glance could not fly up from one working-place to another, from desk to desk, a sober and brotherly glance which guarantees the reality of creation which is a happening—*quantum satis*. . . . A worker can experience even his relation to the machine as one of dialogue, when, for instance, a compositor tells that he has understood the machine's humming as "a merry and grateful smile at me for helping it to set aside the difficulties and abstractions which distorted and bruised

and pained it, so that now it could run free." Must even you
not think then of the story of Androclus and the Lion? [25]

These sentiments could easily be dismissed as a romantic glorification of the proletariat which bespeaks Buber's socialism. Yet
at their core is the recognition of a fundamental truth articulated
through the meaning of the I-Thou dialogue—that unless dignity and humanity be restored to work itself, man will have
paid too high a price for the technological development of society. As all the other twentieth-century thinkers in this book
have noted, this is the question of whether, in creating the
machine to enhance his existence, man will maintain mastery of
his creation or become its slave.

How dialogue is to be practiced by men in their ordinary
tasks, no one can say; and no one can demand dialogue of another, no one can ask for dialogue. All that one can do is to
point to dialogue as a capacity of man, indeed as his *essence.*
Buber comes closest to showing the practical possibilities of
dialogue in the world of affairs when he speaks of an acknowledgment of the human reality in all work and endeavor. This
openness is as real a possibility for the executive, the captain of
industry, as for the worker. Buber writes:

> You ask with a laugh, can the leader of a great technical
> undertaking practice the responsibility of dialogue? He can.
> For he practices it when he makes present to himself in its
> concreteness, so far as he can, *quantum satis*, the business
> which he leads. He practices it when he experiences it, instead
> of as a structure of mechanical centers of force and their
> organic servants (among which latter there is for him no
> differentiation but the functional one), as an association of
> persons with faces and names and biographies, bound together
> by a work that is represented by, but does not consist of,
> the achievements of a complicated mechanism. He practices
> it when he is inwardly aware, with a latent and disciplined
> fantasy, of the multitude of these persons, whom naturally
> he cannot separately know and remember as such; so that now,

when one of them for some reason or other steps really as an individual into the circle of his vision and the realm of his decision, he is aware of him without strain not as a number with a human mask but as a person. He practices it when he comprehends and handles these persons as persons—for the greatest part necessarily indirectly, by means of a system of mediation which varies according to the extent, nature, and structure of the undertaking, but also directly, in the parts which concern him by way of organization. Naturally at first both camps, that of capital and that of the proletariat, will decry his masterly attitude of fantasy as fantastic nonsense and his practical attitude to persons as dilettantist. But just as naturally only until his increased figures of production accredit him in their eyes. (By this of course is not to be implied that those increases necessarily come to pass: between truth and success there is no pre-stabilized harmony.)[26]

I cite this passage at length to show that Buber is sensitive to the full organizational problems that confront any corporate business that seeks to have good operating relations with its "workers." Buber anticipated years ago what is now recognized, that the very economic future of business is directly tied to its social "awareness" and that the public responsibility of a business requires more than a public relations office.

Buber views the problem of the relation between man and work in society within the framework of his primary ideas about God, man, and the interpersonal. Almost all people reflect, more often unconsciously than consciously, religious or theological attitudes in their social and political convictions. And no religious attitude has been more influential in shaping the development of Western social and political thought than the view that the human and divine are not only different spheres but that they are separate. Out of this view has come the belief that the only link between God and the world is the "religious," the impingement on the world of a "revelation," an event of a special "religious experience." Western thinking shows the widening gap between the "secular" and the "sacred," and the result has been the reduction of the secular to the worst conditions of existence: alienation, purposelessness, loss of distinctiveness and quality. With these has come the temptation to abandon the world in lonely romantic acts of withdrawal, of a political or philosophical as well as a religious form; or, by contrast, to seek to exploit the world selfishly. When Buber sees in the possibilities of dialogue an alternative vision of the interrelation of divine and human, he is saying that the problem of man lies not in the religious but in the meeting between man and the world. And for him this meeting is not a narrow, truncated humanism, but an encounter of deep religious significance, where fulfillment and healing occur.

This vision, in biblical terms, is that of God, the Creator, and his creation. Trust in God the Creator is not, as the dominant Christian traditions of Western theology have maintained, the belief in a stupendous act of world-creation ex nihilo by a supernatural being, nor is it the belief showed by many "modernist" thinkers in a world of nature set free from the divine and given to man for his use and enjoyment. For Buber, the belief in God the Creator is the belief in an inner unity in existence that unites God and man *only through the world*. Man's task is man, precisely because through God his father he has man as his brother. The belief in God the Creator is the fundamental belief for recognizing not only the problem of man in the world, but in avoiding despair and retaining hope in confronting and not evading this problem. In light of this, it is interesting to note that Buber cites the New Testament passage wherein Jesus is asked what one should believe, and he answers by referring to the Great Commandment of the Hebraic scripture, that one should love God with all one's heart, soul, and mind, and that one should love one's neighbor as oneself. The focus of belief is thus the triad, God, man, and neighbor—not one without the others.

Although Buber acknowledges that Kierkegaard's analysis of man's existence helped him to see the centrality of the interpersonal in human life, he rejected Kierkegaard's vision of the religious, precisely because it was achieved at the expense of man's human or social relations—thus contradicting the Great Commandment. Kierkegaard interpreted the Christian revelation as a condition fulfilled only by the individual willing to sacrifice the "world," the "ethical," the "everyday," the "domestic." He made of the girl who was his fiancée that necessary sacrifice without which he could not attain faith—though he admitted later that if he truly had faith he need not have given her up. Kierkegaard saw in the story of Abraham's sacrifice of Isaac the paradigm of faith and the rationale for his own act of sacrifice. But, in Buber's judgment, Kierkegaard paid an unnecessary price for faith. One need not, indeed *should not*, make God and man rivals. Kierkegaard saw marriage as an impediment to the religious sphere, hence an impediment to man's highest relation to God; but Buber contends that is precisely the problem with Kierkegaard's vision.

At a time in Denmark when what it meant to be a Christian was confused with "the crowd," Kierkegaard sought clarity by inviting men to return to the austerity and world-denying stance of the monastery. He saw acceptance of the absurd—the Christian paradox of God becoming a man—as the only way to faith. Buber cannot accept Kierkegaard's analysis, because to him God has not given man the right to reject the world by renouncing marriage and committing other acts of social and political negation. God is the Creator as well as the Redeemer, and this means that he rather wishes man to enjoy life with him precisely as his creature—to be related to God *through* the world, therefore through marriage, work, leisure, and sundry other acts. Buber comments on Kierkegaard's misunderstanding of the creature's relation to the Creator:

> "In order to come to love," says Kierkegaard about his renunciation of Regina Olsen, "I had to remove the object." That is sublimely to misunderstand God. Creation is not a hurdle on the road to God, it is the road itself. We are created along with one another and directed to a life with one another. Creatures are placed in my way so that I, their

fellow-creature, by means of them and with them find the way to God. A God in whom all life is fulfilled. A God in whom only the parallel lines of single approaches intersect is more akin to the "God of the philosophers" than to the "God of Abraham and Isaac and Jacob." God wants us to come to him by means of the Reginas he has created and not by renunciation of them.[27]

What Buber is saying, then, is that the structure of human existence as set forth in the myth of God, the Creator, prohibits withdrawal from the human world as an act of faith; in fact, it is faithlessness. For such a decision has God as its goal, as a possession to be acquired by the steadfastness of Kierkegaard's lonely hero, thereby negating God's whole purpose in creation. All men can in God create value and meaning for each other, thereby witnessing as obedient creatures to the power and glory of their Creator. And marriage is for Buber an essential expression of this creativity:

> Marriage, essentially understood, brings one into an essential relation to the "world"; more precisely, to the body politic, to its malformation and its genuine form, to its sickness and its health. Marriage, as the decisive union of one with another, confronts one with the body politic and its destiny—man can no longer shirk that confrontation in marriage, he can only prove himself in it or fail. The isolated person, who is unmarried or whose marriage is only a fiction, can maintain himself in isolation; the "community" of marriage is part of the great community, joining with its own problems the general problems, bound up with its hope of salvation to the hope of the great life that in its most miserable state is called the crowd. He who "has entered on marriage," who has entered into marriage, has been in earnest, in the intention of the sacrament, with the fact that the other *is*; with the fact that I cannot legitimately share in the Present Being without sharing in the being of the other; with the fact that I cannot answer the lifelong address of God to me without answering at the same time for the other; with the fact that I cannot

be answerable without being at the same time answerable for the other as one who is entrusted to me. But thereby a man has decisively entered into relation with otherness; and the basic structure of otherness, in many ways uncanny but never quite unholy or incapable of being hallowed, in which I and the others who meet me in my life are inwoven, is the body politic. It is to this, into this, that marriage intends to lead us.[28]

Personal decision, in Buber's view, that decision which maintains the sacredness of human individuality in the midst of "the crowd," is not a decision *against* the world; it is always a decision in which a man is responsible to the place and people through which he is and has been nurtured, and therefore to which he belongs. This is so even when his decision may be directed in some decisively political way against his communal group. Thus Buber says:

In my decision I do not look away from the world, I look at it and into it, and before all I may see in the world, to which I have to do justice with my decision, my group to whose welfare I cling; I may before all have to do justice to it, yet not as a thing in itself, but before the Face of God; and no programme, no tactical resolution, no command can tell me how I, as I decide, have to do justice to my group before the Face of God. It may be that I may serve it as the programme and resolution and command have laid down. It may be that I have to serve it otherwise. It could even be—if such an unheard-of thing were to rise within me in my act of decision—that I might be set in cruel opposition to its success, because I became aware that God's love ordains otherwise. Only one thing matters, that as the situation is presented to me I expose myself to it as to the word's manifestation to me, to the very ground where hearing passes into being, and that I perceive what is to be perceived and answer it. He who prompts me with an answer in such a way as to hinder my perceiving is the hinderer, let him be for the rest who he will.[29]

Both Buber and Berdyaev adopted one of the most important insights of Kierkegaard's existentialist theology—that knowledge of God is not objective in the sense that one has knowledge of such "objects" as philosophy and world history. Buber and Berdyaev agree that God is a mystery. But, though God eludes the forms of man's knowledge, this does not mean that he is unknowable. Man does have knowledge of God, a knowledge contained in the difference (or lack of difference) God makes in men's lives; which is to say that to know God is finally a matter not of *what* but of *how*, a matter of how man lives in relation to God. Theology, for Buber and Berdyaev, as for Kierkegaard before them, is really theological anthropology: knowledge of God in light of the human response, the character of man's living. Only in examining his own life and consciousness does man come to knowledge of his own being as God's creature, and in that sense come to knowledge of his Creator, God.

The existentialism which Buber and Berdyaev share leads them to a fundamental assumption which shapes their respective theologies. This is the assumption that God and the world are inseparable. In knowing the deepest meanings of the world, including man, one comes to know God; and to know God is not to know a special object, a transcendent being, but rather to be led into a deep, sensitive understanding of oneself, one's fellow man, and the surrounding world. Through the biblical metaphor of creation, this means that to know God, the Creator, is to know God by virtue of what he has created, which is to know God in and through the world; and conversely, to know the creature precisely *as creature* is to be led inescapably to knowledge of the reality of the Creator. According to Buber and Berdyaev, the function of the theologian is not to establish by argument God's reality or existence, nor even to demonstrate that God is related to the world; rather, it is to discern the power and presence of God in all things. Our two authors stand thus opposed to Maritain's revitalization of the old philosophical proofs for God's existence. If God is not a special being, his existence cannot be an object of "proof" or "disproof." Still further, our authors must reject the apologetic purpose of Tillich's theology. Since the meaning of God is inseparable from the deepest meanings of man-in-the-world, one need not "justify" God's relevance or seek to defend a special religious meaning such as "ultimate concern." In ultimate concern, Tillich may have provided a genuine definition of religion, but Buber and Berdyaev are saying that man's relation to God is deeper and wider than ultimate concern, deeper and wider, therefore, than religion.

Buber's notion of the meeting of I and Thou, and Berdyaev's critique of objectification in behalf of the freedom of spirit constitute, in their respective ways, a theology of man's life in relation to God. It was the intention of both theologians to clarify the difference God makes in human life, and thus to discern the value—"God"—in man's daily existence. Both men, in their theological expressions, are phenomenologists of the divine power and presence in man and in the world, seeking to discern, as we said, the meaning of the divine in the world, detecting and identifying that internal bond between Creator and creation. Both Buber and Berdyaev must, in this regard, reject any narrow humanism, as they must also reject atheism. Neither will accept the view that "God" is merely a name for what any man can recognize as ethical values. The individual actually encounters God, meets with the eternal Thou, as Buber puts it, in love, suffering, mutuality, freedom, creativeness, and potentiality in any moment of his ordinary life. In other words, in the most profound and the simplest expressions of man, that Transcendent Mystery is encountered with such power that it is finally unimportant whether the name "God" is given to it. Thus, neither author will recognize atheism. For in the experiences of mutuality, of freedom, of sacrifice, every man encounters the Transcendent Mystery, the eternal Thou, irrespective of what he calls it, and irrespective of whether or not he *chooses* to acknowledge its reality.

At many points the theological reflections of Tillich and Maritain approach the kind of theology of living relation which is represented in the writings of Buber and Berdyaev. Tillich speaks of the ground of being which is manifested in all human acts, and Maritain speaks in similar fashion of the divine act which is reflected in the various acts of man's spiritual self-expression as they are found in social relations, political decisions, moral acts, and artistic creations. In some sense, then, both Tillich and Maritain share the insight common to Buber and Berdyaev, of a fundamental, ongoing relation between God and the world. But neither Tillich nor Maritain achieves that sense of mutuality and reciprocity between God and the world which marks Buber's and Berdyaev's thought. For Tillich and Maritain, the relation between God and the world is largely an external relation where the presence of God is seen negatively: for Tillich in the religious symbols of estrangement; for Maritain as a witness of natural, finite being, to supernatural, infinite being. One recognizes in both instances that Tillich and Maritain are in part motivated by the desire to defend the meaning and relevance of a particular religion, indeed of a particular tradition of that religion. Despite the facts that Berdyaev was nurtured in the faith of Eastern Christianity, and that Buber was a Jew, both seek to articulate the relationship between God and man in terms that recognize the most creative aspects of their historical religions, but which finally lie deeper than religious traditions. They lie in a deep relationship between the divine and the human, man and the eternal Thou—a relationship which is most essentially expressed in the daily perceived meanings of mutuality, creativeness, freedom, sacrifice, and redemptive suffering. These are meanings which have always been expressed in the traditions of religions, but which lie at the core of human existence, and which make it possible for man to encounter that ultimate meaning, the divine.

The common theological outlook of Buber and Berdyaev would appear to have a distinct advantage over that of Tillich and Maritain. In refusing to restrict God to a particular experience and meaning, Buber and Berdyaev remain faithful to the dual character of the biblical witness to creation. On one hand, the creation of the world by God expresses the belief that *all* the world is creaturely. Hence, all of it, not merely some area designated "the religious," enjoys a relation to God. But the second aspect of creation is that the world, precisely because it is God's creation, exists as an independent reality, distinguishable from God, as God is from it. The meeting of God and man in the world can take place only because each continues to exist apart from the other. Thus, the relation between God and man is that of meeting, the dialogue between two actual beings, I and Thou, the communication of different but equally real spirits. Because the relation between God and man is that of an encounter, this relation can exist at any level of man's life in the world; the encounter can occur within any context of experience. It can occur "culturally" as in art and literature, or "ordinarily" as in work, family life, eating, and resting. It is important to recognize that what Buber and Berdyaev affirm is the basic meaning that man's life as a creature of God in the world is only sustained, only preserved in significance by living fully the life of the creature. Buber's theology of I and Thou, as much as Berdyaev's theology of Godmanhood, seeks to elucidate the meanings of man's creaturehood as life in the world and as life in relation to the transcendent Creator.

While Berdyaev's theology of Godmanhood clearly resembles Buber's theology of I and Thou at crucial points, the later development of Berdyaev's thought shows that he grew so pessimistic about the human condition as to produce in his thought a dualism which closely resembles Tillich's notion of the estrangement between essence and existence, ideal creation and actual history. Berdyaev's ambiguous view of Jesus Christ as a spiritual figure able to inspire any and all men—a view which Buber could accept—*and* Jesus Christ as a savior of man, conquering estrangement through his atoning death—a view which Buber could not accept—foreshadows the later development of Berdyaev's thought. Despite this development, the tendency of Berdyaev's overall thought is similar to Buber's: that of a divine-human mutuality in which man, the creature, acts in freedom and creativeness, thereby contributing directly to the life of

God; as God, through his own actions as Creator and Redeemer, gives meaning to the life of man.

We have suggested that the theologies of Buber and Berdyaev are based on a wholistic vision of the world. It is important to ask, finally, whether Buber articulates his vision at the price of recognizing the reality of evil. Clearly, Buber does not put the reality of evil in such metaphysical terms as to suggest that dualism of God versus evil, spirit versus matter, which plagued the thought of Tillich and Berdyaev. In contrast to the Christian theologies represented in this study, Buber rejects the doctrine of original sin developed by Christianity through the centuries. For Buber, nothing can mar God's creation, for if this has happened it would prove to be the death of the Creator, hence the death of God. (This is exactly the conclusion reached by the Jewish death-of-God theologian, Richard Rubenstein, with whom we shall deal in the concluding chapter.) Buber cannot accept the tendency of Christian theology, from Saint Paul to Paul Tillich and Reinhold Niebuhr, to recognize a dark force in human behavior "making man do what he would not do, and not do what he would do." Buber does not minimize the actuality of evil; but, following the wisdom of the Hasidic sages, he views evil in essentially practical and psychological terms. Evil is a human reality to be dealt with finally by man. Man alone can undo what he has done; man alone can achieve that change of mind which was and is the source of his evil—but that he can *change* Buber firmly believes. Evil has set creature against Creator because it has set creature against creature; but, notwithstanding the Christian doctrine of original sin, evil has not destroyed the fundamental relationship between creature and Creator, and hence the relationship between creatures is also intact. The answer to evil is goodness, and goodness is always possible. Buber, like Maritain, believes that the myth of Adam's Fall does not replace the myth of creation; rather, it symbolizes for man the depths of the living relationship between creatures and Creator, ultimately giving him insight into the possibilities of goodness.

VIII

Theologians in a World Come of Age

At the root of theology in the twentieth century is the struggle to come to terms with the erosion of the traditional religious basis of society. This is the complex process we have come to call "secularization."[1] For modern theology, the twentieth century had its symbolic beginning in the Second World War, but secularization began well before 1914.

For fully a thousand years, from 500 to 1500, the beliefs guiding human affairs were religious ones: man is created by God and endowed with a purpose for carrying out his creaturely role on earth; and God had created the church to minister to those needs of man which transcended his earthly obligations: the need for forgiveness of sins, for that grace which redeems man and reunites him with his Creator. During the Italian Renaissance, beginning in the fourteenth century, the first signs appeared of the decline of these beliefs. Reviving the wisdom of classical antiquity, artists and writers discovered that man was interesting in his own right, not merely because he reflected the working of his heavenly creator. In intellectual and artistic terms, the period from the fourteenth to the sixteenth centuries marked the transition from the medieval to the modern world. The political and social causes of this transition were rooted in Luther's revolt against the church. Luther defended the validity of the individual's religious conscience against the church's claim to have exclusive authority over the salvation and eternal destiny of man's soul.

If the Renaissance discovered that man was interesting in his own right, the Reformation went one step further by declaring man's inherent worth. The philosophers and painters of the fourteenth century and the theologians of the sixteenth believed their view of man was essentially harmonious with what they had been taught by the church to believe; but, from the end of the sixteenth century, philosophers, writers, and artists no longer concerned themselves with such a problem. Man's creativity needed no "higher" justification, for it was everywhere in evidence: in his moral insight and freedom for decision, in his powers of political change and reform, in his talent for social organization and economic growth, and in his philosophical ideas and artistic creations.

The movement away from a religious order of life characterizes the Renaissance, the Reformation, and the shaping of the modern scientific mind in the seventeenth century. But what began as the expression of human authenticity rapidly passed into a period of man's autonomy. The industrial and technological revolutions of the eighteenth and nineteenth centuries were paralleled by the political and social ideologies which developed after the French Revolution. We speak of secularization as a complex "process" because it means *both* the liberation of man from systems that suppress and obstruct the expression of his human integrity, *and* the repudiation of all religious visions of man in the name of independence or autonomy.

Secularization has challenged the imagination of the major religious thinkers of the twentieth century by forcing them to come to terms with both the creative and destructive energies loosed by the changing culture of the last five hundred years. Still, even the theologian of the first half of the twentieth century proceeded on the view that man possesses a religious nature, and sought ways to understand the expression of man's religiousness in the symbolic forms of culture; but the theologian of the second half of the century has challenged this perspective.

The pivotal figure in this changing view is Karl Barth. If Barth's use of existential philosophy in many respects set the style for theological reflection in the first half of the century, then his abandonment of existentialism and clear separation of the realm of God from the realm of man have influenced the newer theologies appearing in the second half. Thinkers such as Tillich, Maritain, Berdyaev, and Buber accepted the reality of spiritual depths in man. At the same time, they saw in existentialism an affirmation of what is creative in the secular ethos, the affirmation of man's freedom and humanity. In the ideas of existentialism, these theologians found a way of interpreting man's essential religiousness in relation to a culture which had broken completely with traditional religious forms. But for the theologian of the second half of the century, existentialism and existential theology represent a continuation of precisely that piety or religiosity which was the target of Barth's early thought. The new theologian [2] follows Barth in rejecting the validity of man's religiousness in any form. There is the realm of the human and there is the realm of the divine; both are valid, but they are not linked. The human or secular realm is valuable and meaningful in its own right, and not because it contains spiritual depths disclosing relation to a divine ground or reality.

Here the new theologian parts company with Barth himself, for where Barth argued that the realms of God and man are separate, and then developed a theology exclusively of the realm of God, the new theologian has "stood Barth on his head" and developed a theology exclusively of the realm of man. These newer efforts to wrestle with the meaning of man's secularity, and to construct a theology of what Dietrich Bonhoeffer called a "world come of age," reveal themselves in both Christian and Jewish religious thought at mid-century.

Three men are especially representative of "secular theology": Dietrich Bonhoeffer, Harvey Cox, and Thomas J. J. Altizer. We will then close with two rebuttals to the stance of the secular theologian, one by Richard L. Rubenstein and the other by Bernard E. Meland.

In the world of contemporary theology, Dietrich Bonhoeffer, the German Protestant theologian, has the status of a Christian martyr. His participation in the plot of July 1944 to assassinate Hitler led to his execution by the Nazis in April 1945 at the age of forty. Nothing so powerfully conveys Bonhoeffer's belief in the obligation of the Christian to disavow piety in order to affirm the concrete world of men and events as his own decision to enter into such political conspiracy. In the theology that he set forth in letters to friends and family while in prison before his execution, Bonhoeffer saw the movement of the believer out of the cloister, where he is of no use to God or to man, into the world, where he can be of service to both—he saw this secularization as a meaningful style of Christian existence in the modern world. In Bonhoeffer's theology, the Christian is responsible when he accepts the full burden of being a man in a world of other men. The believer understands that being a Christian is a matter of service, and he learns how to be of service.

One of Bonhoeffer's most provocative notions—a notion greatly influenced by Barth's early polemic against religion—is that religion robs man of responsibility.[3] Religion preserves man in his immaturity by offering him "consolations" for life's woes, by soul-satisfying ministrations of all sorts—especially allowing man to believe that his relation to God is a private and personal affair, sealed off from the events of the world. Religion instills sin-consciousness and the preoccupation with one's salvation, thereby reinforcing man's basic egoism.

In Bonhoeffer's view, the religious attitude has been sustained in our time by theologians like Tillich, who assume in man a basic religious *need* which must be satisfied. Bonhoeffer regards Tillich's identification of religion with the crises of human life as an exploitation of human weakness. When God is identified with the "boundary-situation" of death, loneliness, and meaninglessness, then he is a God whom man discovers not through his own happiness and strength but through his wretchedness and weakness. According to Bonhoeffer, such a theology preys on all that is weak in man, ignoring what is strong and good. Bonhoeffer writes:

> Religious people speak of God when human knowledge (perhaps simply because they are too lazy to think) has come to an end, or when human resources fail—in fact it is always the *deus ex machina* that they bring on to the scene, either for the apparent solution of insoluble problems, or as strength in human failure—always, that is to say, exploiting human weakness or human boundaries.[4]

And in response to theological existentialism, Bonhoeffer says:

> I have come to be doubtful of talking about any human boundaries (is even death, which people now hardly fear, and is sin, which they now hardly understand, still a genuine boundary today?). It always seems to me that we are trying anxiously in this way to reserve some space for God; I should like to speak of God not on the boundaries but at the center, not in weakness but in strength; and therefore not in death and guilt but in man's life and goodness. As to the boundaries, it seems to be better to be silent and leave the insoluble unsolved.[5]

Thus, for Bonhoeffer, the God of religion and existential theology is the problem-solver, the Supernatural to whom man resorts when his questions go unanswered, or when there are gaps in his knowledge.

The traditional image of God is that of an all-powerful deity in relation to whom man can only express reverence. But the image of God presented by Jesus' ministry and his death on the cross is that of a father who suffers for his children. The essence of Christian faith is not the other-worldliness of our traditional forms of worship but the sharing of God's sufferings in Christ through imitation of Christ's own service to man in the world. This is the faith that Bonhoeffer regarded as "secular." He also called it "discipleship," living in the style of Jesus, whom the Gospel writers portray (to use Bonhoeffer's language) as "the man for others." It is the only faith that Bonhoeffer could regard as relevant to a world that had grown out of its religious immaturity and "come of age." Writing from his prison cell shortly before his death, he says:

> . . . I am still discovering right up to this moment, that it is only by living completely in this world that one learns to have faith. One must completely abandon any attempt to make something of oneself, whether it be a saint, or a converted sinner, or a churchman (a so-called priestly type!), a righteous man or an unrighteous one, a sick man or a healthy one. By this-worldliness I mean living unreservedly in life's duties, problems, successes and failures, experiences and perplexities. In so doing we throw ourselves completely into the arms of God, taking seriously, not our own sufferings, but those of God in the world—watching with Christ in Gethsemane.[6]

We have said that Bonhoeffer's "religionless Christianity" was deeply influenced by Barth's early attack on man's religious presumptions. It is important to note that Barth's later dogmatic theology, which puts before man a vast array of theological dogmas on a "like it or lump it" basis, was evaluated by Bonhoeffer as a reversion to religion because of its indifference to the world of human affairs.

Bonhoeffer's criticism of the religious a priori in Tillich's existential theology also applies to the theologies of Maritain,

Berdyaev, and Buber. Here Bonhoeffer raises a serious question
about the relation between the humanity of man—what we
earlier identified as the qualitative or spiritual dimension of life—
and such boundary-situations as death, guilt, and meaninglessness, a question we will deal with more fully at the close of
this study.

Bonhoeffer's criticism of Tillich's theology is aimed at what
he regards as Tillich's "negativism," his preoccupation with the
meaninglessness and estrangement of man's contemporary life.
Bonhoeffer seeks to counter the strong negative judgment on
the human condition expressed by modern Protestant theology
generally. He believes that such a judgment is inconsistent with
a "religionless Christianity" which emphasizes man's involvement in the world, hence the validity of human forms and acts.
Here Bonhoeffer comes very close to affirming the kind of
theological immanentism one finds in Maritain, Berdyaev, Buber,
and, in a highly qualified way, even in Tillich. This is the view
that God is experienced as a dimension within the particularities
and immediacies of the world. But where these authors articulate
this dimension as a "depth" or quality of spirit within life,
Bonhoeffer himself remains unclear.

One must conclude by saying that Bonhoeffer seems to be
of two minds on the relation between God and a world come of
age. He speaks of a world which no longer needs God, and of
the Christian who must get along in the world without God.
But, on the other hand, he criticizes Barth's theology for so
separating God and the world that "the world is in some degree made to depend on itself and left to its own devices, and
that is [a] mistake." [7] The ambivalence in Bonhoeffer's thought
exists because he attempts to develop a theology of secularity
which wants on the one side to avoid plain humanism by affirming the biblical revelation of God in Christ, but at the same
time rejects theologies of the religious a priori in favor of an
ethical Christianity of service. Bonhoeffer expresses this dilemma
for himself when he asks the question, How does one speak of

God in a nonreligious way? [8] It is a question which he does not readily nor clearly answer.

Bonhoeffer's thesis about the man come of age, the religion-less Christian, has been applied to the problems of society by Harvey Cox, the American theologian who teaches at Harvard University, in his widely read book *The Secular City* (1965).[9] Cox believes that the forces of secularization—science, technology, automation, urbanization—are not dehumanizing but in fact liberating. In divesting man of his religiousness, secularization has brought him to a level of responsibility in the contemporary world identified as man's maturity, or coming of age.

Cox, in fact, views secularization as a process in history which has come to maturation in the modern epoch with the ascendancy of the technological society. In the first, tribal epoch of man's existence, man came into being as man through blood and kinship ties. The tribal represents a style of life "in which tradition prescribes the proper relationship with any person one is likely to meet during a normal lifetime." [10] Moreover, "the tribe represents that stage during which man moves from a belief in ghosts and demons to a belief in gods, from spells and incantations to prayers, from shamans and sorcerers to priests and teachers, from myth and magic to religion and theology." [11] In Cox's view, the tribal period of man's existence represents mankind in its infancy.

The next stage in man's growth is identified by Cox as the period of the town. The town is epitomized by the Greek *polis*, or city-state:

> The polis appeared when bellicose clans and rival houses met here and there to form a new type of community, loyalty to whose laws and gods replaced the more elemental kinship ties which had previously held force. The gods of the tribes were demoted and a new religion arose, often centering on a common divine ancestor.[12]

Tribal man was enclosed in the family; all his acts, meanings, and values were those of the family; his contact with the world outside the tribe was virtually nonexistent. "He does not so much live in a tribe; the tribe lives in him," Cox states. "He is the tribe's subjective expression." [13] The appearance of currency and the development of the alphabet marked the transition from the closed world of the tribe to the wider, more open world of the town, for money and written communication increased contact between men. As tribal societies began to break up, the basis of a person's allegiance to the human community changed from blood and kinship ties to the meaning of citizenship, an allegiance which one has in common with other men regardless of one's family. Cox concludes his analysis of town man's existence by saying:

> The age of the towns gave us printing and books, rational theology, the scientific revolution, investment capitalism, and bureaucracy. . . . Calvinist Puritanism . . . was in many ways the prototypical religion of the period. . . . The shaman is the symbol of tribal man. He dances and chants his religion. The Puritan or maybe even the Yankee is his town-culture counterpart. Town man reads the word and hears it preached. Tribal man merges with his daemon and his group. Town man is a discreet individual who reads *Robinson Crusoe*. Tribal man's gods whirl with him in the night of sensual ecstasy. Town man's God calls him from an infinite distance to work soberly in the daylight of self-discipline.[14]

Centuries of tribal society existed before the rise of towns. In some sense the tribal forms of living have never ceased. Not only do tribal societies continue in the modern world, but Cox allows that certain tribal ways can be found within modern towns and cities.

Just as tribe gave way to town, so town has given way to what Cox calls the technopolis. The technopolis is created when technology and urbanization converge with secularization. Thus the technopolis is the culmination of history with respect to man's society or style of living. The character of man's life in the technopolis has changed from what it was in the town. Tribal man was a man bound to the family; town man was liberated from the family by virtue of his place as citizen in the town or city-state. Technopolitan man owes allegiance to no particular city because he belongs to a world community, created by the twin forces of urbanization and secularization.

Cox interprets the historical evolution of man's society toward technopolis as a process of human liberation. Man has become free not only because of the expanded opportunities for human self-expression represented by the technological society; he has also been freed from older, traditional religious restraints. The evolution of technopolitan existence has thus brought about a *humanization* of man, a liberation from restraining and repressive forces, providing man with richer possibilities of action, meaning, and value.

Few would argue with Cox that the secularization of society has achieved a distinct good in freeing man from the inhibiting and controlling power of religious traditions and institutions. But there would be wide disagreement with one of the implications he draws from this thesis: that since secularization is the product of a technologically urban society, one must regard the essential features of that society as themselves good. Here, as we said, Cox opposes the existentialists who also protest the religious oppression of man, but who sense as well the deep wound in the life of modern man. Where Kafka portrayed the dehumanization of man in modern society through symbols of anonymity, impersonality, and purposelessness, Cox contends that anonymity and urban mobility are resources for preserving man's humanity.

Contrasting the rapid change of the cities with the relative stasis of rural life, Cox claims that man has a greater freedom in the city, that anonymity and mobility increase his power of choice and therefore his opportunities for self-expression. In rural existence, where everyone knows everyone else and their place—socially, economically, and psychologically—freedom is relatively fixed. In the rural areas and small towns, one's relationship to others is not a matter of choice; one is compelled to deal with people on a more intimate level than one might have chosen, hence one's freedom of self-expression and quality of experience are reduced.

Countering Martin Buber's thesis that there are two basic modes of human relationship—I-Thou and I-It, the personal and the functional—Cox argues that it is unfair to regard the city as a dehumanized "I-It" world. When most relationships are functional, one has a greater freedom to choose exactly which relationships he will enjoy as I-Thou. In response to Buber's dichotomy of I-Thou and I-It, where the latter, according to Cox, carries the negative meaning of the impersonal and the dehumanized, Cox suggests a third order of human relationship more appropriate to the functional relationships one has in the city; the I-You, wherein one is related to a host of people on the basis of services bought and sold. Technopolitan man is a freer man than his predecessors in tribe and town because he can use his anonymity and mobility creatively; because he is pragmatic, seeking solutions to problems, not contemplating unanswerable metaphysical questions. Technopolitan man is a "doer" whose thought is directed to what he is challenged to do in the technopolis, not a thinker thinking his own thoughts.

In his affirmation of an anti-metaphysical pragmatism, Cox rejects the basic thrust of Tillich's theology and accepts Barth's. Tillich spoke of man's native religiousness, his "ultimate concern," which he expresses symbolically through the diversity of his culture. Man's ultimate concern is accentuated by his response to the experience of estrangement. Cox answers Tillich by saying that man may have been religious or "ultimately concerned" in earlier epochs of human history, but man has grown out of his religiousness, and is no longer suffering from youthful preoccupations with meaninglessness. Cox gives his readers the impression that man in technopolis is simply too busy doing things to ruminate about the ultimate, or to be anxious or existentially worried about meaninglessness.

It is in Barth's theology that Cox finds the more correct vision of God's relation to the world and to man, a vision which more adequately conforms to Cox's own vision of "the secular city." Barth's theology of the Word of God involves that demarcation of the divine and the human which is congenial to Cox. He agrees with Bonhoeffer that Barth correctly saw that God's creation of the world means that the world has been separated from God, given a value which is its own, the value of the secular. Any effort to put God back into the world by some sort of pious act represents an act contrary to God's biblically expressed will. In the act of creation the world was dereligionized, put on its own feet, as it were, and thus challenged by God himself to express this maturity in responsible action. The world was bidden to be itself, to be authentically secular or "worldly."

Cox, like Bonhoeffer, is guided by the spirit of Barth's early polemic against religion. Just as Barth interpreted the messages of the Bible as containing a rejection of man's religious pretensions, so does Cox. For Cox, this means that the Bible turns its back on religion in order to embrace secularization, its antithesis. (The biblical story of creation represents the disenchantment of nature; the story of Exodus represents the desacralization of politics; and the story of Sinai or the giving of the Law represents the deconsecration of values.) Cox's argument is that in the stories of the Bible we have examples of a faith that is clearly separated from the religiousness associated with the great nature-religions of the ancient Near East.

In the act of creation, for example, God declares the world to be his. He gives it to man for his responsible use. The world does not belong to various spirits and gods as in the religions of ancient Egypt and Babylonia. Cox speaks of the biblical story of creation as a *disenchantment* of nature: nature itself is not sacred, it is meant for man, to be investigated, cultivated, put to human use. Man no longer has to fear nature. With the change from the nature-religions to the biblical attitude toward nature, man is free to explore and use nature responsibly. In this change of attitude toward nature, Cox correctly identifies the root of the scientific exploration of nature, an exploration which was ultimately to produce technology.

Similarly, in the story of the Exodus is an act of dereligionization. Cox speaks of the biblical belief in God's liberation of the people Israel from their Egyptian captors as the *desacralization* of politics. In the religious system of ancient Egypt, the Egyptian pharaoh was regarded as a divine being who ruled absolutely and was given unquestioning obedience by his subjects. Thus, when Yahweh rescued the Israelites, it was tantamount to declaring that in human society there is only human politics, no divine politics. The event of the Exodus is an event of political rebellion against the religious pretensions and power of the political establishment. Cox regards the Exodus story as the root of the modern, revolutionary rejection of imperial and ecclesiastical authority. The Exodus is the prototypical event of political secularization. Cox writes:

> The contest between pope and emperor in the Middle Ages is a parable of the futility of any attempt to return to simple sacral politics once the secularization process has begun. The emperor would have liked to be the religious as well as the political sovereign of the West—wistful longings for a "Holy Roman Empire" headed by a monarch with sacral functions indicate this desire. Similarly, many of the popes would have liked to wield the sword of empire as well as the Keys of Saint Peter—theological efforts to subsume the temporal under the spiritual realm testify to this incessant hankering. Neither side won. The pope finally lost his temporal power along with the Papal States, and the emperor lost everything when the Empire itself dissolved.[15]

In the Sinai covenant, Cox sees a *deconsecration of values*, by which he means that moral values have lost their standing as eternal absolutes, and have acquired a new standing as guides for human living in a socio-historical context. The story of God's granting Israel the Commandments, whereby Israel is to be faithful to her deliverer, might be regarded as a triumph of absolute values. But Cox interprets the Sinai event not as a covenant but as a prohibition against idolatry. In the commandments against idols, Yahweh has opposed any effort of man to absolutize himself or the values of his life in the sense of making gods out of them—and this, in Cox's view, includes the laws that govern sexuality, diet, dress, and labor.

In the biblical themes of creation, Exodus, and the Law, Cox finds not only the historical roots of secularization but also the theological sanction for affirming the values of "this-worldliness" —pragmatism, anonymity, political action, social change, and ethical relativism. Biblical scholars have questioned Cox's interpretation of the meaning of the mythic materials of scripture.[16] But what is provocative about Cox's argument is what is also perennially relevant about Barth's polemic against religion (echoing the attitude of the Hebrew prophets)—what God wants from his people is not more temples and burnt offerings but justice to reign among them, that justice which comes only from the willingness to enter into and support social change and reclamation. In the words of the Prophet Amos, Yahweh declares to his people of Israel:

> I hate, I despise your feasts, and I take no delight in your solemn assemblies. Even though you offer me your burnt offerings and cereal offerings, I will not accept them, and the peace offerings of your fatted beasts I will not look upon. Take away from me the noise of your songs; to the melody of your harps I will not listen. But let justice roll down like waters, and righteousness like an ever-flowing stream (Amos 5:21–24, RSV).

It is just here, in the prophetic call for the reform of society, that Cox, following Bonhoeffer, sees the validity and relevance of biblical faith. Cox does not wish to see the eradication of religion so much as the eradication of the religious *attitude*, that attitude described by Bonhoeffer in which man rejects his maturity by his refusal to take responsibility for his worldliness and escapes into religion's traditional other-worldliness. Cox opposes that part of religion which is closed to the world, but he supports that biblically rooted faith which advocates openness to the world.

Cox believes not only that traditional religions have been exclusive, but also that covert religions, or the ideologies of the secular world, represent for their adherents a closed world-view. Thus the secularization process which liberates man from religious tutelage should be distinguished from those secularistic ideologies which, though they may express antipathy toward religion, actually share in religion's closedness.

Cox distinguishes between valid and invalid practices of faith today, paralleling Bonhoeffer's notion of a secular and a religious way of speaking of God. The faith of the Christian church is secular and valid when the church, to use Cox's phrase, is "where the action is." [17] This presupposes knowing where the action is, but Cox assumes that when the church is fully alive to the social and political predicaments of the world, it will have no difficulty finding the action. The church must not be stationary and identified with the social and political establishment; it must be on the move—as the Israelites in the desert were on the move, bringing revolutionary change in the world. In the same vein, Cox advocates the disestablishment of the churches, a minimization of that formal structure expressed in the concerns for the size of congregations and the state of financial resources. This is the return to that spiritual ethos of early Christianity where Christians were to be found meeting spontaneously, in little groups, seeking ways to manifest their faith in the world. Christianity of this kind would mean that the Christian's place is not in church but perhaps on a picket line, or in a civil rights registration drive, or teaching others about the social ramifications of an exploding population. The Christian's witness *as Christian* is thus secular. He understands God to have bidden him in faith to seeking out a life of "worldly faith," as Bonhoeffer put it; and that is what Christian living in the secular city means.

The secular city represents, in one sense, the essential features of technological-urban society. But, more boldly, it represents Cox's effort to assign concrete meaning to the New Testament's myth of the coming Kingdom of God. To some extent, the secular city symbolizes the Kingdom of God being made real on earth in the idealized form of all men fully devoted to reforming the world. Thus, for Cox, in ways reminiscent of the theology of the Social Gospel in America, the myth of the coming Kingdom does not mean the introduction "from above" of a religious order judging and cleansing the corrupt, secular world. It means the transformation from within of a religiously false, other-worldly order into a nonreligious, secular, and authentically human order—by man himself, in faith, through God's help.

Despite his optimism about man's willingness to accept the task of social justice, Cox does not think that this secularized kingdom has been realized, or that its realization is imminent. His decision, however, to identify the forces of secularization in urbanization and technology clearly shows that on his reading of history, man has before him possibilities of self-realization never before present, and that the achievements of technology and urbanization represent the highest possible expression of man's role in creation as God's chosen co-creator in the world.

Thomas J. J. Altizer, the young American theologian trained in the history of religions at the University of Chicago, also rejects religious Christianity in favor of what he calls "Christian atheism." [18] The principal claim of Altizer's theology is that God is dead, and that this should be an occasion for joy rather than lamentation on the part of all believers. To understand what Altizer means by the death of God, it is important to recognize that Altizer's theology represents an effort to incorporate Nietzsche's vision of man into the basic claim of Christian faith that God has appeared in the person of Jesus Christ.

Nietzsche himself rejected the Christian religion because he thought that its practices and its traditions denied the human spirit. Christianity, for Nietzsche, was moralization, negating all that is creative, joyful, strong, and free in the human spirit. One must choose between Christianity and authentic humanity. The Christian religion is so destructive that it makes a tyrant out of its God. In his glorification of the human spirit, and in his yearning for the emergence of a race of fully realized human beings—his so-called supermen—Nietzsche was prepared to pronounce God's death. For the arrival of the superman signals the death of the tyrannical, repressive, joyless, enslaving God of religion.

Altizer accepts Nietzsche's basic view that the God of the Christian religion is a repressive tyrant, thus Altizer rejects centuries of moralization, corruption, and inhumanity on the part of the institutions of the Christian religious establishment—and he finds all this in the traditional theology that God is a transcendent, all-powerful, Wholly Other being. This theology of the power and majesty of God makes God not just "other" than man but basically antithetical to man. In his aloneness, hiddenness, and might, God is *against* man. His opposition to humanity has been mediated by the churches of Christianity. The gospel of such a God is an inauthentic gospel; the authentic Gospel declares such a God to be dead. Altizer contends that the deepest truth of the New Testament lies just here—that God has, in fact, chosen to die in order to remove the great barrier between himself and man. The infinite distance between God and man was closed in the person of Jesus Christ. Jesus Christ represents the full incarnation of God, which means that God took flesh completely in Jesus and thus became one with man. God ceases to be the alien, powerful, world-denying, and man-opposing deity, and in Jesus Christ becomes one with man and the world.

Altizer becomes unclear when he explains what he means by the *death* of God in Jesus Christ. He accepts the findings of New

Testament scholars that, historically speaking, very little is known about the person of Jesus. Thus, when he bids his readers to accept the gospel of Christian atheism, he does not mean to imitate Jesus in the kind of ethical ministry advocated by Bonhoeffer. What he seems to believe, rather, is that the myth of God's self-embodiment in Jesus Christ represents a symbol for the affirmation of the secular in the form of man's physical body. Since God became flesh in Jesus Christ, man need no longer fear his own body; he is free from religious repression of the human body. When God became flesh in Jesus Christ, he "died" as the Alien God, the Wholly Other. The sacred became the profane and therefore ceased to be an alien sacred. The profane, the worldly has now been sacralized, affirmed, made to be good. In the death of God there is no sacred that exists apart from the profane.

For all its iconoclastic references to the "death of God" and "atheism," Altizer's point is really one in spirit with the recurring theme in Buber and Berdyaev: the world of God's creation is incomplete without man's creativity; man is most like God in his freedom for creation; there are spiritual depths in man's feeling, reason, and will.

Altizer regards Tillich as the modern father of death-of-God theology because it is in Tillich's theology, as contrasted to Barth's, that God is rejected as the alien Wholly Other and brought into the profane world as the ground of being. Altizer appears to overlook or undervalue those points where Tillich regards the divine ground of being as transcending every symbolic witness of itself. For, in a very real way, Tillich's godly ground of being is also a Wholly Other, with the characteristics of transcendent alienness and immobility that Altizer deplores. Theologically, Altizer seems more closely akin to Berdyaev and Buber, who think of God not as a "being" but as the dimension of ultimacy which man experiences and to which his own creativeness is a responsive witness. This is the God whose alienness is dead, a sacred dimension which has ceased to be Wholly Other by incarnating itself fully in the world.

Bonhoeffer, Cox, and Altizer agree that religion undermines man's authenticity *as man*. For these thinkers, the preoccupation of traditional religion is other-worldliness: problems are solved not by the application of human intelligence and initiative but by God out of the heavens; the reasons for things lie not in the things themselves but in the realm of the supernatural; the purpose of living consists of preparing for the life in the "other" world; only man's relationship to God is ultimate, and all his other relationships—to wife, family, friends, work—all this-worldly relationships are temporary and provisional. In the minds of these three Christian theologians, the historic Christian community has looked on the realm of the divine as negating the realm of the human. For that reason, they welcome secularization as a healthy cleansing of the life of man in modern society, restoring that realistic perspective expressed by the Bible in which, immediately after the creation, God assigns man the responsibility for living in and through the world. These theologians reject the piety of traditional Christianity in order to affirm this more worldly faith which they regard as more consistent with the real meaning of the biblical revelation of God.

Richard Rubenstein, who was Hillel Rabbi at the University of Pittsburgh and who now teaches at Florida State University, has provided one of the most sensitive critical reactions to the theology of secularization.[19] Rubenstein is fully aware of the "escapism" in religion; he knows that religion can repress human feeling and thought, and that the powerful myths of religion often have not deepened man's vision of reality but have narrowed it, frequently putting religious communities at war with each other.

But any psychological assessment of religion shows that it is so deeply rooted in man's consciousness that to forcibly sever man from religion would deprive him of spiritual values and meanings he cannot do without. Thus, Rubenstein, following the type of analysis established by Freud, understands man to have fundamental psychological needs which can be and have been fulfilled by the rituals of religion. But where Freud believed that human beings outgrew these needs, Rubenstein claims they are an inherent part of man's spiritual or psychological makeup.

What are these needs? They are identified by Rubenstein as "the decisive times and crises of life" which all men experience and with which they must constantly struggle: birth, puberty, marriage, sickness, old age, death, the rearing of children, the changing seasons, the need to express and find catharsis for feelings of guilt, and the need for personal renewal.[20] The religious community arose and developed, and, in Rubenstein's judgment, *must* survive, because it makes it possible for man to cope with these life-crises. It gives a person a way of sharing his life with other persons, thus mitigating the inherent loneliness of human existence. This sharing is possible only through the community into which one was born and by which he was nurtured as a human being; for the Christian this means the church, and for the Jew it means the synagogue.

Bonhoeffer, Cox, and Altizer all celebrate the "death" of God because it is an action in favor of Jesus Christ, who comes before man as the paradigm for a new Christian humanity in a secular age. Bonhoeffer and Cox tend to interpret this humanity along ethical lines—that one must address oneself honestly to the wrongs of the day and seek with patience and humility to right them; whereas Altizer's interpretation appears to be psychosexual. What is important to note in all these thinkers is the shared assumption that God in some sense died *in order* to free man. Rubenstein, too, expresses great sympathy with the death-of-God theology which has emerged in Christian circles, but for him God's death can only be an occasion of lamentation.

Rubenstein sees the death of God as a cultural fact which says more about what men have experienced in the contemporary world than about God himself. He prefers to speak not of the death of God, but says rather that *we live in the time of the death of God*, much as Buber spoke of human existence in the time of the "eclipse of God." God's death is actually a quality of our experience. In Rubenstein's judgment, the symbol of this death is the contemporary experience of massive destructive evil, as seen, for example, in the murder of six million Jews. Such evil is the norm of modern man's existence, certainly the norm of the modern Jew's existence. The issue is put succinctly by Rubenstein when he asserts, "Auschwitz killed God."

Unlike Altizer, however, Rubenstein cannot accept this death as a new source of human freedom and joy. A better guide to the meaning of God's death is not Nietzsche but Ivan Karamazov, one of the tormented heroes of Dostoevsky's novel *The Brothers Karamazov.* According to Ivan, if God is dead all things are possible, man knows no restraint. Rubenstein, as a Jew, wants to say that what really died at Auschwitz was the biblical God, the Lord of History, Israel's Redeemer and Protector. This is the God whom the deuteronomic historians interpreted as the source of the misfortunes of ancient Israel. When Israel was set upon by her neighbors, the deuteronomist stated that God was punishing Israel for her faithless disobedience. According to this biblical belief, God is the author of all that happens in history, and if this belief is affirmed today, then the Jew would have to believe that God is the author of Auschwitz—and this Rubenstein cannot accept.

For Rubenstein, Auschwitz, not the secular city, is the real symbol of what the technological society has produced. Where Cox's secular city reflects an overly optimistic belief in moral progress, Auschwitz shows that man is no better morally than he was five hundred or fifteen hundred years ago. In the secular city, men are no longer concerned with what they *are* in the ultimate sense, but rather with what they are doing. Rubenstein believes that such existentialists as Kafka, Sartre, and Camus have shown in various ways that when the moral history of man culminates in Auschwitz, the deeper question about human action lies in the nature of the human condition, the answer pointing inevitably to what Tillich called "estrangement."

The experience of the death of God drives Rubenstein to seek a new vision of man in the contemporary world. But unlike his Christian theological colleagues, he does not accept a vision that reflects naive optimism about man's future; he accepts only a vision mirroring the realism of existentialism's doctrine of man.

For Rubenstein, this means that man's entrance into the world is as arbitrary as his exit. We are not children born to a loving and protecting Father who receives us back when we die; rather, to use Heidegger's term, we are "thrown" into and out of the world, and our lives bear constantly this quality of arbitrariness, of "thrownness" (*Geworfenheit*). The origin and destiny of man are a profound mystery that possesses all the depths that the biblical writers attributed to God. But it is not the Creator that defines our existence; it is a Holy Nothingness, a Sacred Void out of which we came and to which we return. Only the great religious mystics such as Luria of Safed and Jacob Boehme have given adequate attention to this profound mystery about human existence. "We are alone," Rubenstein says, "in a silent, unfeeling cosmos." [21] It is precisely because we are alone that we are sustained by the historic religious communities into which we are born and which make it possible for us to share our lives with others. For, as he concludes, "We have been cast up absurdly and without reason into a world which knows not warmth, concern, care, fellowship, or love, save that which we bestow upon one another." [22]

In opposition to those theologians who view secularization as a distinct threat to man's humanity, the new younger group of thinkers—Cox, Altizer, and others such as John Robinson, William Hamilton, Paul van Buren, and Gibson Winter,[23] all influenced to some degree by the writings of Bonhoeffer—regard secularization as a condition through which man can discover and express his humanity. The difference is in part a result of the different problems to which the two groups have addressed themselves. But their sharpest disagreement is focused on the nature of religion and its significance for the creative self-expression of man. Let us amplify both points.

The first half of the twentieth century can be regarded as the epoch of world war. It is difficult to imagine what aspect of the history of the past fifty years has not been given shape by the two great wars of this century: dissolution of historic empires, emergence of new nations, development of atomic energy, destruction and dislocation of whole peoples, and the appearance of a technological, urbanized civilization. The great religious thinkers of these decades—Barth, Tillich, Maritain, Berdyaev, and Buber—all did their major work between the world wars. They struggled to understand the impact of modern forces on religious faith, and they sought ways to reconceive the meaning of faith in light of the modern experience.

The philosophy of existentialism proved indispensable to these efforts. Developing from Kierkegaard, Heidegger, and Sartre, existentialism presented a unified picture of the predicament of man in the modern world. Existentialism claimed that the value of the individual is threatened by the forces of the collectivization ruling society and by the irrational powers loosed on the world through war and man's pretensions about his reason and moral sense.

This vision of man floundering amidst the complicated machines and systems of his creation is what the major Jewish and Christian theologians of the twentieth century saw as most relevant to the problem of faith in the modern world. If man is in danger of losing his authentic selfhood because of the civilization he has produced, then his efforts have made him lose touch with the ultimate resources which nurture, sustain, and judge him. Of course, for many religious people the solution to the problem of faith eroding under the pressure of secularity is to pit the church vigorously against the new culture, erecting bulwarks of piety to contest for the souls of men.

Authors such as Tillich and Buber recognized that existentialist philosophy is itself a force of secularization in its clear rejection of traditional piety as an adequate answer to the predicament of modern man. Thus, those theologians who spoke from the existentialist perspective removed themselves from any effort to return to the security of a tradition-enshrined faith. But what is more distinctive about these men is that they also rejected the atheistic and narrowly humanistic answers that existential philosophers frequently gave. The theologians accepted the view that the distinct value of man comes down to the question, Will man or will he not exercise his unique freedom? but they rejected the conclusion that man's freedom is void of ultimate or transcendent meaning. Human authenticity, they claimed, comprises not only a distinctly human structure of freedom but also a distinctly nonhuman dimension, an ultimate ground which man experiences in his life and to which he responds in faith as well as in freedom, an Ultimate Reality which he comes to know in the form of unmerited grace of forgiveness and acceptance and as a measure of judgment on all his actions and creations. Tillich speaks of man's ultimate concern as a "depth" perceived conceivably within any human experience, offering a sense of meaning that transcends man. Similarly, Maritain, in his notion of man's "act of existence," Berdyaev in his understanding of spirit, and Buber in his analysis of the I-Thou—all share the insight that in those experiences that are creative and expressive of man's humanity, there are depths that afford a sense of relation to a more ultimate reality of meaning and value. And even Barth, in the early, "existentialist" phase of his career, wrote of the *no* of man's existence pronounced by God in scripture, which is dialectically related to the *yes* of his grace, and which affords a sense of the transcending reality governing man's life.

Despite the declarations of optimism and the emphasis on man's energies for constructive, enlightened action, writers like Cox and Altizer are not ignorant of, nor indifferent to, the demonic aspects of the technological revolution in modern culture. But their strategy involves a different emphasis. What the young, secular theologians are countering is centuries of religious conservatism, a conservatism expressed intellectually in the theologies of the divine absolute; expressed scripturally in the mythology of miracles and the belief in the three-storied universe consisting of heaven, hell, and earth; a conservatism manifested in fixed and oppressive attitudes toward class, race, labor, money, community, war, and peace, and exhibited in the church's outdated and repressive psychological views toward individuality, family, women, and sex. For many sophisticated religious thinkers (surely echoing the feelings of many church-men and believers), science and technology represent fantastic resources for eliminating the worst aspects of the lives of human beings; and what has made this possible, in no small measure, is the decline of the religious style of life and its replacement with a new ethos.

It is important to recognize that this attitude toward secu-larization on the part of Christian writers like Bonhoeffer, Cox, and Altizer does not involve a repudiation of Christian *faith*. What it involves is an attempt to reform the essential meaning of the Christian message in the light of what these theologians regard as the liberating power of secularization. The emphasis of these new thinkers on ethics and their disparagement of religion is quite deliberate, and it recalls the attitude of the Hebrew prophets who denounced the people of Israel for sub-stituting piety for righteousness before God based on human and social justice.

Here is where we can see the tremendous influence of Barth's theology. The secular theologians adopted Barth's early polemic against religion, and they accepted as a framework in their own thinking that drastic separation between the realm of God and the realm of man which runs through all Barth's thought. On the authority of Barth, for example, Cox can say that the story of Creation in the Bible means that once God's creation was complete, man was given responsibility for the life and well-being of all things earthly, a responsibility which he must exercise under God but without concern for supernatural in-terference. This demarcation of the divine and the human suggests that the essence of what it means to be a Christian today—much like what it meant to be a son of the Covenant in the time of the prophet Hosea—consists of an honest and mature response to the demands of justice between human beings in the world. Ironically, considering the antipathy expressed by these theologians toward existentialism's stress on the irrational, man's guilt, and the value of individuality, their own brands of Christian secularity and Christian atheism come close to that humanism that is at the heart of existentialism. Thus, Cox wishes to affirm that celebration of the human spirit struggling against adversity that he finds in the novels of Camus, but he rejects as immature, or dated, Kafka's vision of the world's essential meaninglessness.

The disagreement between two groups of thinkers over the erosion of religion through secularization can also be interpreted as a disagreement over the main problem. Clearly, Tillich, Maritain, Berdyaev, and Buber saw the problem to be the threat posed by a technological society to all those values understood to be essential to man's humanity. Thus, they saw the problem in largely psychological terms—in terms that emphasize the personal aspects of man as a *self*. It would be wrong to think that these theologians looked on religion in its traditional manifestations as safeguarding man's selfhood. The notion of spirit or spiritual depth so vital to their thought went deeper than organized religion and drew as much from existential philosophy, psychology, and contemporary novelists as it did from the books of the Bible and from past theologians. Traditional faith was not so much rejected by these writers as judged irrelevant. Every effort was made to reconceive faith along lines that would preserve its relevance for the contemporary world.

The younger counterparts of these theologians have also judged the traditional faith to be irrelevant, or, more precisely, an obstacle to the expression of faith by contemporary man. But where the earlier theologian tended to see the problem of faith as spiritual or psychological, the more recent theologian sees it as material or social. Existentialism, which is basically a philosophy of individual self-discovery, is of little help to the secular theologian who sees faith as a challenge to man to accept the burden of being in the world as Jesus, present with and for others. Here, as we said, technology and the forces of secularization have come to be regarded not as an enemy to what makes man human but as friend and ally.

Just here a deeper issue is raised over what exactly is understood by "religion." Tillich and Buber were no greater advocates of piety than Bonhoeffer and Cox, yet it was in religion essentially that Tillich and Buber saw the greatest resource and safeguard of man's humanity. Is religion at the heart of humanity, or is it its negation? The question is put into sharp focus by Richard Rubenstein and by Bernard Meland, the American neo-liberal Protestant theologian whose distinctive contribution to the understanding of man's religious sensibility will bring our investigation to a close.

Rubenstein frequently makes the point that a rational-ethical system of beliefs is simply not adequate to sustain the Jew in his identity as a Jew. The same point is expressed when he says that the Jew cannot be separated from his Jewishness nor, in answer to Bonhoefferian theologians, can there be a "religionless" Judaism. What this means for Rubenstein is that although ethical or intellectual aspects of religion are important to Judaism, at its very core are those elements we recognize as psychic: ritualistic, ceremonial, and emotional. This is the Judaism at the nonverbal level of the unconscious, where a man has been nurtured religiously without being required to confess his belief. Thus the Jew's identity is so deeply, so organically related to the religion of Judaism that, psychologically, he cannot repudiate Judaism without repudiating or effacing his own humanness, for he is ultimately shaped as a human being in and through his religion. Religion makes it possible for the Jew to successfully live through the critical junctures of his life as a human being: birth, death, guilt, sexuality, marriage, and old age. Though Rubenstein, as a Jew living after Auschwitz, believes that he lives in-the-time-of-the-death-of-God,[24] it is precisely because he is a human being that he does not repudiate religion but even more earnestly embraces it.

The question that Rubenstein has raised as a Jewish theologian is whether a man can maintain and express his humanity without responding to those ultimate meanings that lie at the heart of religion. One of these meanings is guilt, which is profoundly experienced as the source of being at fault before a High Judge, a fault which can only be forgiven through some symbolic act of atonement and purification. Bonhoeffer saw such essential religious experiences obscuring man's self-responsibility. But if the feeling of guilt is fundamental to man's psychological makeup, it is hard to understand how man can be fully responsible to himself and to other men without also coming to terms—and that means responding in some way *religiously*—with the reality of guilt. As with guilt, so with other human meanings to which man's responses are basically religious: birth, death, tragedy, and loneliness. (Alfred North Whitehead, the British philosopher, defined religion as "what the individual does with his own solitariness.")

To understand religion in this way is not to suggest that there is or must be an objective reality or cosmic person—God—before whom one is guilty. The psychological meanings of religion may give rise to such a belief, as they have in Judaism, Christianity, and other organized religions, but they do not necessitate such a belief. The central character who reappears in Kafka's novels represents a profound psychological portrait of human guilt; and it is guilt in a godless world. Rubenstein suggests something of the same idea when, in place of Yahweh, the providential Lord of History who died at Auschwitz, he substitutes the Holy Nothingness as the "giver" and "receiver" of all human life. For Rubenstein, men are guilty in relation to each other, but they ultimately experience their guilt in relation to the mysterious nothingness of life and death. The rituals of religion are, for Rubenstein, a way of coming to terms meaningfully with the experience of guilt; possibly the ritualistic act of writing was for Kafka the way of coming to terms with his own vision of guilt.

Religion is man's response to what he experiences as a matter of ultimacy in his life. This is the understanding shared by

Tillich, Maritain, Berdyaev, Buber, and Rubenstein; and it is an understanding present dialectically in the early writings of Barth. Each of these theologians has sought in his own way to come to an understanding of this response, and thus to clarify the meaning of *what* is experienced as ultimate. When the relation of theology to religion is put this way, it will be seen that the theologian's aim is not a pious defense of God, nor a special plea for the validity of religion, but rather the vastly more difficult task of discerning within the data of man's total experience what meaning, if any, can be assigned to the term "God." The resources of philosophy, psychology, sociology, literature, and any number of other intellectual disciplines are utilized in this task, for the guiding insight is that, though religion is the most evident form through which man expresses his sense of ultimacy, it is not the only form.

Thus, one must recognize the difference between religions and the religious. The theological method given precise articulation by Schleiermacher, and applied by theologians from Tillich to Rubenstein and Meland, acknowledges a religious sensibility that is deeper than religion and may or may not take the form of explicit or traditional religious identification. According to Bernard Meland, this sensibility is the awareness that human existence, as demarcated by the mysteries of birth and death, is not wholly at man's disposal.[25] Further, we encounter depths of mystery in our experiences of tragedy, guilt, despair, forgiveness, trust, and in countless other experiences that shape our lives, giving to them what Berdyaev called "spirit" or quality of meaning.

It is not "God" in some pious or simplistic sense of the word that is discerned in the ultimate depths of experience. Rather, there is the suggestion of a relation to "A-More-Than-Human-Reality."[26] That is how Meland identifies the structure of man's religious sensibility. Primarily it is the awareness, through deeply human experiences, of a relation to an Ultimate Reality of grace and judgment. In the experiences of a goodness that comes to us from others in trust, acceptance, affection, friendship, forgiveness, and succor, we have intimations of a sovereign good which acts on our lives. And in the experiences of failure, guilt, and forsakenness, we are also made aware of an ultimate judgment on the inherent presumptuousness of much that man does, and the pretensions of his claims of self-sufficiency. These experiences of depth or ultimacy, taken together with the abiding mysteries of birth and death, suggest to Meland an Ultimate Creative Ground to which all human life is related, and which in turn relates man to man. It is this Ultimate Creative Ground that the Judeo-Christian faith witnesses to in the symbol of "God, the Creator and Redeemer." When Rubenstein speaks of the Holy Nothingness which after Auschwitz must replace the biblical Lord of History, this Holy Nothingness functions very much as Meland's Ultimate Ground does: as a transcendent source of grace and judgment for all human beings mediated through the universal experiences of depth.

For the most part, the secular theologians we have discussed have either ignored or rejected the psychical function of religion. The result is that their own theologies lack critical judgment in assessing the impact of secularization on modern life. Bonhoeffer, Cox, and Altizer all tend to see the dissolution of historic religious structures as a *possibility* for contemporary man, but there is little or no analysis of what *actual* consequences have resulted from the secularization of life through the growth of a technological civilization. Cox speaks in highly ideal if not idealistic terms of what the secular city *can* represent, but hardly in descriptive terms of the *actual* lives of those living in the metropolitan centers of the world.

Meland is one theologian who is sympathetic to the thesis of the secular theologians—that the man of faith today who wishes to be honest with himself must abandon traditional piety and sincerely affirm what is creative and good in the world's culture. But he also argues that this affirmation, if uncritical, can be useless. He recognizes, as the secular theologians do, that the scientific technology which has revolutionized the Western world constitutes a great good for man. But he also sees it as a good not without its own ambiguity,[27] for while a scientific technology can serve man, it can also compel man to serve it. The latter cannot help but occur when techniques of mass production and advertising are developed in order to exploit a mass society and the culture that rises from it. Lost is the meaning of material production for the sake of man's well-being. There emerges the mindless, virtually autonomous cycle of production for its own sake. Human beings are regarded as a market to be artificially created and stimulated in order to receive and justify an endless supply of products, and the techniques and systems of production expand and proliferate as success is achieved.

As it appears less and less that technology serves man, and more and more that man serves technology, the essential exploitation of man occurs: the destruction of any sense that man's work and the product of his work symbolize an act of self-expression. (This was also Marx's prophetic criticism of the Western capitalistic system in its relation to the individual human beings who must live under it.) The sheer complexity, power, and impersonality of the technological basis of modern civilization suggest the opposite: that the life of man is becoming an expression or "aspect" of technology. The danger that this represents to the culture of modern man is that all dimensions of human life will be measured by the cycle of production which now sustains our technological civilization. The effect of this can be seen everywhere: government, law, education, medicine, urban planning, and the arts. At the core of this development is the unspoken attitude that techniques should guide our destiny as a society.

According to Meland, what a technological civilization threatens is the *quality* of human living, reducing all meanings, values, acts, purposes, and goals to the measure of things and their production. But quality does not mean merely an enhancement of life, such as leisure time for recreation and the cultivation of personal interests. What is meant by quality is deeper than this. It is the capacity on the part of an individual human being for achieving meaning through reflection and critical judgment. The expression of that meaning is an act of self-affirmation. Thus quality is not peripheral but really vital to man's humanity. One remembers that Berdyaev called the eradication of quality from modern life "objectification"—a spiritless, purposeless, virtually meaningless existence.

Thus, the ambiguity of technology is that it can provide the goods for meeting the material conditions of life,[28] but it can also tempt, indeed compel, man to believe that the essence of his life resides in the success or failure of the production and use of these goods. Interpreted theologically, this is the denial that anything is more ultimate than man himself, his creative capacities, and the products of his creation. This is the worst feature of secularization, secularization as an ideology. It is fundamentally the denial that man possesses a religious sensibility, a capacity to experience and respond to the mysterious depths of his own existence, to have what Tillich called ultimate concern, and to express this sensibility by qualitative outreaches of his spirit as we discern them in art, literature, religion, or moral beliefs and decisions.

This religious sensibility is a function of the human psyche, lying more deeply in the unconscious life of man than can be suggested by the status of the practice of religion in society, or by the criticism of those practices by the young secular theologians. Yet the relation between the religious sensibility and religions is organic. If secularization threatens historic religious institutions and practices, it thereby threatens the means by which countless human beings give symbolic voice to their deepest feelings about the mysterious and ultimate meanings of living and dying. In fostering pragmatic and utilitarian attitudes, secularization reaches down to the basic sensibility of man and threatens every mode of its expression. We may very well have reached the time when art, music, literature, and architecture, along with religion and other symbolic means of man's spiritual self-expression, may be judged irrelevant to the contemporary culture; or, far worse, they may be made to conform to the measure of "things" and "services." In the minds of many theologians, this would be the ultimate irony for man living in a world he is persuaded to think has come of age.

Theologians from Schleiermacher to Cox have agreed that in the experience of modern man the problem of God is at the same time the problem of man. The loss of certainty about God, church, and Bible reflects, and in part occasions, man's loss of confidence in himself. It is not man's loss of confidence in his powers to acquire scientific knowledge or produce technological advances, but his loss of a sense of personal dignity, a sense of human uniqueness, and a sureness of final purpose or destiny. For, in the minds of theologians, the loss of a certainty about God is at base a loss of a sense of ultimacy which gives depth and purpose to everyday living. As we have seen, religious thinkers have differed for the past 150 years in their interpretations of the meaning of this loss, and they certainly differ in their proposals for struggling with it. But it is impossible to understand religious thinking today without an intimate knowledge of the major theological options laid out by Barth, Tillich, Maritain, Berdyaev, and Buber, and by at least Schleiermacher and Kierkegaard before them.

In response to man's loss of self-confidence through his loss of a sense of ultimacy, the strategy of modern theology has been *apologetic*. It seeks to identify what is meaningful or relevant about God in light of human criteria of relevance and meaning. Despite Barth's efforts to reintroduce the sovereign autonomy of scripture as the only reliable criterion of thinking about God, the general trend in theology from Schleiermacher to the present day has been away from church and Bible and toward cultural experience as the resource and norm for understanding man's relation to God. And so, in responding to the loss of ultimacy, modern theology has reintroduced the question of man himself: his life and death, his experiences of tragedy, joy, guilt, acceptance, loss, and love.

Notes

Chapter I.
The Theology of Feeling: Friedrich Schleiermacher

1. This biographical sketch is based on information provided by Richard Brandt in his excellent study, *The Philosophy of Schleiermacher: The Development of His Theory of Scientific and Religious Knowledge* (New York: Harper, 1941), pp. 1–41.
2. Hugh Ross Mackintosh, *Types of Modern Theology* (New York: Scribner's, 1937), p. 35.
3. Friedrich Schleiermacher, *On Religion: Speeches to Its Cultured Despisers* (New York: Harper Torchbooks, 1958). Introduction by Rudolph Otto, p. vii.
4. *Ibid.*, pp. vii–viii.
5. *Ibid.*, p. xii.
6. *Ibid.*, p. 93.
7. *Ibid.*, p. 72.
8. *Ibid.*, p. 73.
9. *Ibid.*, p. 48.
10. *Ibid.*, p. 106.
11. *Ibid.*, p. xvi.
12. *Ibid.*, p. 49.
13. *Ibid.*, p. 36.
14. Richard Brandt notes that in the second edition of the *Discourses* Schleiermacher dropped the term "intuition," which clearly suggested an object of religious affection, and retained the term "feeling" along with its highly subjective connotations. Brandt, *The Philosophy of Schleiermacher*, pp. 175–184.
15. Schleiermacher, *On Religion*, p. 88.
16. *Ibid.*, p. 97.
17. *Ibid.*, p. 101.
18. Friedrich Schleiermacher, *The Christian Faith*, trans. H. R. Mackintosh and J. S. Steward (Edinburgh: T. & T. Clark, 1928), p. 16.
19. *Ibid.*, p. 17.
20. Mackintosh, *Types of Modern Theology*, pp. 64–65.
21. Brandt, *The Philosophy of Schleiermacher*, p. 141.
22. Schleiermacher, *The Christian Faith*, p. 385.
23. Mackintosh, *Types of Modern Theology*, p. 86.

Notes

24. Kenneth Hamilton, *Revolt Against Heaven* (Grand Rapids, Mich.: Eerdman, 1965), pp. 91–111.
25. Bernard Eugene Meland, *Faith and Culture* (London: Allen and Unwin, 1955).
26. James M. Robinson, *A New Quest of the Historical Jesus* (Naperville, Ill.: Allenson, 1959); Günther Bornkamm, *Jesus of Nazareth*, trans. Irene and Fraser McLuskey with James M. Robinson (New York: Harper, 1960). For further discussion of this question, see Chapter Eight.

Chapter II.
The Theology of the Individual: Søren Kierkegaard

1. Walter Lowrie, *Kierkegaard* (London: Oxford University Press, 1938).
2. Hermann Diem, *Kierkegaard: An Introduction*, trans. David Green (Richmond, Va.: John Knox Press, 1966), pp. 25–26.
3. *Ibid.*, p. 25.
4. Reidar Thomte, *Kierkegaard's Philosophy of Religion* (Princeton: Princeton University Press, 1949), p. 6.
5. *Ibid.*
6. W. T. Stace, *The Philosophy of Hegel* (New York: Dover, 1955), pp. 135–155.
7. Harold Hoffding, *A History of Philosophy*, trans. B. E. Meyer (New York: Dover, 1955), II, 182.
8. *Ibid.*, p. 187.
9. G. W. F. Hegel, *The Philosophy of History*, trans. J. Sibree (New York: Dover, 1956).
10. *Ibid.*, pp. 515–518.
11. Søren Kierkegaard, *Concluding Unscientific Postscript*, trans. David F. Swenson and Walter Lowrie (Princeton: Princeton University Press, 1944), pp. 283–284.
12. *Ibid.*, pp. 317–318.
13. *Ibid.*, p. 200.
14. Hegel, *The Philosophy of History*, pp. 341–457.
15. Kierkegaard, *Concluding Unscientific Postscript*, pp. 169–224.
16. Søren Kierkegaard, "Attack upon Christendom," in *A Kierkegaard Anthology*, ed. Robert Bretall (New York: Modern Library, 1946), pp. 436–439.
17. Kierkegaard, *Concluding Unscientific Postscript*, p. 212.
18. *Ibid.*, p. 211.
19. *Ibid.*, p. 99.
20. Kierkegaard engaged in an analysis of the interior states of the human self as it seeks to become Christian, and proved thereby to be one of the most profound psychologists of the religious temperament. Among the states he analyzed were anxiety (in *The Concept of Dread*, 1844); love (in *Works of Love*, 1847); despair (in *The Sickness unto Death*, 1849); and forgiveness, guilt, aloneness, and erotic pleasure (in numerous essays).

Notes

21. Bretall, ed., *A Kierkegaard Anthology*, p. 192.
22. *Ibid.*, p. 195.
23. Kierkegaard, *Concluding Unscientific Postscript*, p. 108.
24. *Ibid.*, p. 103.
25. Diem, *Kierkegaard: An Introduction*, p. 98.
26. The better known works of the aesthetic mode comprise generally Kierkegaard's early authorship, consisting of his first major works, *Either/Or* (1843), *Fear and Trembling* (1843), *Philosophical Fragments* (1844), and *Stages on Life's Way* (1845). The ethical mode is represented mainly by the monumental *Concluding Unscientific Postscript* of the middle part of Kierkegaard's career (1846) and by sections of books listed by Kierkegaard himself as essentially in the aesthetic mode. The religious mode comprises the so-called late period, and consists of such writings as *Works of Love* (1847), *Christian Discourses* (1847), *The Point of View of My Work as an Author* (1848), and *Training in Christianity* (1850).
27. Søren Kierkegaard, *Stages on Life's Way*, trans. Walter Lowrie (Princeton: Princeton University Press, 1940), p. 64.
28. Søren Kierkegaard, *Either/Or*, trans. David F. and Lillian Swenson (Princeton: Princeton University Press, 1944), I, 57.
29. Søren Kierkegaard, *Fear and Trembling*, trans. Walter Lowrie (Princeton: Princeton University Press, 1941).
30. Thomte, *Kierkegaard's Philosophy of Religion*, p. 60.
31. Kierkegaard, *Fear and Trembling*, p. 78.
32. Kierkegaard, *Concluding Unscientific Postscript*, p. 476.

Chapter III.
The Theology of the Word: Karl Barth

1. Hans Kung, *Justification: The Doctrine of Karl Barth and a Catholic Reflection*, trans. Thomas Calvin, Edmund E. Tolk, and David Granskow (New York: Thomas Nelson, 1964); see esp. bibliography, pp. 304–305.
2. Karl Barth, *How I Changed My Mind*, introduction and epilogue by John Godsey (Richmond, Va.: John Knox Press, 1966), p. 9.
3. Wilhelm Pauck, *Karl Barth: Prophet of a New Christianity?* (New York: Harper, 1931), pp. 55–60.
4. Karl Barth, *Epistle to the Romans*, 6th ed., trans. Edwyn C. Hoskyns (London: Oxford University Press, 1968).
5. Barth, *How I Changed My Mind*, p. 25.
6. Barth, *Epistle to the Romans*, pp. 93f., *passim*.
7. *Ibid.*, p. 10.
8. *Ibid.*, pp. 249, 250, *passim*.
9. Pauck, *Karl Barth: Prophet of a New Christianity?*, p. 65.
10. This is the view, held from the beginning of Christianity, that God himself is the author of the scriptures, having directly inspired the words of the apostles.

Notes

11. Pauck, *Karl Barth: Prophet of a New Christianity?*, pp. 206–207.
12. Barth, *Epistle to the Romans*, pp. 6–11.
13. Pauck, *Karl Barth: Prophet of a New Christianity?*, pp. 106–109, 141–142.
14. Barth, *Epistle to the Romans*, p. 4.
15. Karl Barth, *Church Dogmatics*, I–IV, ed. and trans. G. T. Thomson, G. W. Bromiley, T. F. Torrance, *et al.* (Edinburgh: T. & T. Clark, 1936–1960); Karl Barth, *Anselm: Fides Quaerens Intellectum*, trans. Ian W. Robertson (Richmond, Va.: John Knox Press, 1960).
16. Karl Barth, *Dogmatics in Outline*, trans. G. T. Thomson (New York: Philosophical Library, 1959), pp. 9–14.
17. *Ibid.*, p. 13; Barth, *Church Dogmatics*, IV/1, 722f.
18. Barth, *Church Dogmatics*, I/1, 448f.
19. Barth, *Dogmatics in Outline*, p. 53.
20. *Ibid.*, p. 51.
21. *Ibid.*, p. 70.
22. Barth, *Church Dogmatics*, III/1, 117f.
23. Barth, *Dogmatics in Outline*, pp. 57–58.
24. *Ibid.*, pp. 39–41, 77–79.
25. *Ibid.*, pp. 78–81.
26. Barth, *Church Dogmatics*, IV/1, 161–163.
27. Barth, *Dogmatics in Outline*, pp. 84–85.
28. *Ibid.*, p. 39.
29. John Cobb, *Living Options in Protestant Theology* (Philadelphia: Westminster, 1962), p. 195.
30. Barth, *Church Dogmatics*, III/1, 231f.
31. Barth, *Dogmatics in Outline*, p. 57.
32. Barth, *Church Dogmatics*, I/1, 339–560.
33. Barth's short essay, "The Humanity of God," is often cited as showing a change toward a greater recognition of God's involvement in the world and in the life of man. However, there is no trace in this essay of the belief that what happens in the world has an *effect on God's life;* without such a belief it is hard to understand what could be meant by God's "humanity." See Karl Barth, *The Humanity of God* (Richmond, Va.: John Knox Press, 1957).
34. Barth, *How I Changed My Mind*, p. 44.
35. *Ibid.*, p. 47.
36. *Ibid.*, p. 57.
37. Reinhold Niebuhr, "An Answer to Karl Barth," in *Essays in Applied Christianity: The Church and the New World* (New York: Meridian Books, 1959), p. 176.
38. Barth, *How I Changed My Mind*, p. 63.
39. *Ibid.*, p. 66.
40. Georges Casalis, *Portrait of Karl Barth* (New York: Doubleday, 1963), p. 70.

Notes

Chapter IV.
The Theology of Correlation: Paul Tillich

1. Paul Tillich, *On the Boundary* (New York: Scribner's, 1966), p. 13. This is a revision, newly translated, of Part I of *The Interpretation of History*, written by Tillich in 1936.
2. *Ibid.*
3. Paul Tillich, *Theology of Culture* (New York: Oxford University Press, 1964), pp. 3–9.
4. *Ibid.*, p. 8.
5. *Ibid.*
6. Paul Tillich, *Systematic Theology* (Chicago: University of Chicago Press, 1951–1963), I, 11.
7. Tillich, *Theology of Culture*, p. 8.
8. Paul Tillich, *Dynamics of Faith* (New York: Harper & Row, 1957), pp. 1–8.
9. Tillich, *Systematic Theology*, I, 216–217, 222–227.
10. Tillich, *Dynamics of Faith*, p. 2.
11. *Ibid.*, pp. 109–110.
12. *Ibid.*, pp. 8–12.
13. Tillich, *Systematic Theology*, I, 14.
14. *Ibid.*, pp. 39–40.
15. Tillich, *Theology of Culture*, p. 42.
16. *Ibid.*
17. Tillich, *Dynamics of Faith*, pp. 41–43.
18. Tillich, *Theology of Culture*, p. 56.
19. *Ibid.*, p. 157.
20. *Ibid.*
21. *Ibid.*, pp. 68–75.
22. *Ibid.*, p. 70.
23. *Ibid.*, p. 68.
24. *Ibid.*, p. 75.
25. *Ibid.*, pp. 43–44.
26. *Ibid.*, p. 44.
27. *Ibid.*, p. 46.
28. Tillich, *Systematic Theology*, I, 3–8.
29. *Ibid.*, pp. 15–18.
30. *Ibid.*, pp. 59–66.
31. Franz Kafka, "The Metamorphosis," in *Selected Short Stories of Franz Kafka*, trans. Willa and Edwin Muir (New York: Modern Library, 1952), pp. 19–89.
32. Franz Kafka, *The Trial*, trans. Willa and Edwin Muir (New York: Modern Library, 1964).
33. Tillich, *Systematic Theology*, I, 163.
34. *Ibid.*, pp. 163–164.
35. *Ibid.*, p. 163.
36. *Ibid.*, pp. 186–189.

37. *Ibid.*, pp. 204–210, 236–237.
38. *Ibid.*, pp. 238–247. Tillich claims that all language used to refer to God is symbolic except the language in the assertion "God is being-itself," which does not point beyond itself as a symbol but means exactly (literally) what it says.
39. *Ibid.*, pp. 182–186.
40. *Ibid.*, pp. 185–186; Tillich, *Systematic Theology*, II, 31–33.
41. *Ibid.*, pp. 68–70.
42. Paul Tillich, *The Courage to Be* (New Haven: Yale University Press, 1967).
43. Tillich, *Systematic Theology*, II, 97–180.
44. Tillich, *The Courage to Be*, pp. 163–178.
45. Tillich, *Systematic Theology*, II, 166–167.

Chapter V.
Theocentric Humanism: The Thomistic Philosophy of Jacques Maritain

1. Jacques and Raissa Maritain, *Prayer and Intelligence*, trans. Richard O'Sullivan (New York: Sheed and Ward, 1928); Jacques and Raissa Maritain, *The Situation of Poetry*, trans. Marshall Suther (New York: Philosophical Library, 1955); Raissa Maritain, *We Have Been Friends Together and Adventures in Grace: The Memoirs of Raissa Maritain*, trans. Julie Kernan (Garden City, N.Y.: Image Books, 1961). For a full bibliography of works by the Maritains, see Donald and Idella Gallagher, comps., *The Achievement of Jacques and Raissa Maritain: A Bibliography 1906–1961* (New York: Doubleday, 1962).
2. Charles A. Fecher, *The Philosophy of Jacques Maritain* (Westminster, Md.; Newman Press, 1953), p. 22.
3. *Ibid.*, p. 25.
4. Saint Thomas Aquinas, *The Summa Theologica*, Part One, Question I, First Article.
5. Jacques Maritain, "A New Approach to God" and "Christian Humanism," in *The Range of Reason* (New York: Scribner's, 1952), pp. 92–96, 194f.
6. Plato, *The Republic*, especially Books XXIII–XXV.
7. Aristotle, *Metaphysics*, Book Alpha.
8. Aristotle, *Physics*, Book Two.
9. Aristotle, *Metaphysics*, Book Alpha.
10. John Herman Randall, Jr., *Aristotle* (New York: Columbia University Press, 1960).
11. Aquinas, *The Summa Theologica*, Part One, Question II, Third Article.
12. *Ibid.*
13. *Ibid.*, Part One, Question III, Third Article.
14. Frederick Copleston, *A History of Philosophy*, Vol. II, *Mediaeval Philosophy* (Westminster, Md.: Newman Press, 1965), Chapter XXXIII.

Notes

15. Jacques Maritain, *Existence and the Existent*, trans. Lewis Galantière and Gerald B. Phelan (New York: Vintage Books, 1966), Chapter 1.
16. Maritain, *The Range of Reason*, p. 185.
17. *Ibid.*, p. 191.
18. *Ibid.*, p. 186.
19. *Ibid.*, p. 194.
20. *Ibid.*, pp. 194–195.
21. *Ibid.*, p. 195.
22. Jacques Maritain, *Art and Scholasticism and the Frontiers of Poetry*, trans. Joseph W. Evans (New York: Scribner's, 1962), pp. 8–9.
23. *Ibid.*, p. 9.
24. *Ibid.*
25. *Ibid.*, p. 23.
26. *Ibid.*, p. 31.
27. *Ibid.*, p. 199.
28. *Ibid.*, p. 181.
29. Maritain, *The Range of Reason*, p. 99.
30. Maritain, *Existence and the Existent*, Chapter v.
31. *Ibid.*, pp. 127–128.
32. Jean-Paul Sartre, "Existentialism Is a Humanism," in *Existentialism from Dostoevsky to Sartre*, ed. Walter Kaufmann (Cleveland: Meridian Books, 1956).
33. Erich Dinkler, "Martin Heidegger," in *Christianity and the Existentialists*, ed. Carl Michalson (New York: Scribner's, 1956).
34. Sartre, "Existentialism Is a Humanism."
35. Jacques Maritain, *Approaches to God* (New York: Macmillan, 1967).
36. Jacques Maritain, *God and the Permission of Evil* (Milwaukee: Bruce Publishing, 1966).
37. Maritain, *The Range of Reason*, pp. 224–225.
38. *Ibid.*, pp. 219–222.
39. Jacques Maritain, "A New Approach to God," in *Our Emergent Civilization*, ed. Ruth Nanda Anshen (New York: Harper, 1947), pp. 285–286.

Chapter VI.
The Theology of Godmanhood: Nicolas Berdyaev

1. Matthew Spinka, *Nicolas Berdyaev: Captive of Freedom* (Philadelphia: Westminster Press, 1950), pp. 9–18.
2. *Ibid.*, pp. 19–44.
3. *Ibid.*, p. 51.
4. *Ibid.*, pp. 67–68.
5. *Ibid.*, pp. 84–85.
6. *Ibid.*, p. 85.
7. Nicolas Berdyaev, *The Destiny of Man* (New York: Harper Torchbooks, 1960), pp. 23–35; *The Meaning of History* (Cleveland: Meridian Books, 1962),

pp. 49–63; *The Meaning of the Creative Act* (New York: Collier Books, 1962), pp. 56–105.
8. Berdyaev, *The Destiny of Man*, pp. 103–153; Nicolas Berdyaev, *The Beginning and the End* (New York: Harper Torchbooks, 1957), pp. 141–194.
9. Berdyaev, *The Destiny of Man*, pp. 23–35.
10. Berdyaev, *The Beginning and the End*, pp. 197–254.
11. Berdyaev, *The Meaning of History*, pp. 133–147.
12. *Ibid.*
13. Nicolas Berdyaev, *Spirit and Reality* (London: Geoffrey Bles, 1939), pp. 49–71.
14. Nicolas Berdyaev, *The Fate of Man in the Modern World* (Ann Arbor: University of Michigan Paperbacks, 1961).
15. Berdyaev, *The Destiny of Man*, pp. 28–29; *The Meaning of History*, pp. 49–63.
16. See Berdyaev's analysis of Dostoevsky's thought in his book *Dostoevsky* (New York: Meridian Books, 1957).
17. Berdyaev, *The Destiny of Man*, pp. 23–44.
18. *Ibid.*, pp. 23–44.
19. *Ibid.*; Berdyaev, *The Meaning of History*, pp. 49–63.
20. Berdyaev, *The Meaning of History*, pp. 103–125.
21. *Ibid.*, pp. 126–153; Berdyaev, *The Meaning of the Creative Act*, pp. 89–105; Berdyaev, *The Beginning and the End*, pp. 141–194.
22. Nicolas Berdyaev, *Freedom and the Spirit* (London: Geoffrey Bles, 1935). Quoted by Donald A. Lowrie, ed., *Nicolai Berdyaev: Christian Existentialist* (New York: Harper Torchbooks, 1965), p. 233.
23. *Ibid.*, p. 233.
24. Berdyaev, *The Meaning of the Creative Act*, p. 101.
25. Berdyaev, *The Beginning and the End*, p. 173.
26. *Ibid.*, p. 179.
27. *Ibid.*, p. 250.
28. Berdyaev, *The Destiny of Man*, p. 169; Berdyaev, *The Beginning and the End*, p. 228.
29. See Thomas A. Idinopulos, "Nicolas Berdyaev's Ontology of Spirit," *Journal of Religion*, XLIX, No. 1 (January 1969), 84–93.

Chapter VII.
The Theology of Dialogue: Martin Buber

1. R. G. Smith, *Martin Buber* (Richmond, Va.: John Knox Press, 1967), p. 5.
2. Martin Buber, *The Way of Man*, Foreword by Maurice Friedman (Wallingford, Pa.: Pendle Hill pamphlet, n.d.), p. 3.
3. *Ibid.*, pp. 13–14.
4. *Ibid.*, p. 32.
5. Martin Buber, *I and Thou*, 2d ed., trans. R. G. Smith (New York: Scribner's, 1958).

6. Smith, *Martin Buber*, p. 3.
7. *Ibid.*, p. 14.
8. Buber, *I and Thou*, pp. 7-8.
9. *Ibid.*, p. 63.
10. *Ibid.*, p. 79.
11. *Ibid.*, p. 80.
12. *Ibid.*, p. 87.
13. *Ibid.*, p. 94.
14. *Ibid.*, p. 104.
15. *Ibid.*
16. *Ibid.*, p. 106.
17. *Ibid.*, p. 107.
18. *Ibid.*, pp. 110-112.
19. *Ibid.*, p. 112.
20. *Ibid.*, p. 111.
21. *Ibid.*, p. 118.
22. *Ibid.*, p. 120.
23. *Ibid.*, pp. 117-118.
24. Martin Buber, *Between Man and Man*, trans. R. G. Smith (New York: Macmillan, 1965), p. 35.
25. *Ibid.*, pp. 36-37.
26. *Ibid.*, p. 38.
27. *Ibid.*, p. 52.
28. *Ibid.*, pp. 60-61.
29. *Ibid.*, pp. 68-69.

Chapter VIII.
Theologians in a World Come of Age

1. For serious and responsible efforts to analyze the meaning of secularization, see David Edwards, *Religion and Change* (New York: Harper & Row, 1969); Langdon Gilkey, *Naming the Whirlwind: The Renewal of God-Language* (Indianapolis: Bobbs-Merrill, 1969); Bernard E. Meland, *The Secularization of Modern Cultures* (New York: Oxford University Press, 1966).
2. I have taken this phrase from the title of Ved Mehta's interesting and entertaining account of the mood of contemporary theology. Ved Mehta, *The New Theologian* (New York: Harper & Row, 1965).
3. Dietrich Bonhoeffer, *Letters and Papers From Prison* (New York: Macmillan, 1967).
4. *Ibid.*, p. 142.
5. *Ibid.*
6. *Ibid.*, p. 193.
7. *Ibid.*, p. 145.
8. *Ibid.*, p. 141.
9. Harvey Cox, *The Secular City* (New York: Macmillan, 1965).

10. *Ibid.*, p. 8.
11. *Ibid.*
12. *Ibid.*, p. 9.
13. *Ibid.*, p. 10.
14. *Ibid.*, p. 13.
15. *Ibid.*, p. 26.
16. George W. Peck, "The Secular City and the Bible," in *The Secular City Debate*, ed. Daniel Callahan (New York: Macmillan, 1966).
17. Cox, *The Secular City*, p. 126.
18. Thomas J. J. Altizer, *The Gospel of Christian Atheism* (Philadelphia: Westminster, 1966). See also Thomas J. J. Altizer and William Hamilton, *Radical Theology and the Death of God* (Indianapolis: Bobbs-Merrill, 1966).
19. Richard L. Rubenstein, *After Auschwitz* (Indianapolis: Bobbs-Merrill, 1966).
20. *Ibid.*, p. 222.
21. *Ibid.*, p. 225.
22. *Ibid.*, p. 80.
23. John Robinson, *Honest to God* (Philadelphia: Westminster, 1963); Altizer and Hamilton, *Radical Theology*; Paul van Buren, *The Secular Meaning of the Gospel* (New York: Macmillan, 1963); Gibson Winter, *The New Creation as Metropolis* (New York: Macmillan, 1963); *The Suburban Captivity of the Churches* (New York: Macmillan, 1962).
24. Rubenstein, *After Auschwitz*, p. 151.
25. Meland, *The Secularization of Modern Cultures*, pp. 116–140.
26. *Ibid.*, p. 137.
27. *Ibid.*, pp. 76–115, 141–163.
28. *Ibid.*, pp. 58–75.

Selected Bibliography

Chapter I.
The Theology of Feeling: Friedrich Schleiermacher

Brandt, Richard. *The Philosophy of Schleiermacher: The Development of His Theory of Scientific and Religious Knowledge.* New York: Harper & Brothers, 1941.

Mackintosh, Hugh R. *Types of Modern Theology.* New York: Charles Scribner's Sons, 1937.

Niebuhr, Richard R. *Schleiermacher on Christ and Religion.* New York: Charles Scribner's Sons, 1964.

Schleiermacher, Friedrich. *The Christian Faith.* Translated by H. R. Mackintosh and J. S. Steward. Edinburgh: T. & T. Clark, 1928.

———. *On Religion: Speeches to Its Cultured Despisers.* New York: Harper & Brothers, Harper Torchbooks, 1958.

Spiegler, Gerhard. *The Eternal Covenant: Schleiermacher's Experiment in Cultural Theology.* New York: Harper & Row, 1967.

Chapter II.
The Theology of the Individual: Søren Kierkegaard

Bretall, Robert, ed. *A Kierkegaard Anthology.* New York: Random House, Modern Library, 1946.

Diem, Hermann. *Kierkegaard: An Introduction.* Translated by David Green. Richmond, Virginia: John Knox Press, 1966.

Kierkegaard, Søren. *The Concept of Dread.* Translated by Walter Lowrie. Princeton, N.J.: Princeton University Press, 1946.

———. *Concluding Unscientific Postscript.* Translated by David F. Swenson and Walter Lowrie. Princeton, N.J.: Princeton University Press, 1944.

———. *Either/Or*, Vols. I and II. Translated by David F. and Lillian Swenson. Princeton, N.J.: Princeton University Press, 1941.

Selected Bibliography

———. *Fear and Trembling*. Translated by Walter Lowrie. Princeton, N.J.: Princeton University Press, 1941.

———. *For Self Examination and Judge for Yourselves*. Translated by Walter Lowrie. Princeton, N.J.: Princeton University Press, 1944.

———. *The Sickness Unto Death*. Translated by Walter Lowrie. Princeton, N.J.: Princeton University Press, 1944.

———. *Stages on Life's Way*. Translated by Walter Lowrie. Princeton, N.J.: Princeton University Press, 1940.

Lowrie, Walter. *Kierkegaard*. London: Oxford University Press, 1938.

Thomte, Reidar. *Kierkegaard's Philosophy of Religion*. Princeton, N.J.: Princeton University Press, 1949.

Chapter III.
The Theology of the Word: Karl Barth

Barth, Karl. *Anselm: Fides Quaerens Intellectum*. Translated by Ian W. Robertson. Richmond, Virginia: John Knox Press, 1960.

———. *Church Dogmatics*, Vols. I–IV. Edited and translated by G. T. Thomson, G. W. Bromiley, T. F. Torrance, *et al.* Edinburgh: T. & T. Clark, 1936–1960.

———. *Church Dogmatics: A Selection*. Selected by Helmut Gollwitzer. New York: Harper & Brothers, Harper Torchbooks, 1961.

———. *Dogmatics in Outline*. Translated by G. T. Thomson. New York: Philosophical Library, 1959.

———. *Epistle to the Romans*. 6th ed. Translated by Edwyn C. Hoskyns. London: Oxford University Press, 1968.

———. *How I Changed My Mind*. Richmond, Virginia: John Knox Press, 1966.

———. *The Humanity of God*. Richmond, Virginia: John Knox Press, 1957.

Berkouwer, Gerril Cornelis. *The Triumph of Grace in the Theology of Karl Barth*. Grand Rapids, Michigan: Eerdman's, 1956.

Casalis, Georges. *Portrait of Karl Barth*. New York: Doubleday, 1963.

Cobb, John. *Living Options in Protestant Theology*. Philadelphia: Westminster Press, 1962.

Deegan, Daniel. "The Christological Determinant in Barth's Doctrine of Creation," *Scottish Journal of Theology*, XIV, No. 2 (June 1961), 119–135.

Hartwell, Herbert. *The Theology of Karl Barth: An Introduction*. Philadelphia: Westminster Press, 1964.

Hick, John. *Faith and the Philosophers*. New York: St. Martin's Press, 1962.

Kung, Hans. *Justification: The Doctrine of Karl Barth and a Catholic Reflection.* Translated by Thomas Calvin, Edmund E. Tolk, and David Granskow. New York: Thomas Nelson and Sons, 1964.

Niebuhr, Reinhold. *Essays in Applied Christianity: The Church and the New World.* New York: World Publishing Company, Meridian Books, 1959.

Osborn, Robert T. *Freedom in Modern Theology.* Philadelphia: Westminster Press, 1967.

Pauck, Wilhelm. *Karl Barth: Prophet of a New Christianity?* New York: Harper & Brothers, 1931.

Chapter IV.
The Theology of Correlation: Paul Tillich

Adams, James Luther. *Paul Tillich's Philosophy of Culture, Science, and Religion.* New York: Harper & Row, 1965.

Kegley, Charles, and Bretall, Robert W., eds. *The Theology of Paul Tillich.* New York: Macmillan, Macmillan Paperbacks, 1964.

Kucheman, Clark A. "Professor Tillich: Justice and the Economic Order," *Journal of Religion,* XLVI, No. 1 (January 1966), Part II.

Tillich, Paul. *The Courage to Be.* New Haven: Yale University Press, 1967.

———. *Dynamics of Faith.* New York: Harper & Row, 1957.

———. *On the Boundary.* New York: Charles Scribner's Sons, 1966.

———. *Systematic Theology,* Vols. I–III. Chicago: University of Chicago Press, 1951–1963.

———. *Theology of Culture.* New York: Oxford University Press, 1964.

Chapter V.
Theocentric Humanism: The Thomistic
Philosophy of Jacques Maritain

Evans, Joseph W., ed. *Jacques Maritain: The Man and His Achievement.* New York: Sheed and Ward, 1963.

Evans, Joseph W., and Ward, Leo R. *Jacques Maritain: Challenges and Renewals.* Cleveland: World Publishing Company, Meridian Books, 1966.

Fecher, Charles A. *The Philosophy of Jacques Maritain.* Westminster, Maryland: Newman Press, 1953.

Gallagher, Donald and Idella. *A Maritain Reader.* New York: Doubleday, Image Books, 1966.

Maritain, Jacques, and Maritain, Raissa. *Prayer and Intelligence.* Translated by Richard O'Sullivan. New York: Sheed and Ward, 1928.

Maritain, Jacques. *Approaches to God.* New York: Macmillan, 1967.

———. *Art and Scholasticism and the Frontiers of Poetry.* Translated by Joseph W. Evans. New York: Charles Scribner's Sons, 1962.

———. *Existence and the Existent.* Translated by Lewis Galantière and Gerald B. Phelan. New York: Random House, Vintage Books, 1966.

———. *God and the Permission of Evil.* Milwaukee: Bruce Publishing Company, 1966.

———. *On the Use of Philosophy.* New York: Atheneum, 1965.

———. *The Peasant of the Garonne.* New York: Macmillan, 1968.

———. *The Range of Reason.* New York: Charles Scribner's Sons, 1952.

———. *Scholasticism and Politics.* New York: Doubleday, Image Books, 1960.

———. *True Humanism.* New York: Charles Scribner's Sons, 1938.

———, and Maritain, Raissa. *The Situation of Poetry.* Translated by Marshall Suther. New York: Philosophical Library, 1955.

Maritain, Raissa. *We Have Been Friends Together and Adventures in Grace: The Memoirs of Raissa Maritain.* Translated by Julie Kernan. New York: Doubleday, Image Books, 1961.

Chapter VI.
The Theology of Godmanhood: Nicolas Berdyaev

Berdyaev, Nicolas. *The Beginning and the End.* New York: Harper & Brothers, Harper Torchbooks, 1957.

———. *The Destiny of Man.* New York: Harper & Brothers, Harper Torchbooks, 1960.

———. *Dostoevsky.* New York: World Publishing Company, Meridian Books, 1957.

———. *Dream and Reality: An Essay in Autobiography.* London: Geoffrey Bles Company, 1950.

———. *The Fate of Man in the Modern World.* Ann Arbor, Michigan: University of Michigan Paperbacks, 1961.

———. *Freedom and the Spirit.* London: Geoffrey Bles Company, 1935.

———. *The Meaning of the Creative Act.* New York: Crowell-Collier, Collier Books, 1962.

———. *The Meaning of History.* Cleveland: World Publishing Company, Meridian Books, 1962.

———. *Slavery and Freedom.* New York: Charles Scribner's Sons, 1944.

——. *Spirit and Reality*. London: Geoffrey Bles Company, 1939.

Calian, Carnegie Samuel. *The Significance of Eschatology in the Thoughts of Nicolas Berdyaev*. Leiden: E. J. Brill, 1965.

Idinopulos, Thomas A. "Nicolas Berdyaev's Ontology of Spirit," *Journal of Religion*, XLIX, No. 1 (January 1969), 84–93.

Lowrie, Donald A., ed. *Nicolai Berdyaev: Christian Existentialist*. New York: Harper & Row, Harper Torchbooks, 1965.

Richardson, David Bonner. *Berdyaev's Philosophy of History*. The Hague: Martinus Nijhoff, 1968.

Spinka, Matthew. *Nicolas Berdyaev: Captive of Freedom*. Philadelphia: Westminster Press, 1950.

Chapter VII.
The Theology of Dialogue: Martin Buber

Buber, Martin. *Between Man and Man*. Translated by R. G. Smith. New York: Macmillan, 1965.

——. *Eclipse of God*. New York: Harper & Brothers, Harper Torchbooks, 1952.

——. *I and Thou*. Translated by R. G. Smith. New York: Charles Scribner's Sons, 1958.

——. *The Knowledge of Man*. New York: Harper & Row, Harper Torchbooks, 1965.

——. *The Way of Man*. Wallingford, Pennsylvania: Pendle Hill Pamphlet, no date.

Diamond, Malcolm. *Martin Buber, Jewish Existentialist*. New York: Harper & Row, Harper Torchbooks, 1960.

Friedman, Maurice. *Martin Buber: The Life of Dialogue*. New York: Harper & Brothers, Harper Torchbooks, 1955.

Smith, R. G. *Martin Buber*. Richmond, Virginia: John Knox Press, 1967.

Chapter VIII.
Theologians in a World Come of Age

Altizer, Thomas J. J. *The Gospel of Christian Atheism*. Philadelphia: Westminster Press, 1966.

——, and Hamilton, William. *Radical Theology and the Death of God*. Indianapolis: Bobbs-Merrill, 1966.

Bonhoeffer, Dietrich. *Letters and Papers from Prison*. New York: Macmillan, 1967.

Selected Bibliography

Callahan, Daniel, ed. *The Secular City Debate*. New York: Macmillan, 1966.

Cobb, John. *Living Options in Protestant Theology*. Philadelphia: Westminster Press, 1962.

Cox, Harvey. *The Secular City*. New York: Macmillan, 1965.

Dewart, Leslie. *The Future of Belief*. New York: Herder and Herder, 1966.

Edwards, David. *Religion and Change*. New York: Harper & Row, 1969.

Gilkey, Langdon. *Naming the Whirlwind: The Renewal of God-Language*. Indianapolis: Bobbs-Merrill, 1969.

Hamilton, Kenneth. *Revolt Against Heaven*. Grand Rapids, Michigan: Eerdman's, 1965.

Idinopulos, Thomas A. "Radical Theology, Evil and Freedom," *Scottish Journal of Theology* (June 1969).

Mehta, Ved. *The New Theologian*. New York: Harper & Row, 1965.

Meland, Bernard Eugene. *Faith and Culture*. London: Allen and Unwin, 1955.

———. *The Realities of Faith: The Revolution in Cultural Forms*. New York: Oxford University Press, 1962.

———. *The Secularization of Modern Cultures*. New York: Oxford University Press, 1966.

Nicholls, William. *Systematic and Philosophical Theology*. Baltimore: Penguin Originals, 1969.

Noel, Daniel C. "Still Reading His Will? Problems and Resources for the Death of God Theology," *Journal of Religion*, XLVI (October 1966), 1–23.

Phillips, John A. *Christ for Us in the Theology of Dietrich Bonhoeffer*. New York: Harper & Row, 1967.

Robinson, John A. T. *Honest to God*. Philadelphia: Westminster Press, 1963.

Rubenstein, Richard L. *After Auschwitz: Radical Theology and Contemporary Judaism*. Indianapolis: Bobbs-Merrill, 1966.

Van Buren, Paul. *The Secular Meaning of the Gospel*. New York: Macmillan, 1963.

Winter, Gibson. *The New Creation as Metropolis*. New York: Macmillan, 1963.

———. *The Suburban Captivity of the Churches*. New York: Macmillan, 1962.

Zahrnt, Heinz. *The Question of God: Protestant Theology in the Twentieth Century*. New York: Harcourt, Brace & Company, 1966.

Index

Index

196-197, 203-208; compared to Bonhoeffer, 214-215; compared to Cox, 219; compared to Kierkegaard, 200-202, 203-204; compared to Maritain, 195, 204-205, 205-207; compared to Schleiermacher, 190; compared to Tillich, 190, 195, 204-208; and dialogue, 182, 184-185, 192, 197-199; and evil, 208; and Hasidism, 179-183; and I-Thou, 184-198; idea of God, 189, 194, 205; influences on, 178-179; and religion, 195-196; and work, 198-199; and Zionism, 179-180, 183

Buber, Solomon, 178-179
Bultmann, Rudolph, 25
Business, social responsibility of, 199

Calvin, John, 17
Camus, Albert, 229, 234
Cézanne, Paul, 143
Chagall, Marc, 143
Chain of being, 132-133
Change, 110
Choice, 47, 145-147. *See also* Freedom.
Christ, Jesus: as answer to estrangement, 112, 115-118, 169-170; meaning of, 27-28, 169-170, 173, 174; as the meaning of Creation, 72-75; redemptive power of, 24; role of, in Christianity, 57; as symbol of the secular, 226
Christian, becoming a, 41, 42, 44
Christian Faith, The (Schleiermacher), 17-20
"Christian Humanism" (Maritain), 135
Christianity: antagonism toward, 40; commitment to, 39-41; indictment of, 52; meaning of, 42, 56; as perfect religion, 23; "religionless," 214-215; as religious truth, 38-43; role of Christ in, 57; of service, 215
Church: role of, in mediating grace, 133-134; of today, 223-224
Church Dogmatics (Barth), 67-69, 77, 79, 80
City, as "I-It" world, 219
Cold War, 82
Communism, 84-88, 137, 155
Concern, ultimate. *See* Ultimate concern.

Concluding Unscientific Postscript (Kierkegaard), 33-34
Conflict, of self and society, 161
Conscience, moral-rational, 50-51
Consciousness: religious, 50; roots of religion in man's, 227-228, 237
Conservatism, religious, 232-233
Contemporaneity, with Christ, 53-54
Continuity, human-divine, 60, 122
Correlation, 108
Cox, Harvey, 121, 212, 216-224, 230, 232, 234, 235
Creation: Barth's interpretation of, 71-74, 79; biblical witness to, 206-207; stories of, 70-71, 79. *See also* Myth, of Creation.
Creativity: and God, 14, 143, 148, 166, 189; nature of, 168, 171, 175-176
Culture: and death of God, 228-229; and religion, 28, 30, 92, 101; and the ultimate, 99-103

Darwinism, 136-137
Decision, and struggle, 48
Dehumanization, 108, 159
Demonic, in modern culture, 232
Dependence, as religion, 18, 21
Descartes, René, 135-136, 137
Despair, 46-47
Dewey, John, 137
Dialectical materialism, 155
Dialectical method, 34-36
Dialogue: freedom for, 197; of I and Thou, 184-185, 207; openness to, 198-199; responsibility of, 198-199; theology of, 182, 192; with work, 197-198
Diem, Hermann, 31, 32
Discipleship, 214
Discontinuity, of human and divine, 122
Discourses on Religion to the Cultured Among Its Despisers (Schleiermacher), 5, 13, 15-20
Divine creation. *See* Creation.
Divine humanity, 125, 167, 174
Divinity, omnipresence of, 11-12
Dostoevsky, Feodor, 44, 137, 144, 149, 156, 229
Dream and Reality (Berdyaev), 157
Dualism: of Berdyaev, 175-176; of Plato, 129

Index

Duty. *See* Responsibility.

Egoism and religion, 212
Emotions, religious, 10–11. *See also* Feeling.
Empirical method, of Schleiermacher, 8
Empiricism, 18–19
Engels, Friedrich, 123
Epistle to the Romans (Barth), 63, 65, 67, 80, 82
Escapism, religion as, 223, 227
Essence, dialogue as man's, 198
Estrangement, 119, 147, 219, 229; as basis for religion, 94–95, 111; Christ as answer to, 118, 169–170; in *Guernica*, 103, 105; in industrial society, 98, 106, 108–109; and non-being, 112, 114–115
Ethical mode of existence, 32, 47–50
Evil: Barth's idea of, 77–78; freedom as root of, 166; Maritain's idea of, 148–150; in modern society, 161; reality of, 163, 208
Evolution: creative, 124; of society, 155
Evolutionary monism, 22–23
Existence: Christian, 53–54, 56; contemporary, 98, 196–199; contingent, 131; modes of, 32, 44, 45–51; particularity of, 153; philosophy of, 134; reality of, 37–38; relational character of, 35
Existentialism, 58, 108, 112–114, 211, 230; Cox's view of, 218; and industrial society, 106–107; Maritain's view of, 143–148; and secularization, 231–232, 234–235; and theology, 56, 203–204, 213
"Existentialism Is a Humanism" (Sartre), 145–146
Exodus, biblical story of, 221
Experience, 16, 91–92
Experiential method, 20–22

Faith, 39–41, 133, 201–202, 223–224; Christian, 53–54, 150–151, 214; as distinct from religion, 220–221; dynamic of, 99; in religious mode of existence, 48–51; and secularization, 233
Fall, the. *See* Myth, of the Fall.

Feeling: in aesthetic mode of existence, 45–48; as a passive experience, 8–10, 18; religion as, 12, 17–18, 25–26, 91–92
Ferre, Nels, 25
Fichte, Johann Gottlieb, 6, 12
Finite, and Infinite, 9–10
Freedom: and choice, 145–147; of man, 8, 42, 112–113, 124, 197, 218–219; reality of, 164–165; source of, 162–163, 175–177; use of, 158–159, 166, 174, 232
Freud, Sigmund, 227–228
Freudianism, 136–137, 151–152
Friedman, Maurice, 180

Giovanni, Don, as aesthetic hero, 45–46
Givenness, of human life, 152–153
God: anthropomorphic way of speaking about, 173; authority of, 80; as beauty, 141–142; birth of, 172–173; concept of, 27, 131–132, 165–166, 193–194; as Creator, 14, 143, 148, 189; in daily life, 4, 205; death of, 121, 224–226, 228–229; definition of, 111–112; encounter with, 14–15; experience of, 3–4, 14, 16–17, 190; grace of, 68–77; idea of, 3; image of, 213–214; infinity of, 27; Kingdom of, 172, 175, 176, 224; knowledge of, 63–64, 66, 68, 70, 76–77, 126–127, 128–129, 191–192, 204; law of, 133; love of, for individual, 180–181; and man, 133–134, 151, 181, 189, 200–202, 207, 221, 224, 227; meaning of, 9–10, 19–21, 89, 237; mystery of, 194–195, 204; other self of, 166–167, 168; as problem solver, 213; proofs of existence of, 131, 148, 204; relation of, to evil, 162–163; relation of, to world, 9, 139, 174, 200–202, 204–206, 215, 220; self-manifestation of, 15; self-revelation of, 193–194; self-sufficiency of, 166–167; subjectivity of, 80; superfluity of, 105; symbolic language referring to, 19, 112, 173; as a tyrant, 225; Word of, 64, 67–70, 76
God-consciousness, 27
God-humanity, 172, 174
God-man, paradox of the, 52, 53, 56

261

Index

Index

Maritain, Jacques, 122–153; compared to Barth, 149, 167; compared to Berdyaev, 157, 167, 172, 204–205, 205–207; compared to Bonhoeffer, 214–215; compared to Buber, 204–205, 205–207; compared to Sartre, 147; compared to Schleiermacher, 126; compared to Tillich, 128, 172, 205–207; conversion to Catholicism, 124–125; education of, 123; on evil, 148–150; and existentialism, 143–148; as neo-Thomist, 134; as philosopher, 126–127; on reason, 138–139

Marriage, Buber and Kierkegaard on, 201–203

Martenson, H. L., 33–34

Marx, Karl, 123, 136–137

Marxism, 151–152, 154–156

Materialism, refutation of, 124

Matter and Memory (Bergson), 124

Meaning: of relationship, 188, 190; of religion, 28, 91–93, 235; universalization of, 145

Meaning of History, The (Berdyaev), 156

Mechanization of life, 161

Meland, Bernard Eugene, 25, 212, 235, 237–239

"Metamorphosis, The" (Kafka), 109

Metaphysical philosophers, 98

Middle Ages, 159

Miracles, 16

Modern industrial society, 155, 159–161, 198–199. *See also* Industrialization; Technology.

Modes of existence, 32, 44; aesthetic, 45–48; ethical, 47–50; religious, 48–51

Monism, evolutionary, 22–23

Monotheistic religions, 22–23, 24

Morality and religion, 6–7, 93

Moralization, Christianity as, 224–225

Moravian Brotherhood, 3–4, 24

Music, 46

Mutuality: divine-human, 156–159, 181, 206–208; as interpretation of history, 159; of I-Thou dialogue, 184–185; reality as, 193

Mysticism, 15, 185, 190

Myth: of Creation, 147–148, 208; of the Fall, 114–115, 147, 148, 165, 208

Naturalism, religious, 26

Nature: disenchantment of, 220–221; in I-Thou, 187–188; philosophy of, 35; relation of man to, 159–160

Nazism, 137, 183, 212; and Barth, 82–85; and Tillich, 91

Near Eastern religions, 70–71, 220–221

Need for religion, 228

Negativism, 215

New Being, 116–118

New Testament, 116, 225–226

Niebuhr, H. Richard, 25

Niebuhr, Reinhold, 84–87, 208

Nietzsche, Friedrich, 123, 176, 224–225, 229

Nonbeing, threat of, 110, 113, 114

Notes from Underground (Dostoevsky), 44

Nothingness, 34, 144, 145; holy, 230, 236, 238

Object, of experience, 184, 185

Objectification, 162; as process of history, 240

Old Testament, 94

Ontology, task of, 110–111

Optimism, about man, 136

Other self, of God, 166–167, 168

Otto, Rudolph, 5–6, 12–13

Pagan epoch, 159

Pantheism, 10, 13, 15, 20

Paradox, the, 52–55

Particular and universal, 11

Pascal, Blaise, 144

Patriotism, 96–97

Paul, Saint, 40, 63, 65, 66, 127, 128, 208

Personality, 96–97, 155

Philosophy, 25, 36–37, 134

Picasso, Pablo, 103–105, 108, 143, 152

Plato, 10–11, 98, 129

Plotinus, 129

Politics: of Barth, 82–87; of Schleiermacher, 4–5

Polytheistic religions, 23

Possessed, The (Dostoevsky), 137

Potentiality, actualization of, 130–132

Pragmatism, anti-metaphysical, 219

Propaganda, art as, 143

Psychologism, 15

Psychoneurosis of contemporary life, 96–97, 114

Index

Index

Symbol, American flag as, 102, 103
Symbols: artistic, 102–103; as language of religion, 100–104; power of, 112; religious, 195, 211; types of, 103
Synthesis, 35

Technology: ambiguity of, 240; as a good, 238–239; effect on society, 198, 216, 229, 231, 234. *See also* Industrialization; Modern industrial society.
Technopolis, 217–220
Teilhard de Chardin, Pierre, 174
Theologian, task of the, 107, 204, 211–212
Theology, 14, 89, 213, 215, 241; anthropocentric, 60, 61; crisis, 67; of culture, 101; death-of-God, 228; dialectical, 67, 79; existential, 203–204, 213; of immanence, 17; liberal, 57, 60–61; neo-conservative, 57; secular, 212; of transcendence, 16
Thesis, 34
Thinking, 50–51
Thomism, 125. *See also* Aquinas, Thomas.
Thomte, Reidar, 33, 50
Thou. *See* I and Thou.
Thus Spake Zarathustra (Nietzsche), 176
Tillich, Paul, 25, 89, 90–121, 128–129; on being, 98–99; compared to Barth, 107, 118–119; compared to Berdyaev, 169, 172, 195, 204–208; compared to Bonhoeffer, 214–215; compared to Buber, 204–208; compared to Cox, 219–220; compared to Maritain, 128, 172, 205–207; compared to Schleiermacher, 92, 190; and culture, 99–103; and estrangement, 94–95, 98, 103, 108–109, 111, 112, 114–115, 118, 119; and *Guernica*, 103–105; idea of Christ, 115–118; idea of God, 111–112; and Nazism, 91; and personality, 96–97; and religion, 91–93; and theology, 107–108; and ultimate concern, 93–101, 120
Time and Free Will (Bergson), 124
Town, period of the, 216–217

Traditions, religious, 218
Tragedy of life, 174–175
Transcendent mystery, 205
Trial, The (Kafka), 160–161
Tribal epoch, 216, 217
Trinity: doctrine of the, 80–81; in Hasidic thought, 182
Troeltsch, Ernst, 21–22, 29, 60
Truth: Christianity as, 38–43; as subjectivity, 41

Ultimacy, 94–95, 237–238, 241
Ultimate concern, 93–101, 120, 205, 219, 240
Ultimate creative ground, 238
Ungrund, 164
Unity: supreme, 189; as wholeness, 11–12, 13
Universal, particular and, 11
Universality, 174
Universe, Schleiermacher's concept of, 9, 11
Unmoved mover, 130–131
Urbanization, 216, 218–219. *See also* Modern industrial society.

Van Buren, Paul, 230
Van Dusen, Henry, 25
Verbal inspiration, doctrine of, 65
Void, Sacred, 230

Whence, God as the, 20–21
Whitehead, Alfred North, 174, 236
Wholeness, 11–12, 13
Wholly other, 63, 66, 226
Williams, Daniel Day, 25
Winter, Gibson, 230
Witness, Christ as, of God, 173
Work, relation of man to, 198–199
Workers, in industrial society, 198–199
World: as a community, 218; knowledge of God in relation to, 191–192; man and, 200
World war, epoch of, 231
World War I, 61–62, 82
World War II, 150
Worth, man's inherent, 210

Zionism, 179–180, 183

265

A Note on the Author

THOMAS A. IDINOPULOS was born in Vancouver, Washington, grew up in Portland, Oregon, and studied philosophy at Reed College, where he became interested in religion and theology. He received a Master's degree in the subject from Duke University, and a Ph.D. in philosophical theology from the University of Chicago. Mr. Idinopulos' writings have appeared in such scholarly journals as the *Journal of Religion* and the *Scottish Journal of Theology*. He is now Assistant Professor of Religion at Miami University in Oxford, Ohio, where he lives with his wife Chessie and their two sons.